SECURITY vs. SURVIVAL

edited by
Theresa C. Smith and Indu B. Singh

SECURITY vs. SURVIVAL
THE NUCLEAR ARMS RACE

Lynne Rienner Publishers, Inc.
Boulder, Colorado

Published in the United States of America by
Lynne Rienner Publishers, Inc.
948 North Street, Boulder, Colorado 80302

© 1985 by Lynne Rienner Publishers, Inc. All rights reserved

Library of Congress Cataloging in Publication Data
Main entry under title:

Security vs. survival.

   Includes bibliographical references and index.
   1. Nuclear weapons—Addresses, essays, lectures.
2. Arms race—History—20th century—Addresses, essays,
lectures.   3. Nuclear disarmament—Addresses, essays,
lectures.   I. Smith, Theresa C., 1951-   II. Singh,
Indu Bhushan.   III. Title: Security versus survival.
U264.S43   1985   355'.0217   84-27521
ISBN 0-931477-13-1

Distributed outside of North and South America and Japan
by Frances Pinter (Publishers) Ltd, 25 Floral Street,
London WC2E 9DS England.   UK ISBN: 0-86187-557-5

Printed and bound in the United States of America

CONTENTS

Foreword, *Edward J. Bloustein* vii

Acknowledgments ix

Introduction: Soviet–U.S. Relations and the Prospects for
Arms Control, *Theresa C. Smith and Indu B. Singh* 1

1 Issues in U.S.–Soviet Nuclear Defense Policy, *William A. Colby* 9

2 Perspectives on Limited Nuclear War, *Frank von Hippel* 23

3 Nuclear Arms Futures, *Richard Garwin* 53

4 Central Nuclear War: Comments, Concepts, and Contexts,
   Herman Kahn 77

5 Military Spending and the U.S. Economy, *Judith Reppy* 109

6 Environmental Consequences of Nuclear War,
   Michael Levandowsky 121

7 Medical Consequences of Nuclear War, *H. Jack Geiger* 139

8 A Critical Analysis of the Arms Control Record,
   George Rathjens 157

Selected Provisions of Superpower Arms Control Accords 175

Glossary 185

Index 191

FOREWORD

It is commonplace to observe that nuclear weapons and the risk of nuclear war constitute the greatest threat and the greatest dilemma confronting humankind. Estimates of the likelihood of a strategic nuclear exchange with the Soviet Union range from possible to highly probable; estimates of the impact of such an exchange range from unprecedented catastrophe to Armageddon. Nobody wants a nuclear war, and nobody is quite sure how to prevent one.

Less commonplace is the assertion that it is ordinary individuals who face the threat and must ultimately resolve the dilemma. Many in positions of power argue that most individuals lack the wisdom and expertise to confront nuclear decisions, and many of us accept the argument and turn our efforts (if not our dreams) to other matters. But for a great public university in a democratic society, there is a clear answer. None of us can responsibly evade the obligation to help determine our country's nuclear policy. And no university can responsibly evade the obligation to offer those in its midst—students, faculty, staff, community—whatever knowledge and courage it can muster in pursuit of security *and* survival.

In such an effort, a committee of Rutgers faculty and students mustered considerable knowledge and courage. They brought to the campus an impressive array of expert commentators on the arms race, many of them leading participants in the debate over arms control policy. The eight chapters of this book are drawn from those lectures, as revised and updated by the speakers and the editors.

The lecture series was made possible by the effort and financial support of many inside and outside the university. In their acknowledgments, the editors have thanked their steering committee, their funders, and others who helped. I should like to add my own thanks, not only to those they named, but also to T. C. Smith and Indu Singh themselves. Their leadership gave Rutgers and New Jersey an invaluable series of presentations, which I am delighted to see expanded now in book form for a still wider audience.

Edward J. Bloustein
President, Rutgers The State University
of New Jersey
February 1985

ACKNOWLEDGMENTS

This volume is a result not only of the efforts of the contributors and editors, but also of the skill and expertise of Peter Garik, a physicist; Diane Shatin and Sue Cutter, geographers; Barbara Hopkins, Berne Psaty, and Jeralee May, administrative assistants at Indiana University; and Steven Flinn, a computer systems specialist at Indiana University.

The exceptional interest in the topic shown by Robert Corman, Esq., of the Fund for New Jersey, is appreciatively noted. The editors also heartily acknowledge the friendly assistance and support made available from the earliest stage of the project by the president of Rutgers University, Edward Bloustein, and by the deans of all the colleges at Rutgers, especially John W. Yolton of Rutgers College and Mary Hartman of Douglass. Many thanks as well to the Graduate Student Association and to other student groups at Rutgers University for their varied contributions to *Security vs. Survival.*

Any effort of this scope incurs a great many debts. We are especially indebted to our colleagues at Indiana University who agreed to serve on the steering committee of the Nuclear Arms Race Conference, and to community leaders too numerous to list.

Any merits of our editing are due largely to the enthusiastic support given to this project by the Department of Political Science at Indiana University, and to the atmosphere of cheerful camaraderie prevailing there.

Theresa C. Smith
Indu B. Singh

Theresa C. Smith
and Indu B. Singh

INTRODUCTION: SOVIET–U.S. RELATIONS AND THE PROSPECTS FOR ARMS CONTROL

This volume brings together the work of specialists from many disciplines who have analyzed the driving forces of the U.S.-Soviet arms race, the costs and probable outcome of this competition, and the prospects for controlling it cooperatively through arms negotiations. This interdisciplinary presentation of current issues invites the concerned scholar and citizen to weigh the evidence for policy-relevant arguments in physics, economics, politics, military strategy, environmental science, and medicine. The editors hope that the extensiveness of the book's coverage as well as the government experience of a number of the book's contributors will focus new attention on the policy relevance of scientific research in general and of the social sciences in particular.

These concerns were pressing in the United States during the 1984 presidential election year, when economic and security issues were re-evaluated and when the direction of U.S. arms control efforts for the following several years was determined—albeit indirectly—both at the polls and in anticipation of voter preference. But arms control and arms-racing concerns have now taken on even greater significance as the consequences of neglected opportunities become apparent over time.

More than a decade has elapsed since any significant strategic arms control agreement has been ratified by the superpowers.[1] In the West it may be attractive to blame the Soviets exclusively for the failures of recent arms control efforts. However, there has been a series of Soviet concessions and counter-offers in many of the negotiations (including the Theater Nuclear Forces Talks, the Mutual Balanced Force Reduction Talks, and elsewhere) that might have been productive. Chief among these concessions may be the February 1979 acceptance of limited on-site inspection. On-site inspection provisions are also codified in the Peaceful Nuclear Explosions Treaty signed in 1976 and awaiting U.S. Senate action. Apparently the Comprehensive Test Ban Treaty draft, now delayed, includes as an integral part proposals for an entire network of seismic detection systems to be installed inside each of the superpowers for immediate treaty verification.

Although the impression has been created since the two-track NATO decision of 1979, and especially since the Soviet war in Afghanistan, that Soviet-U.S. relations suddenly reached a new low in the early eighties, this nadir is in fact a logical extension of deteriorating superpower relations over the last decade and more, at least since the Middle East war and U.S. nuclear alert of October 1973, and the U.S. recognition of the Peoples Republic of China in 1972. In this interval the number of nuclear warheads reported in the Soviet and U.S. arsenals has grown. There have been increases in the accuracy of delivery vehicles on both sides and decreases in warning time. (For example, if the targets of the U.S. Pershing II missiles in Europe are in Eastern Europe, warning time is two to three minutes; if their targets lie in Soviet territory, warning time is about five to eight minutes. Similar warning times for the United States could be produced if Soviet submarine attack on the United States is hypothesized.) The Soviet Union has followed the United States in "MIRVing," and announced in October 1984 that it is also following the United States in deploying cruise missiles, while the United States has begun to increase the throwweight of some of its weapons. Some observers conclude that this trading of asymmetries was the central consequence of SALT II after the U.S. failure to ratify. Meanwhile, the militarization of space has continued.

The period from 1973 on has encompassed the resignation of President Richard M. Nixon and the advent of three different U.S. administrations (not including either of Alexander Haig's), with variable and sometimes inconsistent positions on the difficult questions of Soviet-U.S. arms control negotiations. In addition to interruptions and other impediments occasioned by the change of administrations, there are also institutional political arrangements in the United States that may obstruct constructive agreements with the Soviet Union, such as the power of a one-third Senate minority to prevent treaty ratification, as George Rathjens discusses below. Questions remain in the United States as well as in the Soviet Union concerning the influence of the military in arms accords, because the U.S. Joint Chiefs of Staff continue to exercise considerable authority over the terms of agreements signed and ratified by the United States, and the Defense Council may play a similar role in the Soviet Union.

Both difficulty in maintaining a consistent arms control position over time and apparent conflict-of-interest questions raised by the military's role in arms control might develop in the Soviet Union. Since the death of former General Secretary Leonid I. Brezhnev, there has been a considerable degree of consistency in the arms control positions taken by his successors. However, this predictability may not remain an enduring aspect of the Soviet negotiating position in strategic or Eurostrategic talks, when and if genuinely substantive talks on these issues resume.

In an apparent continuation of the Brezhnev attitude of interest in arms control and in detente, Andropov's successor, Chernenko, joined a chorus of Eastern European statesmen in identifying peace through negotiations as "our main task" in late 1984. In his initiative, reported in the *Washington Post* on 17 October 1984, Chernenko listed four options for improving superpower relations, apparently accepting a favorable U.S. response on some or any one as a basis for improved relations and possibly as a basis for the resumption of particular arms control discussions. The Chernenko options, not unusual in themselves, were notable in that they were presented collectively and very directly. They included a moratorium on the militarization of space, a NATO No-First-Use declaration to match the Soviet NFU commitment already made, a superpower nuclear freeze on delivery vehicles and warheads, and U.S. ratification of the 1974 Threshold Test Ban Treaty and the 1976 Peaceful Nuclear Explosions Treaty. General Secretary Chernenko also suggested that the suspended Comprehensive Test Ban Negotiations might be "finalized." The Soviet insistence on removal of U.S. Pershing IIs and ground-launched cruise missiles from Europe as a basis for the Geneva medium-range talks seemed to have faded from the Soviet media by late 1984, which may imply a greater Soviet flexibility on arms control under Gorbachayov. Although General Secretary Chernenko himself referred to the talks as "wrecked" by the United States, in the October 1984 initiative he called the new U.S. missiles only "obstacles" to accord. Foreign Secretary Andrei Gromyko's meetings in the autumn of 1984 with presidential candidate Walter Mondale, President Ronald Reagan, and Secretary of State George Schultz probably indicated a renewed Soviet effort for medium-range or other arms restrictions, emphasized by Gorbachayov's SS-20 freeze proposal of April 1985. This seems especially likely since the Gromyko meeting with President Reagan, which yielded a commitment to discuss arms control in the future. This meeting led to the discussions in principle (as the scope was excessive for substantive progress) of January 1985, which again resulted in scheduled further talks for March 1985. Even though President Reagan took the position in his opening remarks at a press conference on 9 January 1985 that testing (and deployment?) of the Star Wars ballistic missile defense system is not negotiable, these meetings—including those in Vienna on securing a Mideast peace—still suggest that the mid- and late eighties may be propitious for arms control.

Since the Reagan Administration has argued that arms control was not in U.S. interests because of the reputed weakness of U.S. strategic forces, any serious declaratory interest in arms control marks a policy change, even though BMD may not be discussed. However, this apparent major alteration in the U.S. position on arms control negotiations has served prior election year functions. Neither this earlier meeting nor the January meeting seems to have provided a basis for a substantive agreement after March 1985, especially as the publicity surrounding these events in the West may have conveyed a lack of serious interest to the Soviet leadership. That a human rights linkage issue has arisen with respect to the autumn 1985 summit meeting could convey the same message.

It is unclear whether the second cohort of Soviet leadership, which will emerge in the longer term, will agree to the types of concessions mandated by its predecessors (e.g., the exclusion of U.S. forward-based systems from SALT) or whether they will respond to the economic constraints of the Soviet system in the same way. (See, for instance, the resource debates in the 24th Party Congress documents of 1971 and later, which show that there is recognition now in the Soviet Union that continuing emphasis on resource allocations to the military not only may undermine the health of the Soviet economy but eventually will restrict the allocations available for defense.)

The question of whether the Communist Party of the Soviet Union will continue to lose a significant amount of political control over the Soviet military will produce new uncertainties in the superpower relationship over time, which perhaps may extend even to the choice of responsible authorities and negotiators. So there are potential problems for the future of the arms control process itself, including the fact that we negotiate without some useful information. We do not know the boundaries of the Soviet weapons production system; we do not really know what the maximum capacity of the Soviet system for arms racing would be if the military were given free access to resources in a time of perceived maximum threat. The Soviets probably do not know this either. Thus, we do not know precisely the dimensions of the future force "balance" we might prefer to avoid, although it is possible for the United States to take such steps as would increase the likelihood of our discovering this outcome. Notwithstanding its superpower status, the Soviet Union does compete under some lasting economic disadvantages and demographic constraints.

These recent developments in the political leadership and in the economies of the superpowers have further implications for arms control. There may be uncertainties in long-term negotiations produced by changes of administration, and the domestic political support of any political leader may be eroded (again) to the point that draft treaties that are produced will not be given sufficient political support to ensure ratification. Additionally, the arms control role of the professional military in each country may expand. The arms control process itself—that is, the negotiations within each country, as well as those between the countries—appears to be increasingly protracted, allowing for technological change and fluctuations of political fortune to have maximally counterproductive effects on potential agreements or even to supercede them. Further, the undesirable effects of the history of recent arms control in both countries may prove difficult to overcome. On the Soviet side there may be increasing reluctance to negotiate because a not-inconsiderable list of concessions on the part of the Soviet Union has failed to produce a ratified SALT II Treaty, while START proposals, from the Soviet perspective, have been a non-STARTer from the beginning due to the asymmetrical reductions in ICBMs entailed. On the U.S. side it may prove difficult to overcome the popular impression that the terms of SALT II were disadvantageous to the United States. Failure to appreciate the considerable military benefits of SALT II to the United States could pose difficulties for negotiating other partially substitutable accords that, unlike SALT, do take into account U.S. forward-based systems or do consider the possibility that U.S. strategic systems in the North Atlantic are capable of theater missions. The Jackson Amendment poses other severe problems for the United States, because equal security may not be obtainable through equal numbers, regardless of whether warheads, delivery vehicles, launchers, or some other counting unit is the basis of negotiations. A parallel obstacle may exist for the Soviets, as the stock phrase "equality and equal security" may be used as a criterion for acceptable agreements and may be a contradiction in terms under some circumstances. At the same time, although ceilings on allocations to the military are clearly in the interest of both superpowers, if only because of the opportunity costs entailed, there is no compelling evidence that either country is fast approaching a limit beyond which it will make no further societal efforts for defense.

For reasons inextricably interwoven with the stillbirth of detente and with the larger foreign policies of the superpowers, the late seventies and the early eighties have scarcely advanced the central aims of arms control. Nonetheless, both superpowers have recognized for many years the real and urgent need for meaningful arms control, because, inter alia,

— a nuclear war, should one ensue, might not prove to be limitable, and there are no defenses against nuclear missile war;
— demands for alternate use of resources may be increasingly pressing in the United States,[2] as its competitive edge in the world market is lost, and in the Soviet Union, as poor harvests and slower technological development continues as a result of the disappointment of Soviet hopes for Western aid and trade under detente and the historical priority given to heavy industry;
— especially if detente has not been given a genuine opportunity to suc-

ceed, and we return to Cold War (or even Ice Age) conditions, the risks of the arms race can be managed better if the competition moves in a direction made predictable by agreements in force;
— there are domestic political needs to appear responsible in the face of the costs and risks presented by the arms race.

Against this background, the authors of this volume raise several major issues and voice some common concerns. All of the authors, perhaps Herman Kahn chief among them, recommend further research and clearer thinking on arms control and defense issues. Arguing that existing research should be more widely disseminated, H. Jack Geiger and Michael Levandowsky note that the direct somatic effects of nuclear war on the human population, and the indirect effects through our ecological interdependence, would be substantially more serious and pervasive than is usually assumed in nuclear war scenarios.

There is also recognition here, in Frank von Hippel's chapter, that nuclear threats are a fact of the post-1945 world and a concern that, contrary to William Colby's view, nuclear weapons may well be useable. Dr. von Hippel and Dr. Kahn both note that nuclear weapons might be used indiscriminately against civilians, although Dr. Kahn does not find a good argument for a countercity, anticivilian nuclear attack as a first strike, and although Dr. Levandowsky does not find much difference in probable consequences regardless of target.

Many of the contributors conclude that, as there is no possibility of eliminating the real Soviet military threat to the United States, negotiations provide one answer to our security problem that is at least partially substitutable for arms racing, although negotiations may face multiple political handicaps. A number of the authors point to genuine economic needs for savings from military spending in both superpowers, though in Judith Reppy's analysis the United States may be able to afford some aspects of arms racing in the short term or under specified economic conditions. However, Dr. Reppy's work points to a reduction in U.S. ability to compete on world markets as a result of the overemphasis on military spending, especially for research and development of little immediate applicability to the civilian sector in the United States. Economic considerations also appear in some of the authors' discussions of the definition of national security. There is some recognition here, as in former Secretary of Defense Harold Brown's Report to Congress on the 1982 military budget, that a sound economy is a component of national security, and that the buildup that began under President Jimmy Carter and continues under President Ronald Reagan may have adverse effects on the economy through eventual shortages in supply of some skilled labor, through inflation, and through other channels.

There are no advocates of maximum U.S. arms racing represented here. Neither is technology per se advocated in this volume as an answer to the U.S. security problem. Richard Garwin argues not only that new technology is not the answer to the ongoing arms race, but that even for relatively smaller tasks at hand in defense the appropriate technology—which may be lower technology—has often not been chosen; instead there has been some fascination with devices for their own sake, irrespective of a real deterrent or defense need.

Having recommended negotiations, the authors do not agree on methods or structures that are most likely to lead to accord. Mr. Colby argues strongly against unilateral moves on the grounds that these will not be reciprocated, while Dr. Garwin recommends unilateral withdrawal of battlefield nuclear weapons from Europe, even if there is no reciprocal Soviet move. Dr. Rathjens discusses two cases of informal bargains or evidently unilateral actions that were successful, including an undertaking to reduce military spending. However, there is a shared concern that negotiations may be used disingenuously, to prevent an agreement while convincing some part of the public that serious arms control efforts are underway. Other issues, such as verification or political linkage to immigration and to domestic political dissidence, may also be used instrumentally to prevent agreements, in the view of some of the contributors.

Even the most vigorous advocates of arms control express a concern here that the negotiating process does not keep pace with technological innovation or with deployment of new weapons systems. Thus, as Dr. Rathjens implies, if formal negotiations are not productive, tacit bargaining decisions such as those leading to the reciprocated temporary halt to aerial testing preceding the Partial Test Ban (1958-61) may provide a workable and more timely substitute, especially if there is informed public support behind such maneuvers.

The authors of this set of essays do not unanimously concur with the authors of *Common Security,* a report of the Independent Commission on Disarmament and Security Issues, in asserting that the security of nuclear powers is indivisible. These authors do not reach any consensus on whether the world is safer if the Soviet Union is also safer, or whether the world is safer when the Soviet Union is threatened. However, there is a recurring theme in many of these chapters that deterrence theory has been based on overly simple or even misleading assumptions and has been developed to the point of absurdity, so that an argument can be made for or against any weapons system or any arms accord at any time in deterrence-theoretical terms. Similarly, assessments of Soviet strategic forces that impute any set of probable contingency plans—including contradictory ones—can be made in deterrence terms. These conclusions on the lack of rigor in deterrence arguments or on the dependence of deterrence arguments on idiosyncratic historical and other assumptions argue against the overly hasty response to problems that develop only as a result of the exercise of deterrence assumptions on hardware, but that can be made to vanish in the same way; e.g., what constitutes an "irresistible temptation" for a first strike.

Guides to arms control policy are difficult to find, and expertise in this area is difficult to define. This volume is offered in the hope that it will contribute to an informed debate on the superpowers' strategic relationship in the mid- and late eighties. Such a debate is urgently required, for two reasons. First, we are living through a time of a most peculiar confluence of events:

1. The attitude that there could be no victor in a nuclear war, shared by the superpowers during SALT and articulated by Brezhnev and his successors since 1979, has been challenged in the United States. (See Gray and Payne, "Victory is Possible," *Foreign Policy* No. 39, Summer 1980.)
2. Discussions of prevailing in a protracted nuclear war have emerged in the United States at high levels, although they seem to have largely disappeared from authoritative Soviet writing outside the professional military journals since the fifties.
3. The possible use of limited nuclear options has been given renewed emphasis in the United States.
4. The doctrine of inevitability of war between the socialist and capitalist powers, rejected in the Soviet Union since Premier Giorgi Malenkov in the fifties, has begun to be mentioned in the West.

Second, to date we not only have failed to achieve the aims of arms control—to reduce the risk of war, to control military budgets, or to limit damage effectively if war does break out—we have made these aims politically suspect.

Notes

1. SALT I was signed at Moscow on 26 May 1972, ratified, and entered into force on 3 October 1972.
2. While the employment generated by military contracts has served the second and fourth objectives to some extent in the United States, it may do so to a smaller extent over time. This diminishing effect might be expected as the public begins to recognize that, although military spending may generate new jobs easily and quickly, so as to provide maximum political credit to the administration in office at the time, it is an inefficient method of creating new jobs and does not really address the chronic unemployment problem in the United States.

William A. Colby

1

ISSUES IN U.S.–SOVIET NUCLEAR DEFENSE POLICY

William Colby served as director of the U.S. Central Intelligence Agency from 1973 to 1976 under Presidents Richard Nixon and Gerald Ford. Although he opposes unilateral arms control measures, Mr. Colby has endorsed a mutual, verifiable nuclear weapons freeze, disputing the Reagan administration's position on the verifiability of Soviet compliance with arms control accords. He maintains that a nuclear arms accord with Moscow would make it substantially easier to monitor Soviet production, testing, or deployment of new weapons. Mr. Colby joins George Rathjens in pointing out that higher standards of verification are required for treaties than are required in periods when the arms race is not regulated. That is, the United States is willing to risk strategic surprise only when the probability of it is relatively high.

In this commentary, Mr. Colby identifies two dilemmas in superpower nuclear defense policy: first, that both countries feel compelled to maintain stocks of nuclear weapons, although these weapons are unusable, and second, that the arms race is unwinnable, yet the structure of the superpower relationship compels each side to race. He advocates realistic negotiations as the only solution to these dilemmas.

Introduction

We live thirty minutes away from Soviet weapons pointed at this country, weapons that could produce indiscriminate slaughter many, manyfold. Our Soviet colleagues on this small planet sit under a similar threat, from United States weapons. We not only deal with the possibility of that kind of impact on a community such as New Brunswick, Beirut, or Kiev, we deal with it in terms of the impact on an entire nation and even on life on this planet. This is a serious matter. In looking back on Nagasaki and Hiroshima in 1945, we have only to realize that the weapons that produced those scenes were only small examples of the ordinary weapons available today.

For many years we all tended to leave this subject to someone else. It was born in the secrecy of the Manhattan Project during World War II, when it was patriotic not to know anything about it and to protect the secrets of the weapons. It was a follow-on to nonnuclear strategic bombing. Let's face it: there were more people killed by ordinary weapons in Tokyo a few weeks before the Hiroshima bombing than died in Hiroshima. This kind of mass slaughter became more and more acceptable by reason of the examples of Tokyo, Coventry, Berlin, Dresden, and others. There was a logical relationship between that weapon and the prosecution of a war. It was felt that the enemy forces were a legitimate target, but so was the industrial base that generated those weapons and the labor force that worked to produce them. If the families of the labor force lived with the labor force, then they were incidental casualties of the attack on that legitimate target of modern war.

We were also inclined to leave this subject to someone else because this new dimension of nuclear war was so awesome. The weapons were so destructive that the photographs of the mushroom clouds from the explosions at Bikini and other places were etched on a generation's mind as the ultimate in power. It was hardly conceivable to ordinary citizens, and hardly something that they felt they could influence. Thus, it was left to a priesthood who could talk about bombs, throw weight, megatonnage, and different devices; who could expound on counterforce and countervalue operations, and discuss various tactical and strategic uses of these nuclear weapons.

The ordinary citizen left it to that priesthood until about 1979-80, when in the course of seeing the United States begin to rebuild its strength, we also witnessed the failure of the SALT II Treaty. That treaty had been negotiated by three presidents. It presented many tradeoffs, but it was attacked as fatally flawed. The treaty coincided with a solution to one of these technological problems of nuclear warfare: in order to protect the capabilities of our weapons, we would build a great racetrack in the deserts of Nevada and Utah. We would put fifty to a hundred billion dollars into cement to create that racetrack, so that we could somehow devise a weapons system that would be safe against the Soviet weapons system. It would conceal the exact location of our weapons, while reassuring the Soviets that we had no more than the ones we said were there. I think that the American people felt that that scheme just did not make sense. Is this what the priesthood has brought us to, going out in the desert to build something bigger than the Maginot Line, bigger than the pyramids of Egypt, and expecting that to protect our safety? Isn't there a better way?

I think the nuclear freeze movement originated in these feelings of the American people that it was time they took the subject away from the priesthood and began to apply their own good sense to these complicated subjects, to learn enough about them so that they could discuss and evaluate the different proposals, the different theories, the different projects, and make a democratic judgment about the safety of our country and how our country should deal with the world around it.

Are Nuclear Weapons Usable?

There is a better way, I think we have to admit. The history of the last few years suggests that nuclear weapons are unusable, because of the danger of retaliation. We have a large stock of nuclear weapons; the Soviets have a large stock as well. Any use by us or by them would be followed by unacceptable retaliation by the other side.

For moral reasons, also, nuclear weapons are unusable by our country because of the mass destruction they would cause. They would be rejected for the same reason that we rejected those photographs of the Beirut massacre. The indiscriminate nature of nuclear weapons and the moral compulsion brought to bear on our government when faced with the possibility of using them would be such that the government would pause very firmly before moving into it.

There is evidence to buttress this point that nuclear weapons are unusable: over the past twenty-odd years, in the various potential confrontations that have arisen between Soviet and U.S. soldiers, both sides have been cautious that they not begin shooting at each other because of the potential for escalation to the nuclear level that such a situation contains. In crises in Berlin in 1961, in Cuba in 1962, and in the Middle East in October 1973, both nations shied away from the prospect of direct Soviet/U.S. conflict because of the danger of escalation to nuclear levels. This history suggests that, although these weapons are large and seemingly effective, they cannot be used.

The Arms Race Is Unwinnable

The arms race in nuclear weapons is unwinnable. If one side has a slight advantage in one area, the other side will be stimulated to move to catch up and even to go ahead. We saw the shock in the United States when Sputnik was launched into space by the Soviet Union, and we feared the beginning of a great missile gap between the Soviet Union and the United States in the late 1950s. Partly as a result of that fear, President John F. Kennedy proclaimed that we would put a man on the moon in ten years, and we did. In the nuclear field, the Soviets realized their strategic inferiority in Cuba in 1962, and they made a pledge that they no longer would be inferior. They began a weapons buildup aimed at increasing their power to at least equal that of the United States, if not greater. President Reagan says today that the Soviets have a margin of superiority over the United States in these weapons, and that a very large increase in the defense budget of the United States is necessary to eliminate that margin of superiority. I do not believe that the allegation of Soviet superiority is valid.

In the late 1960s, the United States was well ahead on a device called a multiple independently targetable re-entry vehicle (MIRV)—multiple warheads on a missile that could spill out from the end of the missile and land in several different places, a different warhead in each place. We were negotiating the SALT I Treaty at that time, and we decided that we should not put a limitation on the development of MIRVs in that treaty because the U.S. was well ahead, which was an advantage. So we did not put a MIRV limit in SALT I and the Soviets began to work on a MIRV. Today the MIRV is probably the single most dangerous component of Soviet nuclear power that we face. We had a chance to limit it, to prevent its development in the Soviet Union. But we were ahead, we were "winning." And they caught up. This is the second point: if nuclear weapons are unusable, then a race in producing them is unwinnable.

Unilateral Restraints Are Not Feasible

There is another key point about these weapons: although some would disagree, I think it is true that unilateral restraints, by us alone, are unworkable. Restraint will not be reciprocated by the Soviet Union. If we restrain ourselves, there is nothing to indicate, on the record or elsewhere, that the Soviets will restrain themselves. In fact, there are indications that the United States has restrained itself, either for budgetary or political reasons, in various areas and that has by no means been reflected in any kind of similar restraint on the Soviet side. So I think unilateral disarmament is unworkable. Our allies would also be affected if we should unilaterally decide to dispense with these weapons. Such a decision would be interpreted by many other nations and by our potential adversaries as a clear weakening of American will and a weakening of American ability to retaliate, to handle this balance of terror that has lasted so long.

This does not mean that we have to have absolute equality in every one of these weapons. I think "How much is enough?" is a legitimate question. The technicians call this "sufficiency," as compared to superiority or even equality. If you have enough to deter the other side, then it clearly does not matter if he has twice as much, because there is no real utility in the extra amount. There are ways in which one can design strategic forces so that one has enough to deter the other side, without feeling that one has to have exactly the same number and the same types of weapons.

Negotiations as a Solution

If these three propositions are accurate, that nuclear weapons are unusable, that the race is unwinnable, and that unilateral restraints are unworkable, what then is the answer? Must we continue to build these things and risk their use? There is an answer; the answer is negotiation, negotiation with the other side. It is not an easy answer, but it is an answer. In the period after World War I, the world was horrified by the results of the use of poison gas in that war. It was not a very effective weapon and the damage it did to people was horrible. In the late twenties, the nations of the world met and wrote a treaty [the Geneva Protocol of 1925—Eds.] pledging that they would never again use poison gas in warfare.

That particular treaty was flawed because it was not really enforceable; it was only a pledge.[1] But the interesting fact is that a world war took place about twelve years later and poison gas was not used.[2] It was not used partly because it is not very effective, which I think makes the analogy applicable to nuclear weapons. It was not used partly because it was horrifying, and it was not used partly because the other side would have retaliated in kind. I wish I could say that the treaty has worked since it was signed; however, there is some evidence that the Soviets may have been using poison gas in Afghanistan and Laos. Nonetheless, I think the approach of proscribing weapons systems is a feasible one, if the content of the negotiations can ensure that the treaty is enforceable.

We have tried this with nuclear weapons. In 1946 the United States, through Bernard Baruch, came up with an imaginative proposal for dealing with these terrible new nuclear weapons that had been demonstrated in Japan. The United States proposed that it, as the only nation in the world to hold these weapons, would destroy them, would release the secrets, and would no longer keep the advantage in nuclear weapons, if all nations in the world would pledge not to build them in the future, not to have the weapon at all. That was a very imaginative, very wise proposal. If it had worked, we would not have the approximately 50,000 nuclear warheads we have in the world today. But it did not work.

The proposal said that if the United States were to restrain ourselves, we would have to make sure that the other nations of the world restrained themselves as well. Therefore, we insisted that those nations, in signing this proposed treaty under the Baruch Plan, agree to inspections to ensure that they were not secretly building these bombs in some dark corner of their land. Joseph Stalin said that would be a form of espionage by the West into the internal affairs of the Soviet Union; he rejected the idea. As a result, we were unable to continue to develop that particular proposal, and both the Soviet Union and the United States began to build the weapons. Gradually other powers built them too—the Chinese, the British, the French, and the Indians. [The surmised nuclear powers also include South Africa and Israel, and evidently Pakistan is a near-nuclear country.—Eds.]

But the fact is, there have been successes in negotiations on nuclear weapons. In 1972 we signed the SALT agreement, and one of the provisions of that agreement was that neither side would develop a nationwide antiballistic missile system that would protect it from the other side's missiles while its weapons continued to threaten the other side. The United States and the Soviet Union agreed to leave their countries undefended against these weapons, so that the threat of mutual retaliation would ensure that they would not be used. The United States was able to make that agreement because we knew we would be able to tell whether the Soviets were violating it, by our satellite photography, by our electronic surveillance, by all the devices the intelligence community has developed over the years. We could monitor and actually verify whether the Soviets were complying with the treaty. In the years since, we have not developed a nationwide antiballistic missile system, and we are absolutely certain that the Soviets have not done so either. U.S. taxpayers have saved something in the realm of fifty to a hundred billion dollars that would have been spent on such a system, a system that would not have benefited our security, because the Soviets would have built an equivalent one and we would have had exactly the same balance of terror we have today. That is the lesson of these kinds of agreements.

Mutuality

There are two key words in a nuclear freeze proposal: they are "mutual" and "verifiable." Those two words are absolutely essential to any kind of arms control agreement. First, any treaty must be mutual, it must apply, and it must be beneficial to both sides, because it will not be signed if it is not. Clearly, we have concerns about the Soviet Union and they have concerns about us. We are concerned about some of their "monster" missiles—very much in excess of any that we have, very much in excess of anything we thought was necessary, but nonetheless built by the Soviets and now posing a major threat of extensive damage to the United States because of their huge size. We are concerned about improvements made in the accuracy of Soviet missiles, their ability to target and drop on a precise location after a 10,000-mile flight from the Soviet Union. We are concerned that they may be accurate enough to land right on the top of one of the silos containing our missiles. In theory, a mad Soviet president could launch a flight of missiles at the United States, not aimed at our cities but aimed at our missiles, and destroy all of our land-based missiles. Our president, in that half hour in which he had to decide what to do, would know that if he sent any missiles back to the Soviet Union, the Soviets would have an ample supply of additional ones to focus at our cities, and that if he did not respond he would be subject to Soviet control and blackmail. This is the so-called first-strike scenario, in which our land-based missiles are disarmed and we are left only with the weapons of city destruction, the submarines and the bombers.

I have strong doubts about this scenario. We have never seen a test of that many missiles launched at once, and we know how complex a procedure it is to get more than a few up at the same moment. We know the problems: that they will run into each other when they land and blow each other up, rather than landing where they are sent. So far all of the tests have been done horizontally, across the world; there never have been any tests across the top of the earth. There would be dangers in the targeting and consequent inaccuracies. But Soviet missile accuracy is a real concern of the United States. Combined with the monster missiles, the first-strike scenario is a contingency that a sensible United States president must consider.

We are also concerned about the Soviet conventional buildup. The Soviet army has grown and has modernized its equipment. A Soviet navy that used to be a small coastal defense force around the edges of the Soviet Union now is a blue-ocean navy. We are concerned, too, about a Soviet Union that uses its proxies in Africa and Latin America to avoid direct U.S. confrontation but still extends its influence and power.

The linkage of these kinds of problems concerns us when we face the Soviets. But let us look at this from an intelligence officer's view, from the other side—the Soviets have some concerns too. They are extremely sensitive about their security, with some reason. They have been invaded by Napoleon, by Hitler, by the Allies in 1918 to put down the revolution, and in 1854, during the Crimean War. They know the hostility toward their revolution; they think that they are still trying to carry out that revolution, and they are concerned about the possibility of an attack upon them. They are concerned that superior U.S. technology will lead to a breakthrough in a new area of weaponry that will leave them subordinate. Our landing on the moon convinced them that the United States really is a sleeping giant that can rise and make huge progress in technology, once stirred to do so. The Soviets are concerned about the fact that the Americans have allies who also have nuclear weapons—the French and the British. They are concerned about the Chinese and their nuclear weapons. The Soviets feel that they must be concerned about the possibility that nuclear weapons other than those possessed by the United States could be used against them—it is not enough to make an agreement with the Americans. And they are particularly concerned, and have said they are concerned, about a new U.S. weapon that is being deployed in Europe and elsewhere, the so-called cruise missile.[3] The cruise missile can operate at a minimum height, travel 5,000 or more miles, and find, by following the terrain from a map reading on its computer, the exact target it was aimed at over that huge distance. It would be difficult to tell whether such a missile were carrying a nuclear weapon or a conventional weapon, which leads to enormous problems in working out treaties.

So the Soviets have concerns. The point of a mutual agreement must be that we recognize their concerns and they recognize ours. Although this recognition is sometimes difficult in the negotiations, it is essential. Unilateral restraint on our side will not work, and unilateral imposition on them will not work. Therefore, the advantage has to be to both sides. There are real advantages to both sides in security, in savings of resources, and in the reputation of the leaders of the two countries. I think Mr. Brezhnev, at a late point in his life, when he had not much longer to live [Leonid I. Brezhnev died on 10 November 1982—Eds.], looked back at his accomplishments in SALT I and his accomplishments in negotiating the other SALT II restraints (which apparently will not be ratified by the United States) with some pride. We are not sure whether his successors will take the same point of view.

Verification

The other key word in the freeze resolution is "verifiable." The problem of verification is frequently used to indicate that we cannot reach an agreement, as it was used with regard to the Baruch Plan in 1946. But I think it is overly used as a tool to torpedo an agreement that somebody does not want for other reasons. If one stands back from the details of verification—from whether one can see the difference between a nuclear-tipped cruise missile and a conventionally tipped cruise missile—I think that one can make another judgment about verifiability. That judgment has to start from the fact that our intelligence services will cover Soviet weaponry whether there is an agreement or not, because we have to. We have to know what kinds of weapons and forces the Soviets dispose of in order to protect our country, so our intelligence services are not going to be doing anything different, whether there is an agreement or not. We are going to be finding out, with every means we can, exactly the sort of weaponry, the exact sort of forces that they have. We can see from the published records of our listings of Soviet forces that we do not do badly at that; even on particular items that we cannot count precisely, we can make a sensible estimate of how many nuclear weapons the Soviets have. Soviet artillery certainly can be hidden in garages and barns, and yet we have a sensible estimate of the number of pieces of Soviet artillery in Eastern Europe. Similarly, if tanks are not all out in the open, we can still build up a reasonable estimate of Soviet tanks.

The key to the question of verifiability is that this process of learning about Soviet forces is easier with an agreement than without it. An agreement will contain certain features that will facilitate intelligence gathering. The SALT I and the SALT II treaties, for example, called for both sides to stop concealing their weapons. Does that mean they would never try? No, it does not. But when we have seen certain concealments we have demanded that they be removed, and they were removed. The SALT treaties provide for certain measures enabling us to make inquiries. There are cooperative measures incorporated in some of these treaties, including even the on-site inspections that Stalin rejected, which appear in the Peaceful Nuclear Explosions Treaty that we negotiated but have not ratified. The Soviets have indicated they may accept some varieties of on-site inspection. [Including inspection of the controversial Krasnoyarsk radars alleged to constitute an ABM Treaty violation—Eds.] There are also electronic and other sensors that can be placed in key spots to give us a direct report of important information. For example, a cruise missile with a nuclear tip could have a certain device on it that would be visible from the outside, whereas conventionally armed cruise missiles would not carry the device.

The Soviets can cheat on a treaty, but they cannot cheat very effectively for very long. If they try, they will be caught. The key is to set up a method of communication to discuss suspicions that something is wrong. Either side can demand that the matter be investigated and can demand to be reassured that there is no cheating. If we question the Soviets today about some new weapons system of which there is nothing mentioned in our treaties, they will tell us that it is none of our business. But if we go to them and ask about something that is covered under a treaty, it is up to them to satisfy us that our suspicions are unfounded.

In the history of SALT I there have been a number of these incidents. Once we saw some covers being put over missile silos in Siberia and we asked about them. The Soviets said, "We're doing a little construction work there, and it's cold up there in the winter, so we had to put those covers on." We replied, "The rule says no concealment; take them off," and they took them off. The Soviets added, incidentally, "There are some covers on some of your silos." We said, "Well, we're doing a little work on them, and it's pretty cold up there." "Take them off." They came off. That kind of communication cannot exist in the absence of a treaty, and it can apply to a variety of weapons systems.

Let us admit, however, that the Soviets could cheat on a treaty. Could they do so on a scale that would be significant? If they are limited to a thousand weapons and they produce three more, that is not significant to the protection of our country. If, however, the Soviets develop a hundred or two hundred additional weapons, I think the quality of our surveillance coverage is such that we would detect it, and be warned of the growth of any strategic threat. We are not in a law court; we are interested in protecting our country. And protecting our country involves reducing the threat through agreement, as well as catching every last violation on their side.

There is one more dimension, although I do not think we can rely on it totally. If the Soviets should develop a large-scale cheating scenario in total secrecy underneath some mountain in the Urals in violation of the treaty, a Soviet citizen might come to us and tell us about it. The Soviets have to consider that possibility, because that is exactly what happened during 1961-62, when Colonel Oleg V. Penkovski became appalled at the leadership that Nikita S. Khruschchev and his co-workers were providing to the Soviet Union and the threat the Soviet Union was creating to the world's safety. Penkovski contacted British and U.S. intelligence, to warn us and to give us some confidential politico-military information. Although I do not think we can count on every colonel doing this, I think the Soviets would have to include defection among their concerns if they tried to mount a cheating operation large enough to be effective.

A Mutual, Verifiable Nuclear Freeze and Reductions

I believe a freeze resolution can be both mutual and verifiable. It cannot be automatically verifiable, but we can include the kinds of provisions that will make it verifiable.

Public pressure has shown itself to be effective in this area; the freeze movement already has had an impact on arms control. The movement, I think, is largely responsible for the character of President Reagan's proposal in the Strategic Arms Reduction Talks (START), which began formally in June 1982.[4] This proposal would make substantial reductions in the warheads of both sides, and would reduce the number of land-based weapons. The European antinuclear movement was certainly directly responsible for President Reagan's proposal of the so-called Zero Option. This option proposed that, if the Soviets would remove their missiles (the SS-20s, the SS-4s, and SS-5s) from Eastern Europe, we would not produce the new cruise missiles and the new Pershing IIs for Western Europe; we would both do away with that kind of a force.

That proposal contradicted the president's initial belief that we had to build up our forces to negotiate; and it led him to take a position that the United States would be willing to negotiate so we would not have to build our forces. I, for one, think the latter is the correct approach.

I think we are in a situation in which the good sense of the American people can be brought to bear on this subject, reducing the influence of the nuclear priesthood. It requires work of those who would be involved—studying these weapons, their characteristics, and the counts, in order to make sensible suggestions and to support sensible approaches. An intellectual approach is necessary because emotional approaches—being horrified and not wanting to have anything to do with nuclear weapons—are not going to work. The progress that we have seen already offers hope for the future.

A few years ago, some of the great powers, particularly the United States, were talking about nonproliferation, the idea that these terrible nuclear weapons should not be given to any other countries beyond the two superpowers. The late Indira Gandhi had a rather interesting reaction to that. She said, "You know, I really don't accept that you two superpowers can give me lectures about not developing nuclear weapons when you can't get your own race of thousands of these under control." [India detonated its first nuclear device in 1974—Eds.] I think that a forward movement by us toward a mutual and verifiable freeze, and mutual and verifiable reduction, is the way to lead this world away from the terrible nuclear danger. The freeze is a way to stop further development while we work on the reductions. It is well known that you cannot put a car into reverse directly without stopping it. I think it is important to stop the nuclear buildup so that we can reduce it and reverse it. The freeze is something that can apply mutually, will benefit both the United States and the Soviet Union, and is verifiable.

To paraphrase what Georges Clemenceau once said about war, nuclear war is not only too important to be left to the generals, it is too important to be left to the priesthood and to our governments. It requires the full involvement of all of our citizens in support of a movement in the right direction to limit and eventually to eliminate this threat to us all.

Editors' Notes

1. A No-First-Use pledge.
2. Although they are not numerous and thus do not detract from Mr. Colby's argument, allegations that the United States, Japan, and the Soviet Union used chemical

agents in World War II have appeared sporadically, as have reports of biological warfare and germ experimentation by the Japanese in Manchuria in 1943-44. (See Hersh [1969]; and Powell [1981].) For a Soviet source see the summary of the trial of twelve Japanese servicemen on biological weapons charges (*Materials on the Trial of Former Service Men of the Japanese Army Charged with Manufacturing and Employing Biological Weapons* [1950]. Moscow: Foreign Languages Publications.).

3. Deployment in Europe of 464 U.S. GLCMs (ground-launched cruise missiles) and 108 Pershing IIs pursuant to the NATO two-track negotiate-and-deploy decision of 1979 began in the autumn of 1983. Deployment of Soviet SS-20s, which superceded the SS-4s and SS-5s, began in 1976-77 and seemed to have been almost completed by 1979. Though not first-strike weapons in some views, the Pershing and the cruise missiles have a circular error probable (CEP) of 40-50 meters. These new U.S. weapons in Europe reduce Soviet warning time to approximately five to ten minutes, compared to the half-hour expected warning time in the event of a large, fixed-site ICBM attack. Responding to place the United States "in an analogous position," the Soviet Union reports that it has deployed cruise missiles on submarines off the eastern coast of the United States, producing a comparably reduced warning time in the United States. Further reductions in warning time could be achieved by means of depressed-trajectory SLBM launching by either side.

4. START talks began formally in June 1982, with Ambassador Edward Rowney representing the United States.

Editors' References

Arms Control and Disarmament Agency (1982). *Arms Control and Disarmament Agreements: Texts and Histories of Negotiations.* Washington D.C.: U.S. Government Printing Office.
Brown, Harold (1967). *Report of Secretary of Defense Harold Brown to the Congress on the Fiscal Year 1982 Budget, Fiscal Year 1983 Authorization Request and Fiscal Years 1982-1986 Defense Programs.* Washington D.C.: U.S. Government Printing Office, 19 January.
Burt, Richard (1982). *Arms Control and Defense Postures in the 1980s.* Boulder CO: Westview Press.
Hersh, Seymour M. (1969). *Chemical and Biological Warfare: America's Hidden Arsenal.* Garden City NY: Anchor Doubleday.
Lambeth, Benjamin (1978). *The Political Potential of Equivalence: The View from Moscow and Europe.* P-6167. Santa Monica CA: RAND.
―――― (1980). "Soviet Strategic Conduct and the Prospects for Stability." RAND R-2579-AF. Santa Monica CA: RAND.
―――― (1982). *Trends in Soviet Military Policy.* P-6819. Santa Monica CA: RAND.
Panofsky, Wolfgang K. H. (1971). "Roots of the Strategic Arms Race: Ambiguity and Ignorance," *Bulletin of the Atomic Scientists* 27:15-20. June.
Powell, J. W. (1981). "A Hidden Chapter in History," *Bulletin of the Atomic Scientists* 37:8:44-52. October.
Russett, Bruce M. (1983). *The Prisoners of Insecurity: Nuclear Deterrence, the Arms Race and Arms Control.* San Francisco: W. H. Freeman.
Sigal, Leon V. (1984). *Nuclear Forces in Europe: Enduring Dilemmas, Present Prospects.* Washington D.C.: Brookings.

Stockholm International Peace Research Institute (1977). *Strategic Disarmament, Verification and National Security.* London: Taylor and Francis Ltd., and New York: Crane Russak and Co., Inc.

Frank von Hippel

2

PERSPECTIVES ON LIMITED NUCLEAR WAR

Frank von Hippel, a theoretical physicist, is a professor of public and international affairs at Princeton University and an affiliated faculty member at the Princeton University Center for Energy and Environmental Studies. During the past ten years, his research has focused on the technical basis for energy and nuclear weapons policy alternatives. Dr. von Hippel publishes widely in professional journals on the topic of the nuclear arms race. He is a member of the board of directors of the World Resources Institute and has served on the Three Mile Island Public Health Fund Advisory Board.

In this chapter, Dr. von Hippel clarifies some of the jargon used to discuss nuclear war and presents calculations showing that the ICBM window of vulnerability is fictitious. He documents repeated threats of use of nuclear weapons in U.S. post–World War II foreign policy. Some of these threats were made in response to events that are now regarded as less significant or even, as he suggests, relatively trivial. This history of U.S. threats of first use of nuclear weapons and other considerations leads Dr. von Hippel to argue that superpower nuclear war, if it happened, probably would not be meaningfully limited. However, even if it were limited, its consequences would be likely to be more severe than is generally appreciated. Thus, the political objectives of any such war, especially in Europe, could be achieved more cheaply and effectively through negotiations.

Nuclear Threats

Since the end of World War II, the United States has used threats of the first use of nuclear weapons as the ultimate backup to the defense of its vital interests around the world. During the period of U.S. nuclear superiority, which ended in the mid-1960s, the United States used such threats relatively frequently. For example, President Eisenhower threatened to use nuclear weapons if the Chinese and the North Koreans did not agree to an armistice in the Korean War (Eisenhower, 1963:180), and President Kennedy made more veiled threats about the possibility that the 1961 Berlin crisis might lead to nuclear war (Kennedy, 1961:533-540). The United States even used nuclear threats in fairly trivial crises, for example, during the Quemoy/Matsu crisis of 1958. In this case, General Chiang Kai-shek of Taiwan stationed approximately a third of his army on two small islands off the coast of mainland China. When the mainland Chinese responded by bombarding the islands with artillery, the Eisenhower administration threatened to use nuclear weapons against the PRC if the bombardment did not stop (Halperin). The fact that since World War II the United States always considered the threat of nuclear attack usable as the ultimate "big stick" may be one of the reasons why U.S. foreign policy has not always been thought through very carefully.

A classic case of the brain-numbing effect of the availability of nuclear weapons is recounted by Theodore Sorensen, a close advisor to President Kennedy, in his book *Kennedy*. Just as Kennedy took office, a crisis occurred in Laos, originating in a struggle for power involving three factions. One of these factions was backed by the Central Intelligence Agency (CIA), one by the U.S. Department of State, and one by the Soviet Union. When the Communist faction appeared to have its competitors in full retreat, the U.S. Joint Chiefs of Staff wanted to send in the Marines, and a crisis arose.

> President Kennedy was reluctant to commit troops, his administration recently having surmounted the Bay of Pigs crisis, an embarrassingly unsuccessful invasion of Cuba that had been organized by the CIA. He therefore asked each member of the Chiefs of Staff to give him in writing his detailed views on where our intervention would lead, who would join us, how would we react to a massive Red Chinese response, and where it would all end (Sorenson, 1965:644).

Sorensen reports that, when the requested assessments came in:

> The majority appeared to favor the landing of American troops in Thailand, South Vietnam, and the government-held portions of the Laotian panhandle. If that did not produce a cease-fire, they recommended an air attack on the Pathet Lao [Communist] positions and [use of] tactical nuclear weapons on the ground. If North Vietnamese and Chinese then moved in, their homelands would be bombed. If massive Red troops were then mobilized, nuclear bombings would be threatened and if necessary then carried out. If the Soviets then intervened we should "be prepared to accept the possibility of general war." But the Soviet Union,

> they assured the President, "can hardly wish to see an uncontrollable situation develop." At least that was their judgment, and the President had relied on their judgment at the Bay of Pigs (Sorenson, 1965:645).

Kennedy did not take the advice of the Joint Chiefs in this instance. Instead, he asked the Russians, in effect, whether they cared about Laos. They expressed indifference, and Kennedy proposed a coalition government for Laos. After various further maneuvers, during which Kennedy made clear that he would not accept a Communist military takeover without U.S. intervention, a coalition government was in fact established (Sorensen, 1965:645-648).

Despite the Joint Chiefs' willingness in 1961 to invoke the danger of nuclear war, much had transpired since the days of U.S. nuclear superiority when, for example, Vice President Nixon had been able to tell the *New York Times* (in 1954):

> Rather than let the Communists nibble us to death all over the world in little wars we would rely in the future primarily on our massive mobile retaliatory power which we could use in our discretion against the major source of aggression at times and places that we choose (Freedman, 1983:86).

The Kennedy administration marks the beginning of the period of the "balance of terror," when the United States was no longer immune from the threat of nuclear retaliation. After this, threats of nuclear war took on more the flavor of a game of Chicken.

> "Chicken" is played by two drivers on a road with a white line down the middle. Both cars straddle the white line and drive toward each other at top speed. The first driver to lose his nerve and swerve into his own lane is a "chicken"—an object of contempt and scorn—and he loses the game. The game is played among teenagers for prestige, for girls, for leadership of a gang, and for safety, (i.e., to prevent other challenges and confrontations) . . .
>
> Some teenagers utilize interesting tactics in playing "chicken." The "skillful" player may get into the car quite drunk, throwing whiskey bottles out of the window to make it clear to everybody just how drunk he is. He wears very dark glasses so that it is obvious that he cannot see much, if anything. As soon as the car reaches high speed, he takes the steering wheel and throws it out of the window. If his opponent is watching, he has won. If his opponent is not watching, then he has a problem; likewise if both players utilize this strategy (Kahn, 1965: 10-11).

Limited Nuclear Attack

The above passage from Herman Kahn's 1965 book, *On Escalation*, would be funnier if it did not describe so accurately the basic assumption that underlies U.S. nuclear strategy. The presumption is that threats and even limited nuclear attacks might be effective because the other side might not be willing to escalate to the next step toward a nuclear holocaust. In effect, U.S. policy is based on the hope that the other side may be less crazy than the United States is.

Kahn's 1965 book describes a 44-rung "escalation ladder," with nuclear use first beginning at rung 15, Barely Nuclear War. The idea of a formal escalation ladder is the reductio ad absurdum of nuclear strategy. Nevertheless, it has provided a framework for debates about limited nuclear war ever since. In a world in which each superpower has on the order of ten thousand nuclear warheads mounted on long-range delivery vehicles and a similar number mounted on shorter-range systems, Kahn's successors— those whom Fred Kaplan has called the "wizards of Armaggedon"—have plenty of material with which to dream up scenarios for limited nuclear war (Kaplan, 1983).

But could nuclear war be limited once the threshold had been crossed? Those who think that "credible" nuclear threats are essential to keep the Soviets in check tend to answer this question with a qualified "yes," while those who fear that the most likely outcome of the nuclear arms race is "a nuclear war no one wants" tend to be more pessimistic.

The pessimists point to the absence of any agreed-upon firebreak between different levels of nuclear use after the threshold between conventional and nuclear weapons use has been crossed. They also dwell on the reciprocal pressures in a crisis for preemptive attack and for using before losing vulnerable nuclear weapons. The optimists think that the prospect of the catastrophic consequences of all-out nuclear war would have a sobering effect on nuclear decision makers even in the midst of limited nuclear war.

Recently, however, as the U.S. government has begun thinking through more seriously how a limited nuclear war could be conducted, some technical problems have received more attention. Most prominent among these is the problem of command and control of nuclear weapons after the nuclear explosions have begun. There are far fewer nuclear command headquarters to be destroyed than nuclear delivery vehicle sites. Their communication links are necessarily relatively "soft" and in many cases can be incapacitated by area effects such as the electromagnetic pulse (EMP). As a result of this vulnerability, it has been argued that the use it or lose it pressures would be much greater for a command and control system than for the nuclear weapons themselves. John Steinbruner, an expert on command and control, has concluded, for example that

> once the use of as many as ten or more nuclear weapons directed against the USSR is seriously contemplated, U.S. strategic commanders will likely insist on attacking a full array of Soviet targets. Political motives for engaging in limited strategic attacks will not likely prevail against the risks of leaving a vulnerable command system exposed to counterattack from a severely provoked enemy (Steinbruner, 1981: 22-23).

The Reagan administration has requested twenty billion dollars to improve our nuclear command and control system, but experts in the field estimate that even that amount would at most increase the endurance of our command control system by a few hours (Zraket, 1981).

Steinbruner said that the Soviets would be "severely provoked" if the United States exploded ten nuclear warheads over their country. No doubt the United States would be similarly provoked by a Soviet nuclear strike. This does not rule out the use of nuclear weapons outside the superpower territories, however, and, in fact, most scenarios of limited nuclear war begin with the use of nuclear weapons in a theater outside of the territory of the superpowers. Probably ninety percent of such scenarios involve the first use of nuclear weapons in the Germanies, to stop a Soviet invasion of Western Europe.

Of course, from the German point of view, the idea that the United States and the Soviet Union might organize a nuclear war that would be limited to the Germanies has not been very appealing. Indeed, the primary argument made by the West German government in favor of the cruise missiles and Pershing II missiles currently deployed in Western Europe rests on the fact that the missiles could reach the Soviet Union. According to the establishment view in West Germany, this fact increases the probability that an invasion of West Germany would escalate into an all-out nuclear war between the United States and the Soviet Union and, by reinforcing that deterrence coupling, decreases the likelihood of the invasion (Kaiser, 1982).

Unlimited Nuclear War

Considering the large, although controversial, probability that nuclear war between the superpowers could not be limited, it might be useful to insert here a few illustrations of the consequences of an all-out nuclear war. Figure 1 (Casper, 1981, Slide 53) shows the launch of a Titan II missile. This is a rather old missile, but the United States still has about fifty of them. Each carries the largest warhead in the U.S. active nuclear stockpile—a nine-megaton (million-ton) TNT-equivalent monster.

Figure 2 (Glasstone, 1977, Fig 2.18a) shows the fireball from a warhead with a yield of approximately the same megatonnage exploded near the surface. The fireball is about three miles across.

Figure 3 (FEMA, 1979:10-11) shows a map shaded in by the Federal Emergency Management Administration (FEMA) to show how FEMA imagines the Soviet Union might target its warheads in an all-out attack. FEMA believes that the shaded areas would be subject to at least 50 percent or greater probability of receiving blast overpressures of 2 psi (pounds per square inch) or more (FEMA, 1979:iii). In this same scenario, approximately one-half of the households in the entire United States would be subjected to blast overpressures exceeding 5 psi (Haaland, 1976, Fig. 3.2).

Figure 4 (Glasstone, 1977, Figure 5.55 and Figure 5.57) shows before and after pictures of an ordinary wood-frame house that was exposed to a 5 psi blast wave during a nuclear test that took place on the U.S. Atomic Energy Commission's Nevada Test Site during the late 1950s.

Three Levels of Limited Nuclear War

Returning now to limited nuclear war, let us consider its consequences at the three levels that are most frequently discussed in the literature:

1. The intercontinental missile duel;
2. Antitank warfare using battlefield nuclear weapons; and
3. Theater nuclear war using intermediate-range nuclear weapons.

The human consequences of such nuclear exchanges are infrequently discussed in the military literature, but it is essential to understand them in order to decide whether the military value of these nuclear wars could possibly be worth the consequences—even assuming that nuclear wars could be kept limited.

1. The Intercontinental Missile Duel

The hypothesis that intercontinental nuclear missiles could be used to attack each other in a manner analogous to the artillery duels of World War I has most recently been debated in connection with the "window of vulnerability." My own acquaintance with the issue began after the potential for civilian casualties associated with such exchanges became the subject of heated debate as a result of an obscure statement in the Annual Defense Department

Figure 1. Launch of a Titan II missile.

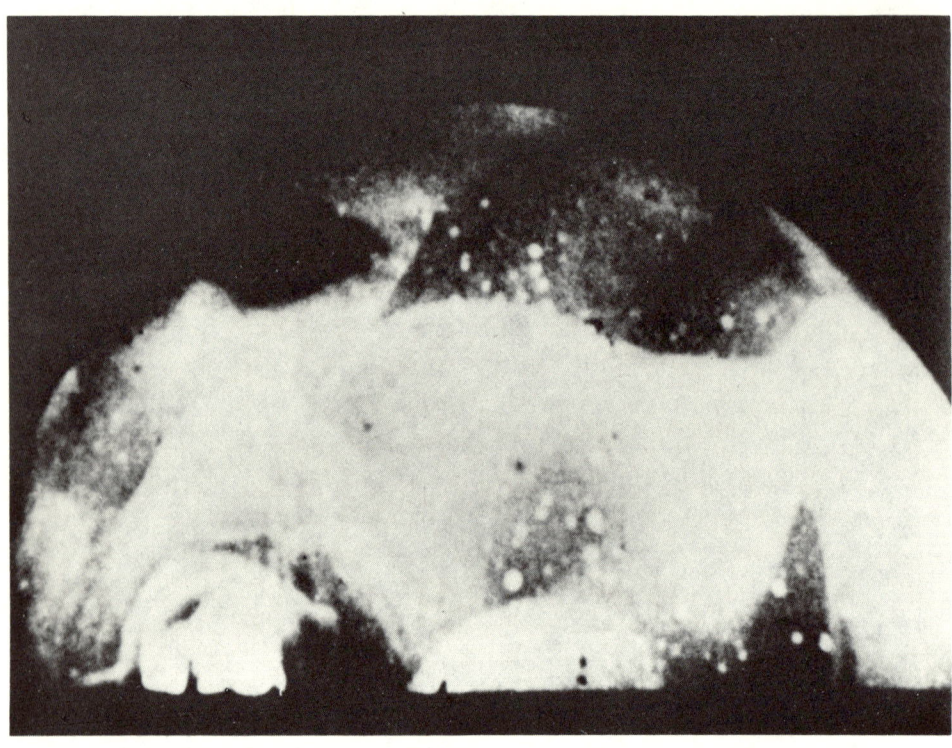

Figure 2. Fireball formed by a nuclear explosion in the megaton energy range near the earth's surface. The maximum diameter of the fireball was 3¼ miles.

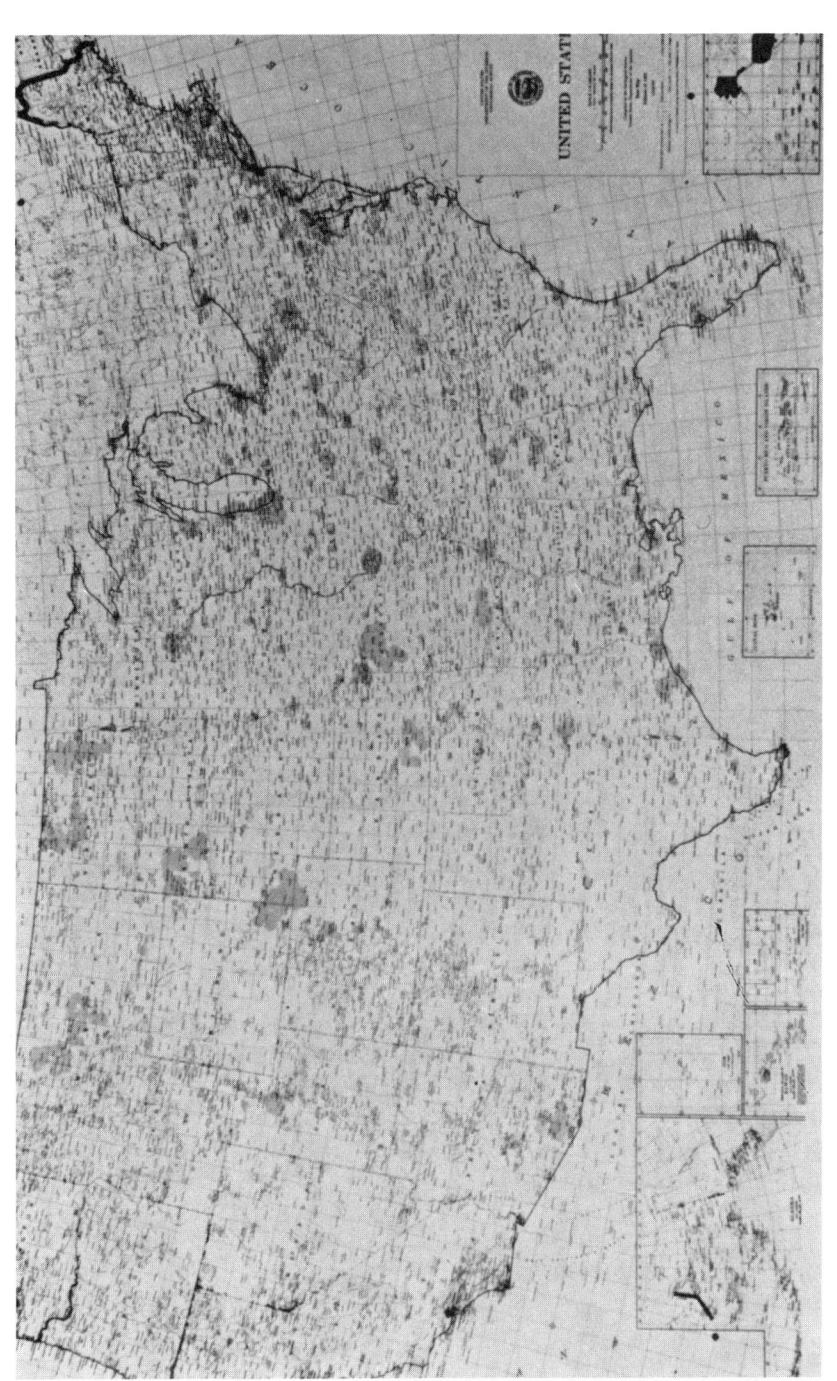

Figure 3. Map shaded in by the Federal Emergency Management Administration (FEMA), showing how FEMA imagines the Soviet Union might target its warheads in an all-out attack on the United States.

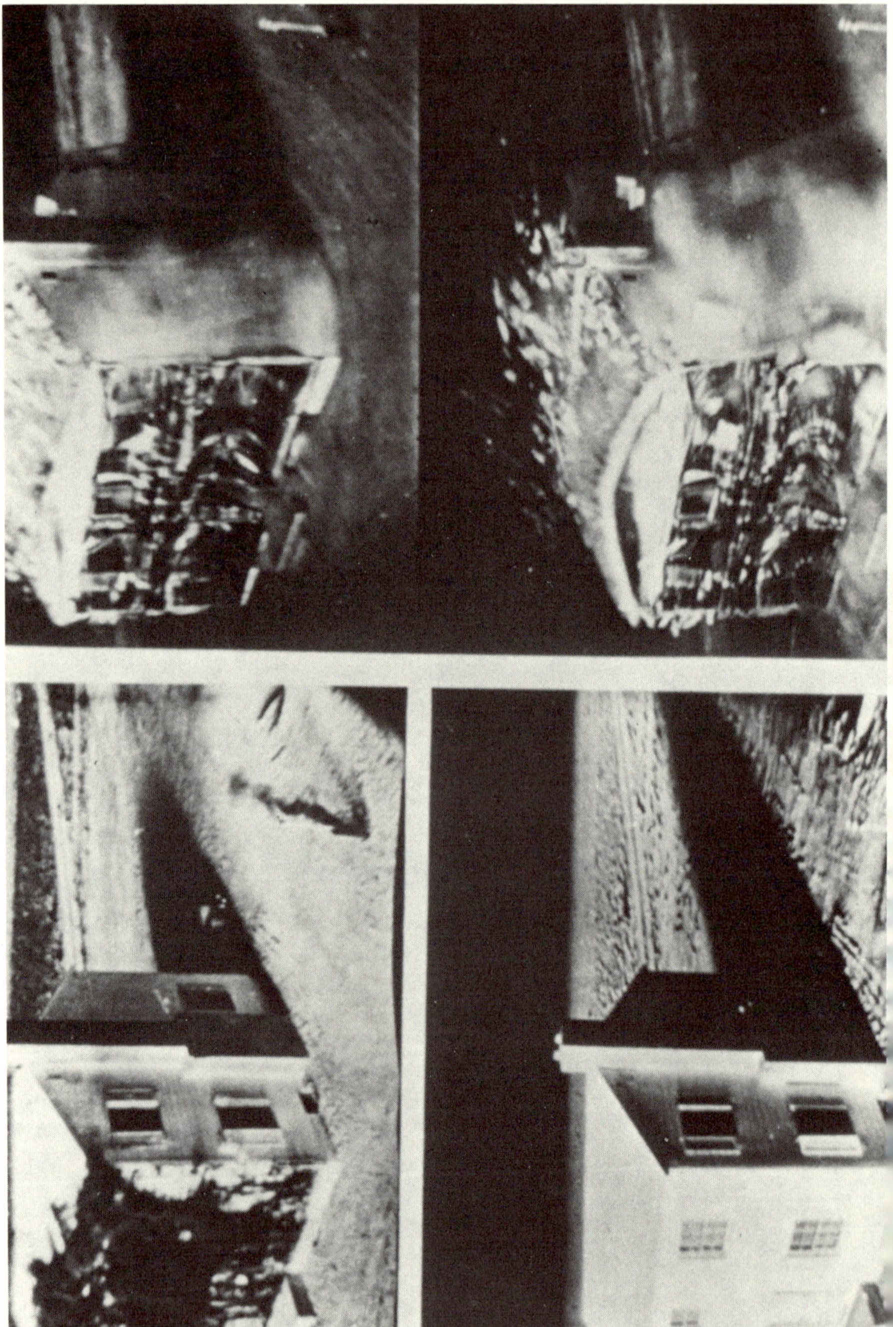

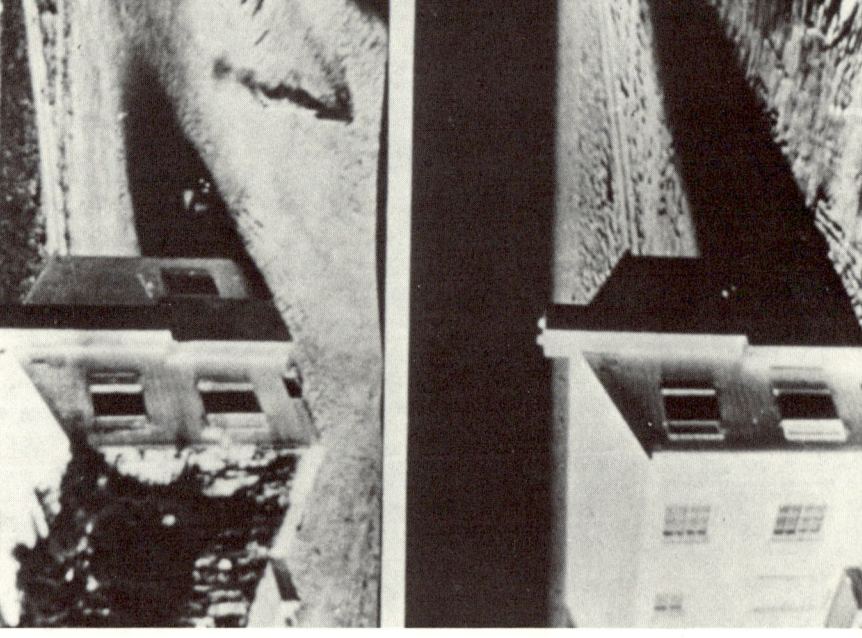

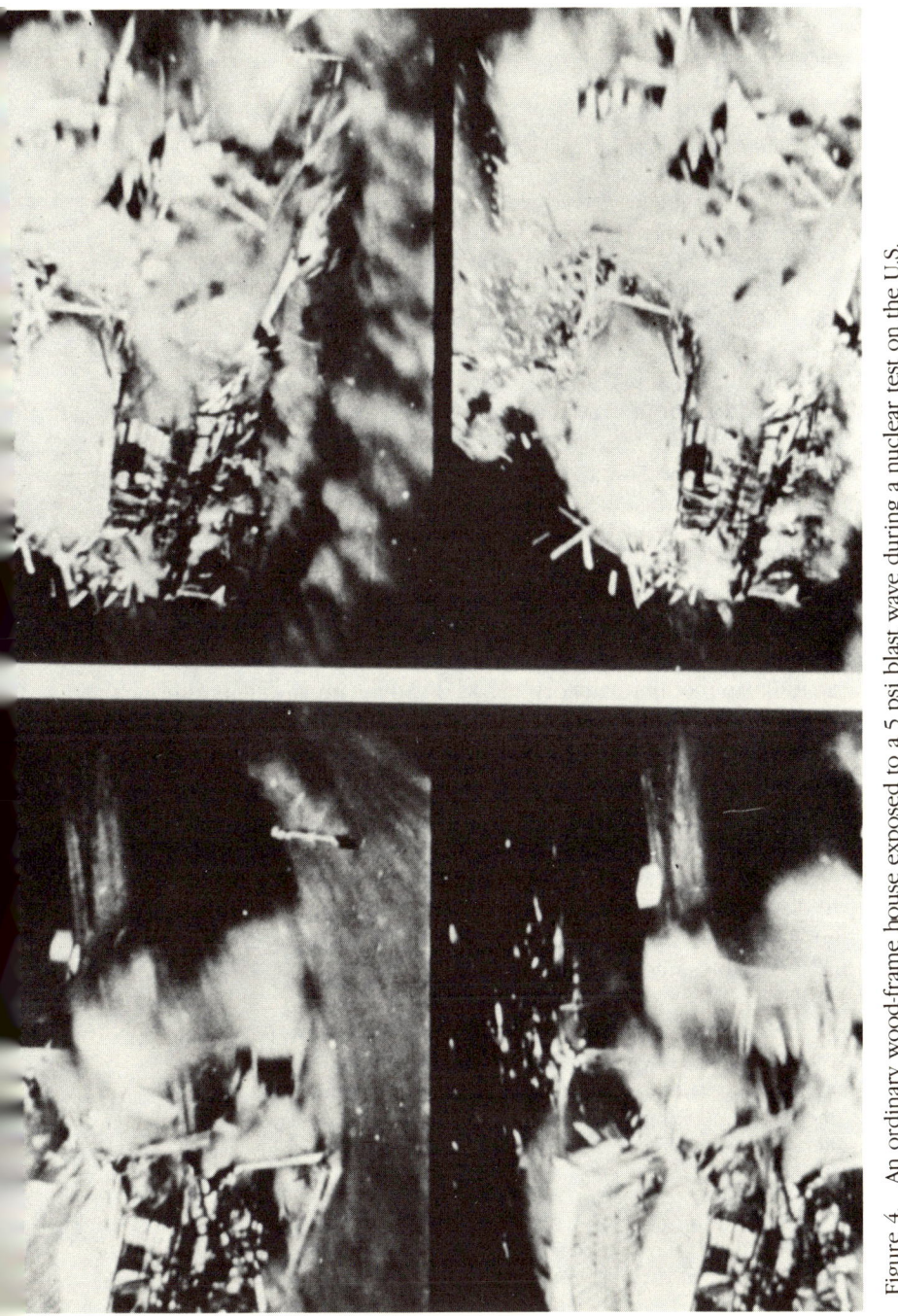

Figure 4. An ordinary wood-frame house exposed to a 5 psi blast wave during a nuclear test on the U.S. Atomic Energy Commission's Nevada Test Site during the late 1950s.

Report for Fiscal Year 1975, issued by James Schlesinger, President Nixon's secretary of defense.

> Since we ourselves find it difficult to believe that we would actually implement the threat of assured destruction in response to a limited attack on military targets that caused relatively few civilian casualties, there can be no certainty that, in a crisis, prospective opponents would be deterred from testing our resolve. Allied concern about the credibility of this particular threat has been evident for more than a decade. In any event, the actuality of such a response would be utter folly except where our own or allied cities were attacked (Schlesinger, 1974:37).

Assured destruction, as used here, means an all-out attack on the social infrastructure of the Soviet Union. Behind the jargon, Schlesinger was, in effect, expressing the concern that the U.S. threat of assured destruction against the Soviet Union might not be an adequate deterrent to Soviet limited nuclear attacks against the United States, because it would be insane for the United States to attack Soviet cities in response to anything less than a Soviet attack on our own or our friends' cities.

Secretary of Defense Schlesinger was particularly concerned about the emerging Soviet capacity to attack U.S. missile silos. He therefore argued that the most effective deterrent against such attacks would be an improved U.S. capability to mount retaliatory attacks on Soviet missile silos. Although there has always been considerable skepticism in the Congress about this argument, it did not stop Schlesinger from initiating the programs that are now producing a new generation of super-accurate ballistic missiles such as the MX and Pershing II.

An alert Senate staffer noticed Schlesinger's discussion of the thinkability of limited nuclear war. As a result, Secretary of Defense Schlesinger was invited to discuss his ideas in a hearing held by a subcommittee of the Senate Foreign Relations Committee. During the hearing, Senator Stuart Symington asked Schlesinger:

> ... you talk about a "response to a limited attack on military targets that caused relatively few civilian casualties." Do you really believe that such an attack against the United States is possible, and just what do you mean in numbers by "relatively few civilian casualties"? (Senate Foreign Relations Committee, 1974a:19).

Schlesinger responded:

> I think hundreds of thousands of casualties as opposed to tens and hundreds of millions must be regarded as relatively few in number. But I

am talking here about casualties of 15,000, 20,000, 25,000—a horrendous event, as we all recognize, but one far better than the alternative (ibid).

After the hearing, the secretary was asked to return to provide Department of Defense (DOD) estimates of U.S. casualties that would result from a full spectrum of Soviet limited attacks against the United States. When Secretary Schlesinger complied a few months later, the greatest attention was given to an estimate of 800,000 U.S. fatalities resulting from a Soviet first strike against the 1,000 Minutemen silos on the Great Plains (Senate Foreign Relations Committee, 1974b:13). For comparison, the total number of U.S. military deaths during World War II was 292,000.

Even these revised estimates turned out to be too low, however. When, at the insistence of Senator Clifford Case of New Jersey, the Congressional Office of Technology Assessment (OTA) set up a panel to review the DOD casualty calculations, the panel questioned a number of the assumptions on which the calculations had been based. In particular, the panel challenged the DOD assumptions that:

1. All the Soviet warheads would be exploded in the air over the missile silos. This would result in reduced levels of radioactive fallout downwind, but it also would result in much less confidence in silo destruction—presumably the purpose of the attack; and
2. Everybody in the fallout zones would find the best available shelter against radiation levels and would stay in those shelters as long as necessary.

When the DOD analysts replaced these assumptions with less optimistic ones, their fatality estimates rose into the millions (Senate Foreign Relations Committee, 1975:19).

Of course, it would not make sense to attack U.S. missile silos without attacking, at the same time, the U.S. nuclear bomber bases at which about one-half of our ballistic missile submarines may ordinarily be found, and the command and communications systems that control U.S. nuclear forces. Many of these facilities are located near heavily populated areas. As a result, the number of casualties caused by a first strike against U.S. strategic nuclear forces would probably number in the tens of millions—on the order of one hundred times U.S. losses in World War II. [See also the discussion of longer-term indirect effects due to the associated destruction of economic and environmental support systems (Katz, 1982; Peterson, 1983; Turco, 1983).]

Nevertheless, the planning for missile duels continues. Recently, Richard

DeLauer, the Reagan administration's under secretary of defense for research and engineering, expressed the fear that

> increases in nuclear hardness of Soviet ICBM silos and other important facilities have reduced our ability to put those targets at risk. Knowing this, the Soviets felt less constrained from adventurism around the world.... (DeLauer, 1982:39).

DeLauer was arguing for the MX missiles, which will allow the U.S. to threaten a first strike against the Soviet land-based missiles more effectively—and thereby presumably "sober them up" when they start thinking about "adventurism around the world."

Figure 5 (*Aviation Week,* 1979:40,41) shows a practice U.S. strike against three imaginary missile silos. Figure 5a shows the launching of two Minuteman III missiles from test silos at Vandenberg Air Force Base, California. Figure 5b is a time exposure photograph of the six warheads from these two missiles, white-hot from air friction, descending on their targets 7,000 miles downrange near Kwajalein Atoll. The warheads are paired up in case one of the missiles should fail or should be inaccurate; one warhead from each of the two missiles has been assigned to each target.

Figure 6 shows three warheads, such as those whose trails appear in Figure 5b, at rest inside the nose cone of a Minuteman III (Caspar, 1981, Slide 55). The warheads are about five feet tall and two feet in diameter at the base (Cochran, 1983:75). Depending upon whether they are Mark 12 or Mark 12A versions, each of these warheads has a yield of about 170 or 335 kilotons. (The yield of the Hiroshima bomb was approximately 15 kilotons.) The warheads are conical to allow them to come down through the atmosphere at many times the speed of sound. This design makes them more difficult to intercept and less affected by unpredictable winds. The object on which the warheads are mounted is called a bus. It contains a small rocket motor and a number of small jets. The bus can put each warhead on a distinct ballistic trajectory toward targets more than one hundred miles apart. This capability explains why the warheads are called Multiple Independently Targeted Reentry Vehicles or MIRVs.

Figure 7 (Senate Foreign Relations Committee, 1975:51 and Drell, 1976) shows why the number of fatalities expected following an attack on U.S. missile silos is so large. The locations of the Minuteman missile fields, which contain 150-200 silos each, are shown by full squares. The Titan II fields, with about a dozen missile silos each, are designated by empty squares. As a result of the overlap of the fallout patterns of 300-400 one-megaton warheads, the region of lethality downwind from a Minuteman base can extend one thousand miles. What could be accomplished at such a horrendous cost?

Figure 5a. Practice launch of two Minuteman III missiles from test silos at Vandenberg Air Force Base, California.

Figure 8 (Feiveson, 1983) is based on a figure used by former President Carter's secretary of defense, Harold Brown, to show the developing window of vulnerability of U.S. land-based missiles. Given the projected steady improvement in the accuracy of Soviet missiles, the Soviet Union would in a first strike be able to destroy a larger and larger fraction of our Minuteman missiles. In this figure, the numbers on the vertical axis of the graph, which were deleted in the published version for security reasons, have been restored using simple calculations based on leaked values of estimated Soviet missile accuracies published in *Aviation Week* and *Space Technology*.

Although Figure 8 makes the window of vulnerability look rather serious, Figure 9 (Fieveson, 1983) shows that, when it is put into a larger context, it is not. The basic points shown by Figure 9 are that, one, the warheads on U.S. land-based missiles represent only 25 percent of the U.S. strategic warheads actually deliverable on the Soviet Union [excluding warheads in reserve—Eds.] and two, overall, even after a Soviet (or U.S.) first strike, either country

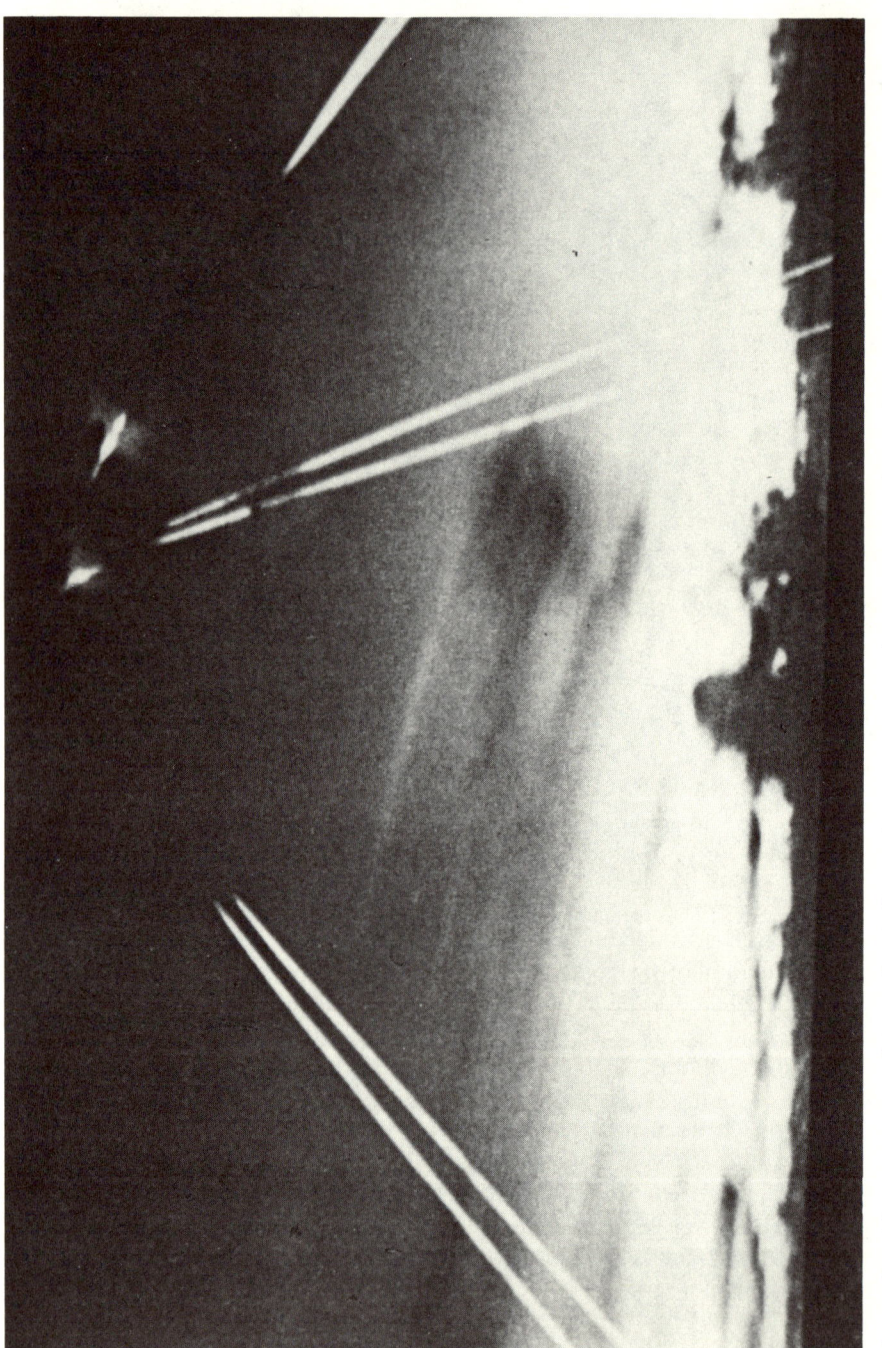

Figure 5b. Time-exposure of six warheads from Minuteman III missiles in Figure 5a descending on their targets near Kwajalein Atoll.

Figure 6. Three warheads at rest inside the nose cone of a Minuteman III missile.

Figure 7. Fallout from an attack on U.S. missile silos.

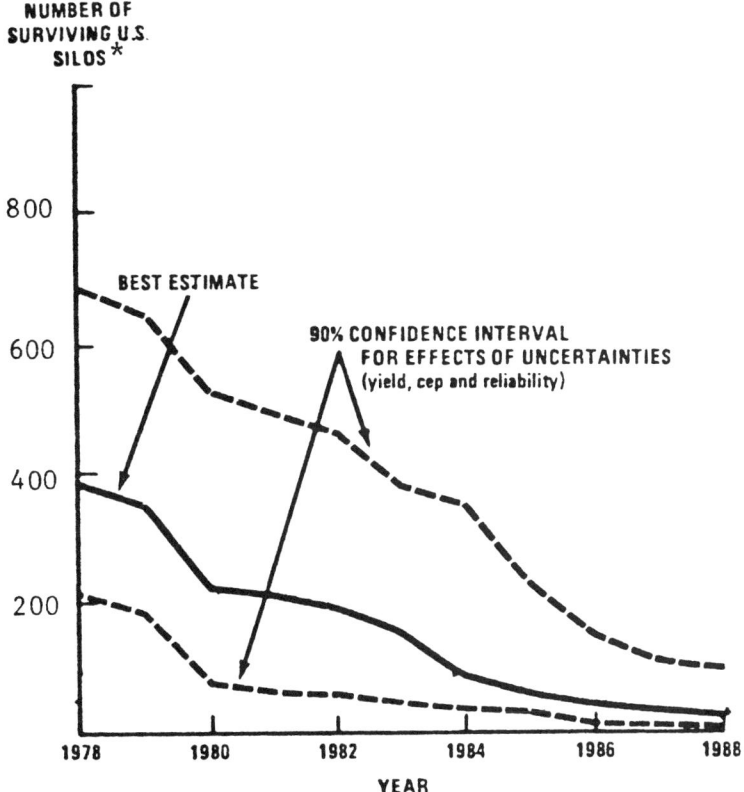

*Numbers suppressed in unclassified original. Our restoration.

Figure 8. The "survivability" of U.S. ICBM silos. (U.S. Department of Defense, 1979)

still would have enough warheads to destroy the other many times over. The results shown in Figure 9 were obtained by my colleague, Harold Fieveson, using assumptions deduced from the results of related calculations made public by the Department of Defense.

The bar charts at the top of Figure 9 show first the approximate number of warheads currently in the superpower arsenals (about 10,000 each) and then estimates of how many would remain, given either a Soviet or U.S. first strike. The bottom row shows the same three situations measured in terms of something called equivalent megatonnage (EMT).[1] This measure makes the Soviets appear marginally superior, as it is believed that on average their warheads are somewhat more powerful than ours.

This exercise shows the futility of either side's mounting a first strike.

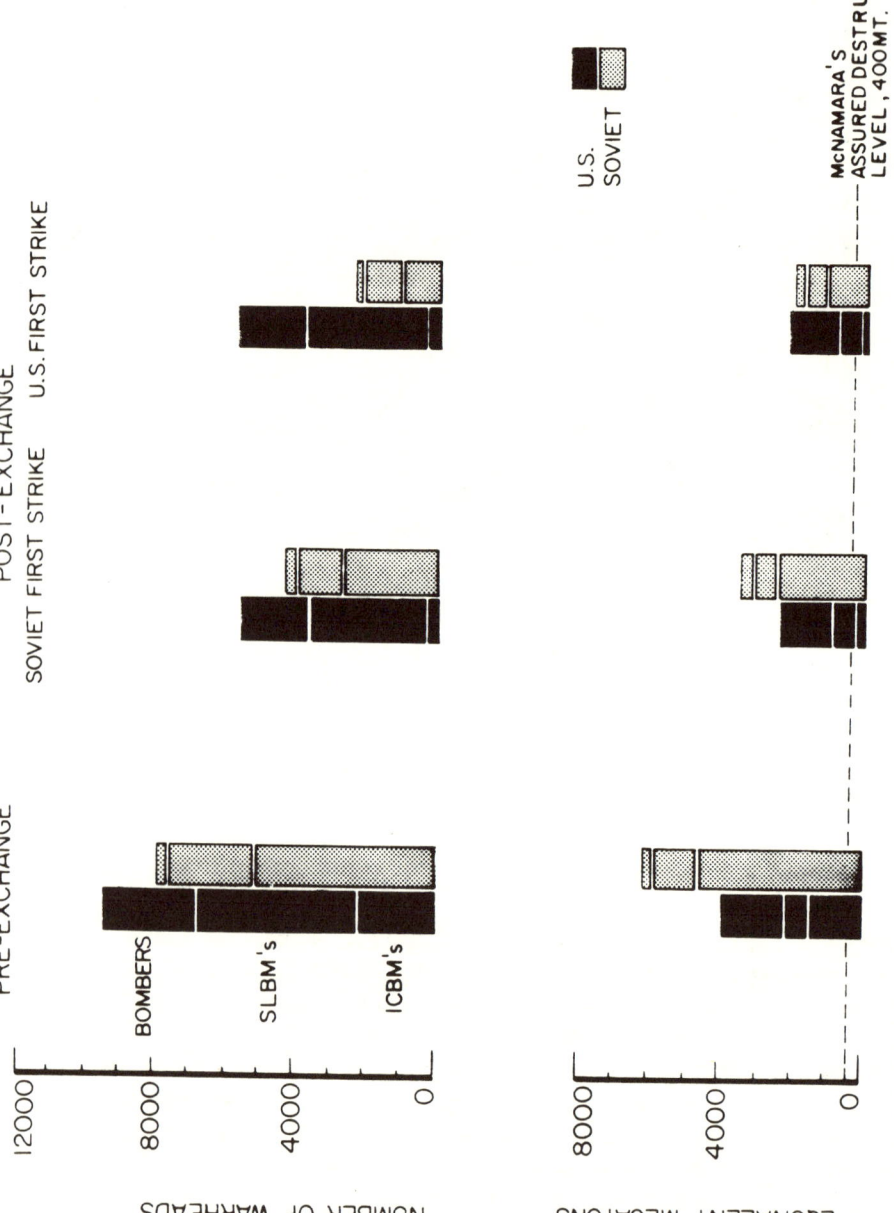

Figure 9. Calculated results of strategic counterforce exchanges, 1982 forces, with both sides on generated alert.

This conclusion can be reached by comparing the heights of the bars in the second row with the height of the line near the bottom. This line corresponds to 200 equivalent megatons—enough, according to calculations published by the DOD in 1968, to destroy 72 percent of Soviet industrial capacity and 52 million of its people (McNamara, 1968:57). What is the point in killing tens of millions of people with a first strike if afterwards your enemy can still destroy you many times over?

2. Antitank Warfare Using Battlefield Nuclear Weapons

The basic rationale given for U.S. threats of first use of nuclear weapons in Europe is the alleged massive Soviet superiority there in conventional forces. These arguments on Soviet superiority are not beyond challenge, however. For example, though it is often pointed out that the Warsaw Pact has twice as many divisions in Central Europe as NATO, it is seldom mentioned that NATO has on average almost twice as many fighting men per division. Furthermore, approximately half of the Warsaw Pact divisions are non-Soviet. It is not clear what weight should be assigned to them [or to the minority nationality groups—Eds.], especially in a prolonged battle. Similarly, though it is often pointed out that the Warsaw Pact has two-and-a-half times more tanks and artillery in Central Europe than NATO has, it is not generally known that when the Department of Defense, in a classified study, added up the total firepower of both sides, it found that they were about equal (Mearsheimer, 1982).

In any case, in the 1950s, the United States began introducing tactical nuclear weapons into Europe. Recently the total number of U.S. tactical nuclear weapons in Europe has been officially given as 5,845 (Halloran, 1983). The Soviet Union likewise has thousands of nuclear weapons for use against Western Europe (Arkin, 1982, Box 2).

Figure 10 (Casper, 1981, Slide 22) shows a nuclear artillery piece being tested in Nevada in 1953. This was an eleven-inch gun, now a museum piece, that fired shells with a yield equal to the Hiroshima bomb. The smaller (six- and eight-inch diameter) varieties of this weapon currently deployed in Europe can fire nuclear warheads with yields up to 12 kilotons (for the eight-inch gun) almost 20 miles (Cochran, 1983:300-310).

Figure 11 (Casper, 1981, Slide 51) shows the Lance battlefield missile. It has a range of seventy-five miles and it can carry warheads with yields up to about 100 kilotons (Cochran, 1983:72-73, 284-286). It would presumably be used to strike second-echelon Warsaw Pact divisions.

In order to reduce collateral (i.e., unintended) damage to the cities, towns, and villages that dot the European battlefield, the United States has

Figure 10. Test of a nuclear artillery piece in Nevada in 1953. The gun fired shells with a yield equal to the Hiroshima bomb.

Figure 11. Lance battlefield missile. It has a range of 75 miles and can carry warheads with yields of up to 100 kilotons.

developed low yield (1,000-ton TNT-equivalent) nuclear weapons that emit large amounts of lethal radiation (enhanced radiation warheads or devices). Figure 12 shows the areas subjected to various effects from such a neutron warhead exploded at an altitude of about 0.5 kilometers. The innermost dark circle, which has an area of about a square mile, is the area of desired military effect. According to the 1976 edition of the *U.S. Army Field Manual*, in this area it is believed that soldiers would receive a dose of radiation sufficient to make them only "partially effective... due to vomiting, diarrhea, and other radiation symptoms" during the period of hours to days before they died (U.S. Army, 1976:22). The largest circle in Figure 12 shows the area of about two square miles over which the radiation dose would cause death from radiation illness within a somewhat longer period—about two months.

The average population density in the Germanies is about a thousand people per two square miles—about the same as New Jersey—while, on average, one would expect to catch no more than a few tanks in the central area shown in Figure 12. Since there would be tens of thousands of tanks and other armored vehicles involved in a full-scale war in the Germanies, the use of neutron bombs against a significant fraction of them could therefore result in millions of collateral deaths. Fortunately, it appears possible to destroy tanks with conventional precision-guided munitions (PGMs) with much less collateral damage than this (Zimmerman, 1984).

3. Theatre Nuclear War Using Intermediate-Range Nuclear Weapons

Should nuclear war appear imminent in Central Europe, it is likely that attempts would be made to destroy the nuclear weapons before they could be used. The expectation that this would happen would tend to be self-fulfilling, because both sides would be placed into a use-it-or-lose-it situation. And, when the decision was made to proceed, the other side's nuclear weapons would be the highest-priority targets.

Figure 13 (Arkin, 1982) shows the locations of most of these targets in the two Germanies. The "As" denote airfields, the "Ms" denote the sites for battlefield missiles such as the Lance, and the "Ss" denote nuclear weapons storage depots. The circles indicate the approximate sizes of the areas of destruction by blast and heat (about fifty square miles each) associated with the 200-kiloton airbursts. Two hundred kilotons is a mid-range value for the yield of the intermediate-range warheads that would probably be used against such targets.

Figure 14 shows the population density distribution of the Germanies. If Figures 13 and 14 are superimposed, it becomes apparent that many of the

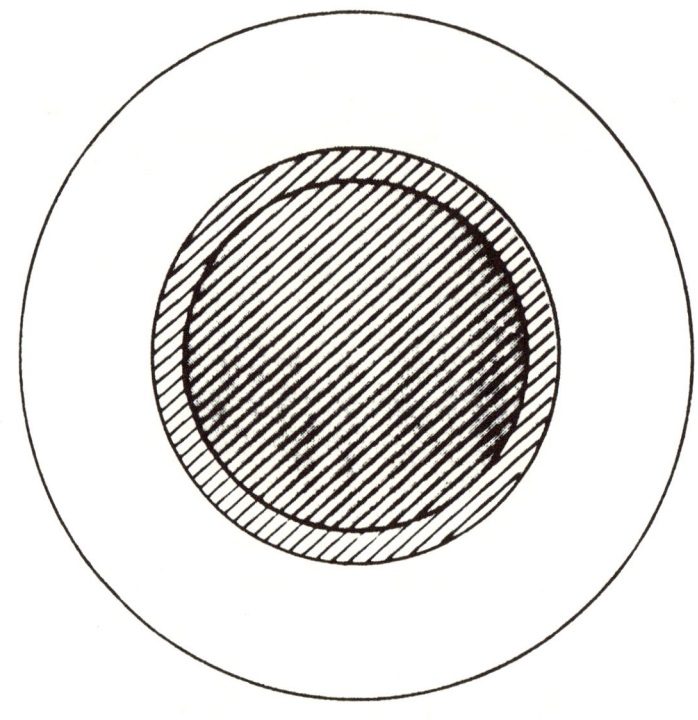

450 METER ALTITUDE BURST

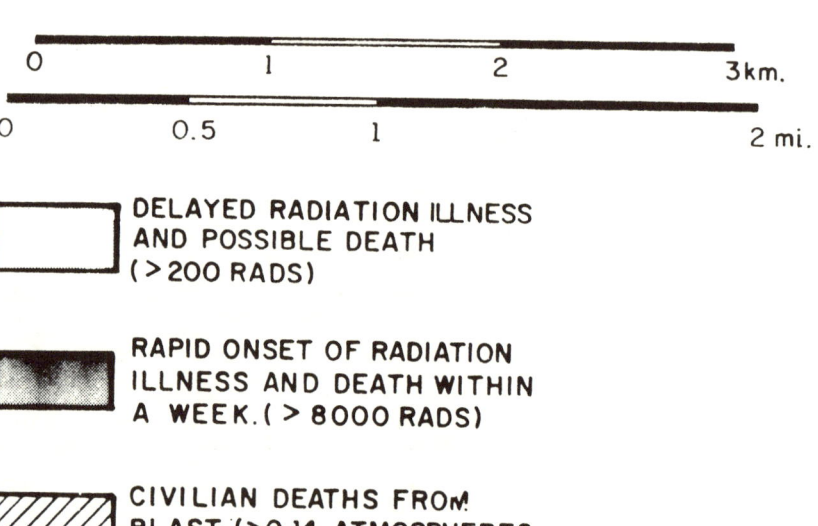

Figure 12. Effects of a 1-kiloton neutron warhead.

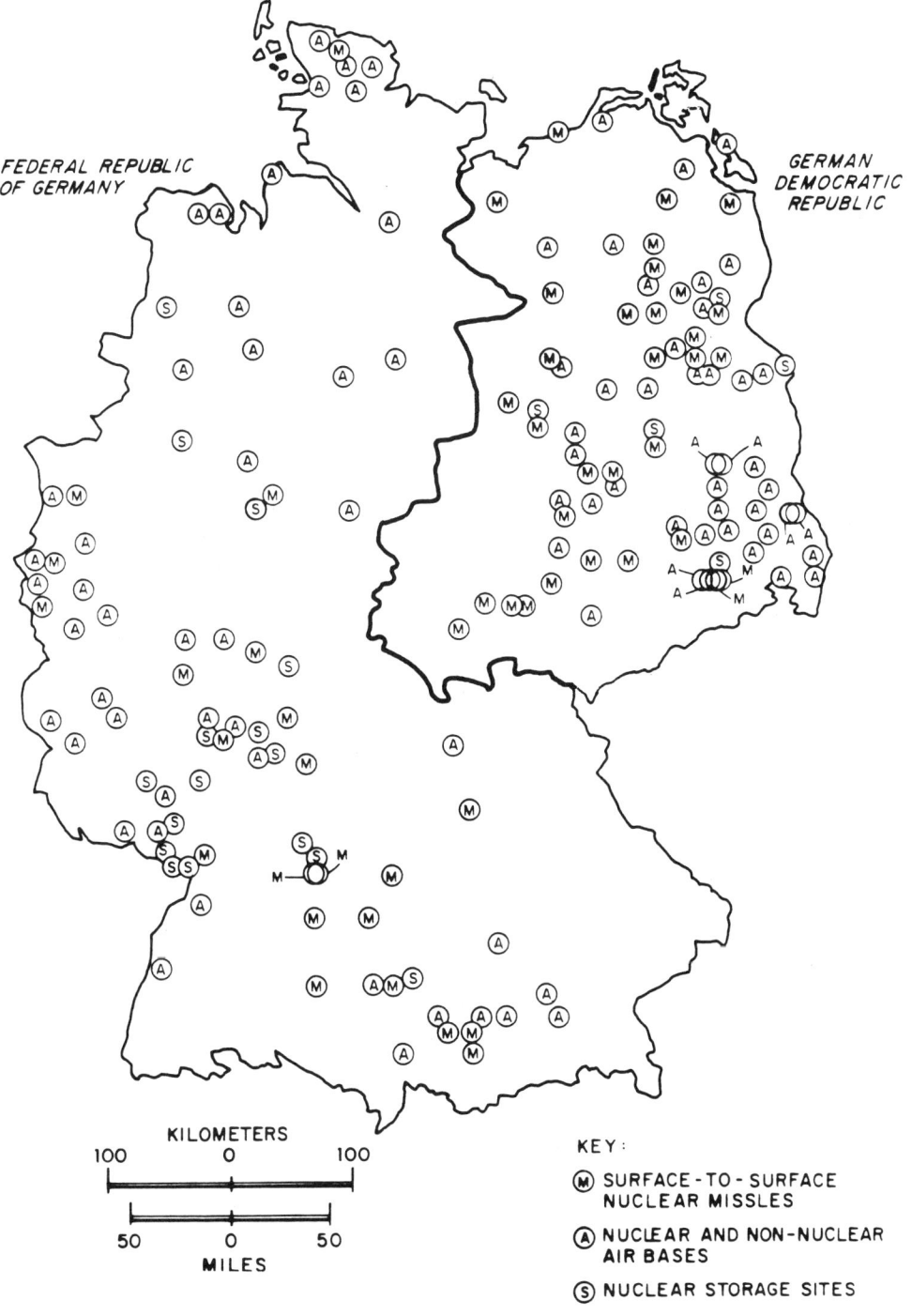

Figure 13. Targets of preemptive attacks.

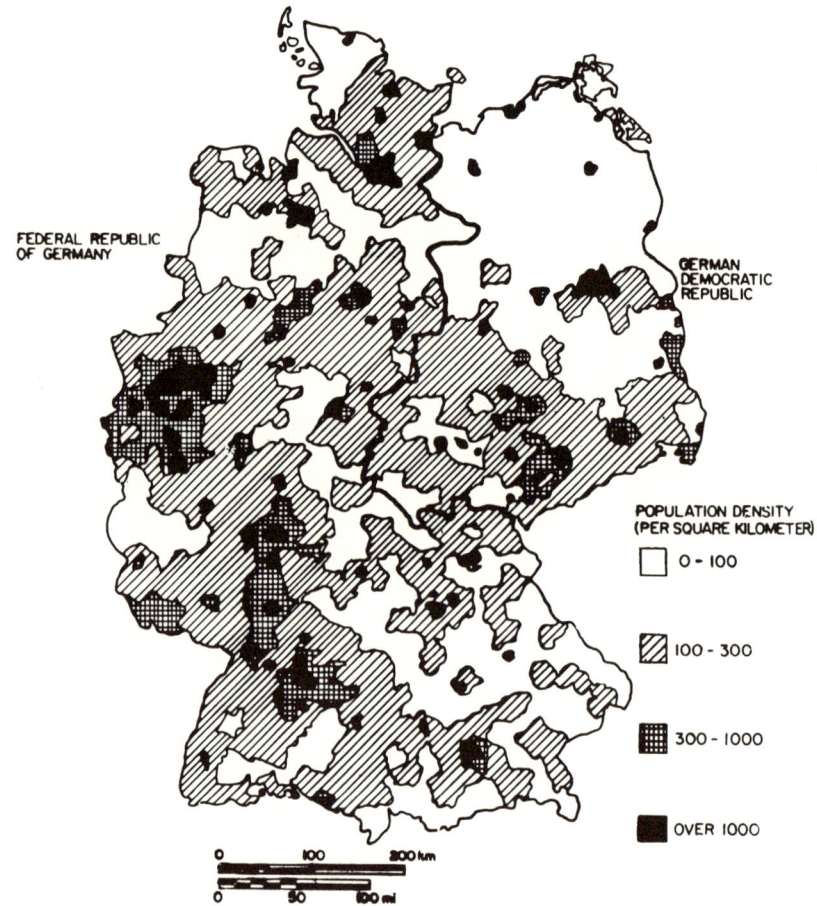

Figure 14. Population density map of East and West Germany.

nuclear targets are in densely populated areas.

Figure 15 shows a typical pattern of areas of lethal fallout that would result if the nuclear explosions occurred at ground level. Depending upon the assumptions used, two to ten million fatalities would result from these attacks, involving only a few hundred out of the thousands of nuclear warheads targeted on Europe (Arkin, 1982). Once again, all that would be accomplished would be the elimination of some of the excessive numbers of nuclear weapons emplaced there. One would think that it might be preferable to do this by negotiation.

Appendixes

A Thought on the Use of Jargon

In the professional literature on nuclear warfare, the accidental destruction of one nuclear warhead by the nearby explosion of another warhead from the same side is described as "fratricide." But if a city is destroyed unintentionally during a nuclear attack on a nearby airfield, that is called "collateral damage." Obviously, language is being used here in a way that desensitizes its users to the real meaning of what they are discussing. This is one reason why the sensitization campaigns that have been undertaken by the Physicians for Social Responsibility and others are so important.

An Analogy for the Balance of Terror

Imagine two superpowers as two men locked in a basement flooded knee-deep with gasoline. Each man tries to intimidate the other by threatening to light the gasoline. But one is slightly more worried than the other because he has only six matches while his adversary has ten.

Editors' Note

1. Equivalent megatonnage (EMT) is a measure of the blast effect of nuclear weapons, and is defined as the two-thirds power of the yield.

Figure 15. Fallout pattern from preemptive nuclear attacks with 200-kiloton groundbursts on 171 military targets in East and West Germany.

References

Arkin, William S., Frank von Hippel, and Barbara G. Levi (1982). "The Consequences of a 'Limited' Nuclear War in East and West Germany," *Ambio* 11:2-3:163 and "Addendum," *Ambio* 12:1:57.
Casper, Barry M. (undated). Nuclear War Graphics Package. Northfield MN: Federation of American Scientists, Nuclear War Education Project.
Cochran, Thomas B., William M. Arkin, and Milton M. Hoenig (1983). *Nuclear Weapons Databook*, Vol. I: *U.S. Nuclear Forces and Capabilities*. Cambridge MA: Ballinger.
DeLauer, Richard (1982). *Astronautics and Aeronautics* May:39.
Drell, Sidney D., and Frank von Hippel (1976). "Limited Nuclear War," *Scientific American* November:27
Eisenhower, Dwight D. (1963). *Mandate for Change*. Garden City NJ: Doubleday.
Feiveson, Harold, and Frank von Hippel (1983). "The Freeze and the Counterforce Race," *Physics Today* January:36.
FEMA (1979). *High Risk Areas for Civil Nuclear Defense Planning Purposes*. Washington DC: Federal Emergency Management Administration, Report TR-82.
Freedman, Lawrence (1983). *The Evolution of Nuclear Strategy*. New York: St. Martins.
Glasstone, Samuel, and Philip J. Dolan, eds. (1977). *The Effects of Nuclear Weapons*, 3rd edition. Washington DC: U.S. Departments of Defense and Energy.
Haaland, Carsten M., Conrad V. Chester, and Eugene P. Wigner (1976). *Survival of the Relocated Population of the U.S. After a Nuclear Attack*. Oak Ridge TN: Oak Ridge National Laboratory, Report No. ORNL-5041.
Halloran, Richard (1983). "Report to Congress Provides Figures for Nuclear Arsenal," *New York Times* 15/11/1983:A15.
Halperin, Morton H. (undated). *The 1958 Taiwan Straits Crisis*, declassified study cited in Daniel Ellsberg undated. Nuclear Armaments. Berkeley CA: The Conservation Press:4.
Kahn, Herman (1965). *On Escalation: Metaphors and Scenarios*. New York: Hudson Institute.
Kaiser, Karl, Georg Lebr, Alois Mertest, and Franz-Joseph Schulze (1982). "Nuclear Weapons and the Preservation of Peace," *Foreign Affairs* Summer:1157.
Kaplan, Fred (1983). *The Wizards of Armageddon*. New York: Simon and Schuster.
Katz, Arthur M. (1982). *Life After Nuclear War: The Economic and Social Impacts of Nuclear Attacks on the United States*. Cambridge MA: Ballinger.
Kennedy, John F. (1961). *Public Papers of the Presidents*. Washington DC: U.S. Government Printing Office.
McNamara, Robert S. (1968). *The Fiscal Year 1969-73 Defense Program and the 1969 Defense Budget*. Washington DC: U.S. Department of Defense.
Mearsheimer, John (1982). "Why the Soviets Can't Win Quickly in Central Europe," *International Security* 7 Summer:3.
Peterson, Jeannie, ed. (1983). *The Aftermath: The Human and Ecological Consequences of Nuclear War*. New York: Pantheon.
Senate Foreign Relations Committee (1974a). *US-USSR Strategic Policies*, sanitized record of a hearing before the Subcommittee on Arms Control, International Law and Organization, March 4, 1974.
——— (1974b). *Briefing on Counterforce Attacks*, sanitized record of a hearing be-

fore the Subcommittee on Arms Control, International Law and Organization, September 11, 1974.

——— (1975). *Analyses of Effects of Limited Nuclear Warfare,* committee print prepared for the Subcommittee on Arms Control, International Organizations and Security Agreements, September 1975.

Sorenson, Theodore C. (1965). *Kennedy.* New York: Harper and Row.

Steinbruner, John D. (1981-82). "Nuclear Decapitation," *Foreign Policy* Winter:16.

Turco, R. P., O. B. Toon, T. P. Ackerman, J. B. Pollack, and Carl Sagan (1983). "Nuclear Winter: Global Consequences of Multiple Nuclear Explosions," *Science* 222:23 December:1283.

U.S. Army (1976). *Field Manual: Operations FM 100-5.* Washington DC: U.S. Government Printing Office.

Zimmerman, Peter (1984). *Princeton Center for Energy and Environmental Studies Report.* Princeton: PCEES.

Zraket, Charles A. (1982). "C3 [Command, Control, and Communications] Systems for the President and Military Commanders," Proceedings of the National Security Issues Symposium: Strategic Nuclear Policies, Weapons and the C3 Connection. Bedford MA: MITRE Corporation, October 13-14, Document M82-30:87.

Richard Garwin

NUCLEAR ARMS FUTURES

Richard Garwin is an IBM fellow and science advisor to the director of research at the Thomas J. Watson Research Center in Yorktown Heights. In addition, he holds appointments as adjunct professor of physics at Columbia University, adjunct research fellow at the Center for Science and International Affairs at Harvard University, and Andrew D. White Professor-at-Large at Cornell. Dr. Garwin has been director of the IBM Watson Laboratory and professor of public policy in the Kennedy School of Government at Harvard. Since 1950 he has worked extensively with the U.S. government on matters of security and arms control, serving on the President's Science Advisory Committee during the Kennedy, Johnson, and Nixon administrations. Dr. Garwin has made substantial research contributions to a variety of problems in physics. He also publishes on nuclear weapons issues and contributes testimony before Congress. In this chapter, his concern is with technical developments in the arms race.

Dr. Garwin begins by advancing some sweeping proposals for arms reductions that would revitalize the bilateral discussions on these issues that had been broken off with the death of detente (1973 and after). These measures are argued to be in the national interest of the United States, and they would also clearly have the secondary effect of greatly improving U.S.–Soviet relations:

1. *Temporarily reduce the numbers of warheads in the U.S. and Soviet arsenals to 1,000 on each side and eventually to much smaller numbers.*

The views expressed in this chapter are those of R. L. Garwin and not necessarily those of IBM or of Columbia University.

2. Ratify a comprehensive test ban treaty and stop modernizing nuclear weapons.
3. Negotiate and ratify an ASAT (anti-satellite war) treaty to halt the militarization of space.
4. Withdraw and recycle U.S. battlefield nuclear weapons.

While reducing its reliance on nuclear weapons in foreign policy through these arms control measures, the United States should, in Dr. Garwin's view, improve its conventional forces.

Dr. Garwin focuses on three prospective applications of technology to the arms race and assesses the feasibility of each:

1. ASW (antisubmarine war) techniques
2. BMD (ballistic missile defense) systems including space-based and ASAT systems.
3. New types of nuclear weapons

The limits of submarine detection are such that submarines not in port are likely to remain essentially invulnerable for some time, auguring for increased deployment of strategic forces at sea. BMD systems are subject to three criticisms, any one of which is sufficient to kill the system: the associated radars are soft targets; optimistic assumptions about system leakage of incoming missiles are unfounded; assumptions that the Soviet Union will not make equal use of space are counterfactual. New types of nuclear weapons, neither atomic nor hydrogen warheads, are not promising and could be easily countered using methods that already exist.

Dr. Garwin concludes that a societal defense against nuclear weapons is technically infeasible, and that technology—especially technology divorced from the task at hand—is not the solution to the problems posed by the arms race. Instead he proposes positive steps in defense management, advanced C^3I (command, control, communications, and intelligence), and arms control.

Elements of an Arms Control Proposal for the 1980s

My view differs from that of the late Herman Kahn. Before I describe an ideal arms control package for strategic forces, I will describe a merely adequate one, which is, even so, too much to wish for (Garwin, 1983[1]). In the near term the United States and the Soviet Union could perfectly well reduce the number of nuclear weapons each country has from approximately 20,000 to base 400 nuclear weapons on small submarines, a few missiles per submarine. Another 400 would be deployed on land-based missiles, but instead of large missiles such as the 100-ton MX that the United States plans to build, with ten warheads per missile, these would be small missiles of only about 10 tons each, carrying one warhead and housed in individual silos, perhaps near the present Minuteman fields. Another 200 could be placed in air-launched cruise missiles of the kind the United States already has, which will no doubt evolve with time. Instead of basing nuclear weapons twenty or thirty to an aircraft, the United States could put two on a smaller aircraft. Then the United States could capitalize on the fact that the cruise missile does most of the job [of traveling long distances and evading air defense—Eds.], so that aircraft carrying nuclear weapons do not have to be designed for penetrating, and the crews do not have to be trained for flying over enemy territory. The superpowers would then have a reduced reliance on nuclear weapons, which is the whole idea.

Nuclear weapons would have one function—retaliation. Their purpose would be to deter Soviet attack on the United States or on the West. In the nuclear realm, that is what I think we should have.

The United States also needs to put more emphasis on command, control, and communications (C^3) of the nuclear force. That must start with the president's knowing more about the effects of nuclear weapons and being in closer contact with the status of missiles—whether they have been launched—knowing that the weapon that gets there first is the weapon smuggled into Washington, not the weapon fired from submarines. We should understand that threats are overemphasized and overdetailed, and that people think too deeply and not sufficiently broadly. That is what we should have: a retaliatory nuclear force with enhanced C^3.

Because nuclear weapons, in my view, have such a limited utility, the United States does not need to continue developing new and better nuclear weapons. The United States particularly does not need several other countries in the world developing their own nuclear weapons. The most effective means to prevent horizontal proliferation is to have a comprehensive nuclear weapons test ban (CTB), prohibiting all nuclear explosions anywhere (Garwin, 1983 [2]).

The United States could also try to avoid some totally unnecessary avenues into world war. One of those ways to war would be to give in to the attractiveness of war in space, asserting that the United States is more advanced than the Soviet Union; in space the United States can destroy Soviet satellites and can put up more effective satellites afterwards. What is wrong with war in space is that the United States and a number of other countries have very valuable civil and military assets there, but no weapons. It should be kept that way. The United States should take advantage of the Soviet draft treaty of August 1981 in the U.N. Committee on Disarmament, (Garwin, 1983 [3]) to negotiate a treaty banning weapons in space and banning the acts of deliberately damaging or destroying satellites. There would be no more testing in space of antisatellite weapons; there would be no antisatellite mines, which will surely be developed if either side deploys laser battle stations. In fact, a ban on weapons in space is my highest priority in arms control.

There is no room in my allotted thousand weapons for battlefield nuclear weapons. One thousand is a great many weapons. When Robert J. McNamara was U.S. secretary of defense, he suggested that 400 weapons would be enough to provide a capacity for assured destruction of the Soviet Union and thereby to deter attack. But weapons are not totally proof against destruction before they are launched, and so one may want to have more. In any case, I do not say that the United States should live forever with a thousand weapons; we can reduce, eventually, far below that.

The United States should, on its own initiative (Garwin, 1980), withdraw and recycle battlefield nuclear weapons. Recycling means converting nuclear weapons into stockpiles for nuclear reactor fuel without necessarily renouncing battlefield nuclear explosions. Battlefield nuclear weapons are a provocation if they are overrun; the field commander will demand the release of those weapons so that he can use them. The United States government would no doubt instruct the field commander that he is only a small part of the overall West, and that it is not in Western interests to grant him the release of those weapons. Field commanders would be very unhappy that they were not supported to the utmost. The United States has its weapons under control secure enough so that they could not be used if the order to use them did not come; however, we do not know whether the same is true of the Warsaw Pact countries, or the French, or the British. If the submarines became vulnerable, and if the ICBM silos—no matter how many there are—could also become vulnerable to attack by acccurate multiple reentry vehicles on the Soviet side, in that instance it may be asked whether the United States should have the ability to launch its missiles under attack before they are destroyed. I do not think the occasion will ever arise, but it will be safer to have this option if the Soviet Union ever demonstrates the capability to destroy submarines, which it is far from doing now. I do not think the Soviet Union will ever be able to do it against a concerted effort on the part of the United States to maintain its submarines invulnerable. The Soviets would still be deterred from attacking if they knew that the missiles could not be destroyed, but only the silos.

In the near term it is harder to obtain all of these new objectives immediately. The United States does not need new systems and should have no programs to build MX missiles or B-1 aircraft or Stealth aircraft. They are unnecessary, and they detract from more urgent defense needs, such as improving the conventional forces and paying the money to reduce the cost of defense.

Recent Developments

The MX

The reason for building the MX was the vulnerability of the Minuteman to the large number of Soviet missile warheads with improving accuracy. Five years of desperate search for MX missile deployment modes has demonstrated that there is no land-basing mode that will provide enduring survival for a large missile. Some of the details of the Dense Pack proposal for close-spaced basing, which the Reagan administration appears to be favoring, will be discussed below.

I believe it was the Carter administration that coined the term "window of vulnerability," probably in response to the argument that even if Minuteman were vulnerable, the remedy for its vulnerability would not come into effect until 1986, 1988, or 1990. There was thus a window of time during which the missiles would be vulnerable. This was not a time of peril; it was just a logical problem. But if it is said that it is terrible to allow Minuteman to become vulnerable, the U.S. Congress's concern will be aroused and it will buy the MX.

Now it is alleged that the United States has vulnerable Minutemen and will have to live with them for ten years. Former U.S. Secretary of Defense Harold Brown addressed this problem before he left office, concluding that Minuteman vulnerability was important only if and when U.S. submarines also became vulnerable. Thus the reason that the United States needed a replacement for the Minuteman was to guard against the eventuality of U.S. submarine vulnerability. It is known that U.S. submarines will be invulnerable through the 1980s, and perhaps through the 1990s as well, but we cannot be absolutely certain. Because the 1990s mark the end of our vision of submarine invulnerability, Secretary Brown felt that the United States needed to begin MX construction as soon as possible. But this position is very distant from the simpler statement that one could not tolerate Minuteman vulnerability.

I am not a fan of technology for its own sake. One should concentrate on the tasks—the things that one wants the armed services to do—and not on the tools. As the MX controversy shows, too much U.S. concentration and too much of the U.S. budget decision making goes into deciding on tools without reference to what they are supposed to accomplish. In 1978, the Department of Defense and the air force sent over to the House Armed Services Committee some support for building the MX missiles—which is the U.S. 100-ton, 10-warhead land-based missile—and supported basing it, at that time, in the deceptive basing trench or racetrack mode. MX basing went through so many cycles that it is difficult to remember exactly which mode was favored at that time. The reason for favoring the trench or racetrack basing mode was that, even though there would be only 200 missiles compared with the 1,000 Minutemen, these 200 missiles could be maintained invulnerable if they were hidden over a large area among 5,000 possible aim points, so that the Soviet Union did not know where they were. The chief of staff of the air force sent over a ten-point set of objectives for the replacement for the Minuteman missile. He thought that the only solution that met these objectives was the basing of MX missiles on land in a multi-protective shelter system. When Sidney Drell of Stanford University and I examined these objectives, we concluded that there is a much better way of fulfilling them, which is to put the MX missile (if one insists on building such a big missile) on small submarines. A large missile does not fit a small submarine the way the United States carries its ballistic missiles now, in vertical launch tubes inside the submarine. However, the missile could be laid down in its capsule in the water alongside the submarine. According to our calculations, two of these missiles, which weigh 175 tons each in their capsules, could be carried on a submarine weighing 500 to 1,000 tons, compared with the 8,000-ton Poseidon submarines, and the 18,000-ton Trident submarines.

Dr. Drell and I found that the small-submarine basing scheme satisfied every one of the ten objectives on the list at least as well as the land-based MX, and most of them better. These objectives included accuracy, controllability, cost, readiness, and especially endurance and survivability. So we proposed the submarine basing system (SUMS) mentioned below, after a good deal of study for the Department of Defense, and SUMS received nothing except scorn. It was scorned by the air force. It was scorned by the Department of Defense without further study. It was scorned by the navy. The navy, of course, did not really want anything to do with solving this air force problem—the Minuteman missile's vulnerability—and to suggest that small submarines might be the way to deploy ballistic missiles at sea would have had an unpredictable but no doubt negative effect on the navy program to build very large submarines, which was the next step in the evolution of the submarine-launched ballistic missile program. Consequently, the air force was quoted as saying that the small submarines would be inaccurate and "vulnerable to atomic tidal waves." The Department of Defense eventually quantified its scorn.

It is very difficult to meet with these people to argue, or to get their arguments in print. The air force, for instance, would never send a representative to appear on a platform with Sidney Drell or with me in Utah or Nevada, but wanted instead to provide a spokesman to come the next day and answer questions. We had to deal with the state governors for a change, because the MX required so much land in the West. General Kelly Burke of the air force had written to Governor Scott M. Matheson of Utah to answer some of the questions the governor had asked him about the MX. Governor Matheson had introduced an innovation in strategic planning. The governor had requested that his questions be answered in a letter, not with briefing charts this time, because he would like to study the response. The response, of course, was published in the *Congressional Record;* thus, there was a chance to analyze the assumptions made by the air force in this case.

Let us examine those air force assumptions. At that time the MX missile was to be deployed in some 5,000 shelters. This was to solve the Minuteman vulnerability problem: build a new missile and put it in a deceptive basing mode. Various people, including Senator Mark Hatfield of Oregon, observed that since the problem was a basing vulnerability and not a deficiency in the missiles themselves, the Minuteman missile could be redeployed into those same shelters. Then how many shelters would be required to provide the same kind of survivability? The air force answered that it would cost more; even though the Minuteman already exists and is smaller than the MX, it would cost about 20 percent more to redeploy them.

To reach this conclusion the air force went through a calculation that was deceptive, although not incorrect. It proceeded as follows:

Compare 200 MX missiles with 2,000 warheads against some Soviet threat that might destroy a certain fraction of the 5,000 shelters and that same fraction of the 200 missiles hidden among the shelters. As an alternative, take 550 Minuteman III missiles that exist in silos in the northern states and put them into a system. They only have 1,650 warheads to begin with, so many more shelters would be needed to guarantee that a smaller fraction of those Minutemen would be destroyed by the Soviet threat.

To make the problem simpler, suppose the requirement was 1,650 surviving warheads. (The MX had 2,000 to begin with; 350 of them could be allowed to be destroyed. This means that about 17 percent could be destroyed by the Soviet threat.) If there were 5,000 shelters, one would assume that the Soviet Union could launch about 1,000 warheads at those 5,000 shelters. To preserve all 1,650 warheads from the total of 1,650 Minuteman warheads originally deployed would take millions of shelters to increase the odds sufficiently. You could not afford to lose even one warhead—that was the deceptive assumption.

A small threat and a small enough number of Minuteman III missiles had been assumed so that the Minuteman option would have cost 20 percent more than the MX and would have required 12,000 shelters instead of 5,000 shelters. The air force never had imagined that instead they could put in more Minuteman III missiles, which are already in inventory, and build substantially fewer shelters. I cannot believe that the United States Air Force has so little imagination. The game was to make this system appear as expensive as possible so that the air force could proceed to build the system that they had planned. This strategy confused the secretary of defense and it confused the president; it confused all of the officials who were supposed to make the decisions. I am grateful for Governor Matheson, who said that, since defense is almost as important as daily business, we should get the terms in writing so that we can look at the contract.

I do not think much of the current foolishness for deploying the MX missile, because of the history of several years' desperate search for a home for the MX missile. Now there is discussion about basing 100 MX missiles in very hard silos. Minuteman silos are reputed to be 2,000 pounds-per-square-inch (psi) hard, which represents an overpressure of 300,000 pounds for every square foot. It is a pretty tough silo. But a nuclear explosion at a distance of 300 meters or approximately 1,000 feet can provide that overpressure. Furthermore, by 1986 or 1988 the Soviets could have much greater accuracy than that. So the new silos are going to be stronger but they will still not be sufficiently strong. They may be 10,000 pounds-per-square-inch hard; they may even be 20,000 psi. But if they are eight times as strong, this would only mean that the Soviets must improve their accuracy by a factor of two. And that they can do.

So there is no hope of making silos survivable by making them hard enough. The report of the President's Commission on Strategic Forces—the Skowcroft Commission—in April 1983 endorsed this view of ICBM invulnerability, although it proposed the deployment of 100 MX missiles in silos!

Silos do, however, become harder than the incoming reentry vehicles that shield the nuclear weapons on their way to their targets. Consequently the air force and the Department of Defense suggest putting the shelters close enough together so that an explosion over one of them will destroy the reentry vehicle that is about to destroy a neighboring silo. Therefore, there will not be a second explosion; and the neighboring silo will be protected. That would, in fact, work if the Soviets did not modify their tactics or their strategic forces. The air force argues that if it cannot be proven that this system will not work in thirty days we must deploy it. But the Soviets will have years to find out how to ensure that it will not work.

There are at least five reasonably easy ways to destroy this system. The easiest way is to attack it in just the way a rival would have attacked the multiple protective shelter system: with reentry vehicles on a mile spacing that would only destroy about 10 percent of the silos at a time. An adversary would have to return after approximately one hour to destroy another 10 percent. The endurance of this basing system would be five to ten hours maximum, without requiring any changes in the Soviet force. To keep the missile from being launched in these ten hours, the adversary would have to explode another warhead above the silo field approximately every minute. Since the deployment area is so small, this other missile for pinning down or for destroying MX missiles that were launched during the period does not have to be very high-yield or accurate.

There are many other ways to attack Dense Pack. It will not work and so it should be dropped; it does not improve the credibility of the U.S. government. There is no reason to build an MX missile irrespective of its basing mode. An MX itself is not so bad. It does not have to have silo-killing capability. But the Reagan administration has already made the firm decision to put the Trident II and the D5 missile into development, which removes the last vestige of necessity or desirability for the MX. There is no sense in developing two brand-new missiles when one will do. The United States does not need the D5 missile either, but that is a separate issue.

Technology in this case really is not a solution [See Spinney, 1984—Eds.]. The philosophical attractiveness of "perfect defense" seems to be overcoming the unfortunate fact that defense good enough to protect society against large numbers of nuclear warheads is a technical infeasibility, given the options available to the offense. The solution, as in many other instances, is lower technology, not high technology.

An Alternative to the MX Basing Mode and Antisubmarine Warfare (ASW)

The Drell-Garwin small submarine system (SUMS) uses diesel-electric submarines. These could be bought off of the production line in West Germany, although it probably does not make sense to buy them from the Federal Republic of Germany, because they would have to be modified by the time the missiles in their capsules are available. But the United States could also build new submarines.

Other technologies that affect submarines and antisubmarine warfare (ASW) influence the basing mode choice. It is perfectly grammatical to say that antisubmarine warfare capability can improve with time. After all, it cannot get worse; in the future we will know everything we know now and more besides. Assuming that antisubmarine capability improves, the submarines can use countermoves. While at sea they can become quieter; noisemakers and decoys can be deployed. (Strategic submarines are always vulnerable in port.) The United States could also attack the adversary's ASW capabilities. There are many options. It has been said that the oceans are becoming transparent; the oceans are not becoming transparent. As a U.S. admiral in charge of submarines remarked recently about the oceans, "The more we learn about them, the more opaque they become." One can see a little farther through the oceans if one uses blue-green light rather than ordinary sunlight, but one still cannot see more than 300 meters. Despite increases in the sensitivity of detectors of the light sources, it is like seeing deeper into the ground with light; more light simply does not help.

However, sound travels through the whole ocean. The United States is learning more all the time about the use of sound for submarine detection. Presumably the Soviet Union is learning more also. Specialists know what can be done with acoustic tracking. The oceans may in some instances prove to be less suitable hiding places for submarines.

Submarine commanders have instruments for locating turbulence, for sensing temperature differences, and for hiding in places in the ocean that are particularly problematical for detection. In the Swedish Archipelago, for instance, it is difficult to detect submarines. Who knows what goes on up there?

The under secretary of defense promised that after he persuaded the air force to reexamine air basing of the MX in large aircraft, he would request that they study this proposed small submarines basing mode. The air force set its own rules in studies of air basing of the MX missile and, as usual, inflated the specifications imposed on an undesired basing system. The air force asserted that the air-based MX had to survive in nuclear war for one or two months. That requirement meant that the airplanes would be launched on warning of attack. They would carry their missiles from the main operating bases. In cases of no attack or of false alarm, they would land again at the main operating bases. But if there were a nuclear attack in which the main bases were destroyed, the planes would land at dispersed bases—thousands of them, which would have to be equipped for refueling and for maintenance. Then, because the maintenance would not be very good after nuclear attack on the United States, the effectiveness of the air-based MX would decline with time. Therefore, the air force would have to make many more of the air-based MX initially. In one way or another the price of this system was inflated to approximately $60 billion. The White House Review Committee, in which I participated, asked the air force why these requirements for 30-60 day survivability were necessary. Suppose instead that the airplanes were to last only about ten hours, or as long as Dense Pack, and suppose that the airplanes did not have refueling capabilities. If there were no nuclear strike, they simply would land on the main operating bases. If there were a nuclear strike, the planes would have to launch their missiles in ten hours or the United States would lose use of them. But the air force found air basing unacceptable because it did not promise enduring survival for the MX missile.

Even the proponents of Dense Pack basing for the MX missiles do not claim that it will survive more than the five or ten hours I have indicated. It is perfectly clear that the Soviets can attack and destroy it, as I have suggested, in that amount of time.

If the question is whether an air-launched MX is more vulnerable than a silo-based MX, it should be remembered that these airplanes are not the 1981 airplanes of the Townes Panel, which would fly all the time and would therefore not depend on warning time for survival. The air-launched MX of 1980 and before sat on airfields and took off when there was warning of submarine-launched ballistic missile attack. The weapons would not be vulnerable after airfield escape or while they were flying. So an airplane that could get off and fly out was needed. Even though the Soviets could barrage the fly-out corridor of the aircraft, and would destroy some fraction of these planes, a sufficient force could be guaranteed if allowances were made for that loss, just as sufficient submarine forces can be guaranteed even assuming that the submarines in port are vulnerable.

If they were both vulnerable and silo-killing, would they not provoke attack? The answer would be affirmative, if they were the only strategic weapons the United States had and if they were genuinely vulnerable. But if they are immersed in a larger strategic force that is not overall vulnerable, such as the U.S. submarines, then empirically we have experience that such weapons do not induce attack. Both of the superpowers have those weapons; their submarines in port are vulnerable.[1]

Imagine a historical period during which both superpowers had only slow-fueling ICBMs that needed liquid oxygen pumped into them, unlike the present ICBMs. In this era it took two hours to fuel an ICBM and one half hour to fly them. If there had been accurate missiles in those days and if the strategic force consisted only of MIRV'd missiles, not bombers, with the same number on each side, then that situation, in which each side could have disarmed the other if it preempted, would have been totally unstable. A rational leader would not even have to wait for a crisis; all he would have to do was to think, "If I go first, I can destroy him now . . . ."

So in the case of MX basing proposals, it is as if there were a tennis tournament in which an unknown, who may not even know how to play tennis, comes in to the finals. His opponent dies laughing, and the one who does not know how to play emerges the victor. The rules should have been the same for Dense Pack as for other proposed basing modes. When the rules were bent to fit Dense Pack, all the other basing systems that had been rejected under the old rules should have been re-evaluated to see how they stood up under the new rules. The air force never did that re-evaluation, although I did receive an apology instead from the under secretary of the Department of Defense. He said that the air force did not know anything about submarines and did not want to learn anything about submarines; the air force could not be made interested in submarines as an option for MX basing.

However, the air force did not know anything about underground silos in the 1950s. Many in the air force fought silos hard—they felt their place was flying in the sky, not lurking in silos in the ground. Now the air force loves silos. Had they tried submarines I think they would have liked them; they even would have found out how to communicate with submarines. As it stands, they do not know that either.

Submarines "listen" very well; they have real-time, continuous communication, radio reception from special low-frequency transmitters in the 10 kilohertz range. If those very vulnerable transmitters are destroyed, the United States has long had aircraft flying continuously that can be sent to communicate through the same low-frequency transmitters. One can communicate with these airplanes through satellites just the way one would "talk" to the missiles on land. They can be talked to by other aircraft. And if those aircraft were destroyed, in one way or another the submarines would sense their destruction. The submarines would then listen to satellites. So submarines can receive orders very well. They cannot talk back very much, but a missile in the field does not have very much to say. A submarine on patrol does not say much either.

For these reasons I see future strategic forces moving largely to sea. That does not mean that the United States has to give up land-based forces. It used to be said (one of the greater sillinesses) that if any part of the strategic force were vulnerable to the extent that there was an unfavorable exchange ratio, that unfavorable exchange ratio would be an irresistible temptation to the Soviet Union to attack. (An unfavorable exchange ratio for the United States would exist if the Soviets could, in an attack, destroy more U.S. warheads than were used in the Soviet onslaught.) The unfavorable exchange ratio argument alleges that Minuteman, when it became vulnerable, created an irresistible temptation to the Soviets and should have been replaced forthwith. Each Minuteman missile, of which the United States has 450 with only one warhead, would require attack by two missiles because of the potential unreliability of the Soviet missiles. So those are not vulnerable. In comparison, the Minuteman III, of which there are 550, has three warheads, but has a low yield and relatively poor accuracy. According to this principle of irresistible temptation, the Soviets would risk the outbreak of nuclear war for the destruction of the Minuteman III's 1,650 warheads by 1,000 high-yield warheads.

If an unfavorable exchange ratio is an irresistible temptation, U.S. submarines are very provocative. About 30 percent of the U.S. submarines are in port at any one time, where they are very vulnerable; they can be rolled over or broken when they are on the surface. Two warheads could destroy two or three submarines full of nuclear weapons. These submarines carry sixteen missiles, with ten warheads per missile on the average, so three submarines would have approximately 500 warheads on board. That target would present an unfavorable exchange ratio, because only two adversary warheads (or even conventional explosives) could destroy 500 of the U.S. warheads. Yet no one had cared to comment that submarines in port are an irresistible temptation to the Soviet Union to attack.

These are examples of arguments that have no validity, but do have currency. They are just like advertising: they are used because they sell, not because they are true.

Prospects for Ballistic Missile Defenses

There are uses for ballistic missile defenses. Hans Bethe and I published an analysis of antiballistic missile (ABM) systems in 1968 in *Scientific American*, which concluded that the Safeguard (ABM/BMD) system for defending the United States would not work.[2] It would not work because a fraction of the available threat directed against the few essential radars, which were soft targets, would destroy those radars. The proposal had been to use that system for defending Minuteman, because Minuteman was assumed vulnerable to missiles that in fact did not at that time have the capability of destroying them. But Safeguard would not work in defending the Minuteman system, even though one could allow some leakage of Soviet reentry vehicles through the system. The vulnerability of the new radar system was just as great. If the Soviet Union wanted to destroy the Minuteman, and had 1,000 or 2,000 warheads to do that, it would take a very small number of warheads directed at the radars. Even if the United States had enough intercepters, eventually a warhead would leak through to destroy the radar and the system would be gone. The vulnerability of radars has always been the problem in ballistic missile defense.

These arguments used to be confined to the government; they never got out to the people. Now it is alleged that if the United States has three layers of defense, and if it is assumed that each layer has 20 percent leakage, then leakage through the second system would be 20 percent of 20 percent, or about 4 percent; leakage through the third layer would be 20 percent of that, or .08 percent. It would be less than 1 percent of the initial numbers of incoming missiles. If the United States could achieve three such layers, each with 20 percent leakage or less, one could create a ballistic missile defense system that would protect the missiles very well, so it is alleged, even against very large forces. (There still remains the question of defending the whole

United States.) One cannot argue with those numbers or that logic except to point out that there is no basis for assuming a 20 percent leakage (20 percent ineffectiveness) instead of an 80 percent leakage. And if leakage is 80 percent, multiplying .8 by .8 by .8 for the layered defense system leaves approximately 50 percent of the reentry vehicles coming through, if the system works at all. So too much is made of assumptions and repetition of assumptions.

One of these proposed ballistic missile defense systems is called High Frontier. It is a re-run of a ballistic missile defense system discussed in the fifties and sixties, in which a large number of satellites would orbit the earth, each carrying many little homing vehicles. There would be detectors to see Soviet missiles in their boost phase, when the rocket engines were still going. If these protective satellites were close enough, they could launch small rockets against the Soviet boosters and destroy them. There is a great deal concealed in those assumptions, however. The existence of an overall system with communication is assumed. It is assumed that, although the Soviet Union cares enough to launch a nuclear strike against the United States, the Soviet Union does not care enough to destroy this defensive system. Yet the defensive system is totally visible in space; it is there for a long time; the Soviet Union can decide when it wants to strike, and will no doubt put small space mines next to each of these weapon-carrying satellites, to detonate those mines at the time it launches its missiles. Thus, unstated for the potential effectiveness of this system is the requirement that the United States convince the Soviets that only the United States can use space; that the Soviet Union cannot get as close to the United States in space as it can on the sea, where the admiralty rules for many centuries have permitted its ships to accompany our ships.

Soviet ships are present in United States naval task forces near United States carriers. At the outbreak of war the Soviets could destroy the United States aircraft carriers. It is all totally legal, all except the [preemptive—Eds.] destruction. So it would be quite new and unprecedented to allege that space is different from the oceans and that the United States plans to own space. I can hardly believe that the Soviets would let the United States do that. War in space will begin the moment the United States makes that proclamation and, incidentally, well before the United States deploys that ballistic missile defense system.

Professor Bethe and I concluded that silos can be defended because there are so very many of them and because it is a matter of indifference whether 30 percent or 70 percent of them are destroyed. The problem with attacking defended silos is that the Soviet Union cannot concentrate all its force on every silo, as it could in destroying a command post (no matter how hard it is), or a few cities. Therefore, not-very-effective defenses—if they are inexpensive and if there are many silos—can defend those silos. But packaging ten warheads on a single missile means that the number of bases is reduced by a factor ten from a situation in which there was one warhead per missile. That is why my future missiles will have one warhead and will be very small.

The Role of Third-Generation Nuclear Weapons in Ballistic Missile Defense (BMD)

Consider third-generation nuclear weapons. Edward Teller for some years has been discussing superweapons—beyond fission weapons, beyond thermonuclear weapons—that somehow will be an antidote to other nuclear weapons and will make us all safe from attack. Because he is expecting this superweapon to be developed, according to Dr. Teller under no circumstances should the United States become party to a comprehensive test ban (CTB), because a CTB will keep the United States from achieving this defense-emphasis strategic posture. Judging from the newspaper coverage, these third-generation nuclear weapons would only work in space. At best (and this is only the beginning of the argument, so do not conclude that I advocate them), they would defend only against ballistic missile attack. They would not defend against cruise missiles, or bombers, or smuggled bombs, or many other threats that could emerge. But these suggested new weapons will not work even in this limited context, in my opinion.

There are, first of all, enormous technical problems in developing nuclear weapons. I cannot present the details of these development problems in print, even as Dr. Teller cannot. I have looked at the new weapons proposals and they are not promising. They would fit into a ballistic missile defense system only by replacing the kill vehicles; they would not replace the sensors; they would need the same kind of communications; they are just as vulnerable or more vulnerable to space mines. If they are deployed permanently in space, if they are launched at the time of detection of a Soviet missile launch, then they will not have line-of-sight communication with the missiles in their boost phase. There are, in short, a great many technical problems with them. Finally, they are too easy to counter, even if technically they would work, and I think there is a great problem as to their technical capability in competition with the ordinary use of nuclear weapons to destroy other targets including offensive missiles.

There are a great variety of threats in society. Any one of us can kill any other of us any day. We really do not worry that the average neighbor who has a capability to destroy us is going to do it; first, because he has no reason and second, because even if he does have some mild justification, there is a deterrent. There is a system of justice. It does not work very well, but it works well enough to counter the small provocation and incentive that people have to damage one another. This does not hold for insane people; it does not hold for professional murderers either.

However, it is true that the capability to destroy does not necessarily instill fear. Now, because there is no world law and there is no punishment from other authorities, the United States must take care of itself or of its allies on the international scene. But the fact that the Soviet Union has for more than twenty years had the ability to destroy the United States has not affected the lives of most United States citizens—even of those of us who work at trying to ensure that the country survives and preserves its way of life. If an argument concentrates only on Soviet capability and does not examine the context, then the only considerations are that the Soviet Union will have to make a decision to use its forces, and it is deterred if and only if the United States is perfectly clear about the damage that will be done to it in return. If every day one emphasizes only that they are able to destroy us, then one may cause some concern.

To my mind that is irresponsible. There is no way to eliminate the Soviet capability to destroy the U.S. government and many of the American people. We live in a real world in which the U.S. deterrent is the ability to damage the Soviet Union in return. However, the United States would want to make sure that its forces are not released by accident and that Soviet forces are not released by accident. The United States would want to ensure that nuclear weapons do not come into action through escalation because nuclear weapons are used in response to some small provocation.

Herman Kahn argued that if the United States were dominant at every level of escalation, the Soviets would not begin the exchange. I had asked Dr. Kahn since 1980 to suppose that the United States were not dominant at a certain level; what then is problematical about relying on the next level as a deterrent, or finally relying on strategic weapons to threaten as much damage to the Soviet Union as they could cause with their short-range weapons? My answer is that nothing is wrong with that, and it provides a clearer means of deterring Soviet attack than to try to match them at every step, as would be done in a strategy of escalation dominance.

I have discussed some of the technologies in space, submarines, antisubmarine war, ballistic missile defenses, new basing modes, and new nuclear weapons. I do not think any of these will save us. We must face the problems of vulnerability and of living with vulnerability. We must decide as people and as a nation which positive steps to take, preferably in cooperation with the other nations of the world and not in competition with them. I do not think there is anything to offer instead of this recognition of vulnerability and of the need to try to deal with it at minimum cost in a way that creates minimum concern, so that we can pay attention to the good things of life instead of to these problems.

Some Positive Steps: Information and Accountability

One has to demand of one's representatives in Congress that they show an understanding of strategic questions and of the cost of strategic programs, and that they can explain why they vote as they do. Usually the response to this demand is that voter ignorance prevents. At a meeting in Los Alamos in the summer of 1980, the chief of staff of the House Science and Technology Committee said that U.S. representatives and senators really do know better than their voting records on defense issues would suggest. They do not vote out of ignorance. Although they know that it does not make any sense to build a B-1 bomber or an MX missile, and that neither program will solve the Minuteman vulnerability problem, their constituents do not know. And their constituents would not "let" them vote the right way.

There is a campaign consideration that holds that doing something is better than just standing there, and so Congress builds missiles, gives jobs, provides continued competence, and increases strength irrespective of how this strength is reflected in improved security. The fact that jobs are not created but are actually taken away by increasing defense outlays is ignored. If the question is analyzed, per defense dollar fewer jobs are generated—if that is what you are interested in—than if that dollar were spent building roads, hospitals, schools, or automobiles. Alternatively, defense money could be saved for people to spend on whatever they want—beer, movies, or travel.

Some years ago I tried to understand why the U.S. Congress was so irresponsible in some cases. It appeared that in representing all the people, the president really had the ability to lead the Congress, but he did not actually do so because the president was too often running for reelection. It would be a much better system if the United States allowed only a single presidential term. A six-year term would be preferable, so that a president would take the first year to learn the job and be on the job for three years or five years, seeking a place in history rather than on the ballot in the next elections. One may think that this concern for reelection does not really drive presidents, but there is evidence to the contrary. Hamilton Jordan wrote an article in *Life* magazine in 1981 in which he reported that only eighteen months into the Carter administration, even if President Carter was not considering the next election, Jordan was. Jordan said that he spent most of his time on the election. Immediately after President Carter said that Jordan was the most valuable person in Washington, working in the White House, Jordan was transferred to run the reelection campaign, which was not the most valuable thing he could have done. I would ask presidential candidates to commit themselves to one term, although experience with these commitments is not good. President Gerald Ford, when he was approved by the Senate to replace President Nixon, said that he would not run for reelection. I believe Jimmy Carter said when he was running for president that he did not believe in second terms. John Anderson, in his campaign for the presidential nomination, did not commit himself to one term only, although he had said that he would. I think that the one-term presidency would help considerably.

People must understand that there is a capability for great destruction. Those who are in charge should deny that one side can have security by means of the threat of destroying the other side. Everything is extremely insecure. The U.S. posture—that we do not deter attack unless we can fight the Soviet Union three months after we have exchanged most of our weapons, and that we actually have to use the nuclear weapons planned for protracted war—is an extraordinarily insecure posture that could very well lead to war in one way or another. This must be made a primary concern rather than something one thinks about only at 3:00 in the morning.

Some Positive Steps: Improve the Command, Control, Communications, and Intelligence System (C^3I)

To reduce the danger of false alarms, the United States must work on the command, control, communications, and intelligence system (C^3I) so that it is more sensible. False alarms (positive system failures) do not reach all the way to the end of the system, to the point at which the alert is sounded warning that a massive attack is underway. They are in an early stage. And one can have, in computers or other systems, error detection systems and error correction systems with several channels. The system must be arranged so that a real raid would appear in more than one channel, and that anomalies that did not appear in all channels would not be rejected, because sensors may fail negative, in which case a real raid might not be seen. It is perfectly feasible to do that. The United States should pay more attention to these systems and in particular should be more open about evaluating them. I have made some proposals in this area.

Finally, the question comes down to the president's making the decision as to whether there is an attack and, if so, what his response will be. The weak link, in my opinion (and I say this generically and not in respect to this president) is at the level of the presidency. The weakness lies mostly in decision making, not so much in getting the word back to the forces. One has to ask what happens if the alert comes when the president is ill, out of the country, out of communication, or has been killed by a smuggled weapon. Who takes over? If the president is known dead, there is a legally prescribed devolution of authority; the vice president is next and so on. But if the president is known or believed to be alive, he is presumably the only one who has the authority to make such a decision responding to a warning of nuclear attack. He should be empowered to delegate that responsibility. In fact he can delegate it, but he should take this problem seriously and delegate, so that there is more than one center of decision. However, when the president is in communication it should be his sole responsibility, and at such times others should not have the ability or the authority to launch nuclear weapons.

Then there is the terrible question of madmen. If countries care about their security and their survival, they will pay attention to the way in which the decision is made to launch weapons or to decide that there is an attack. The United States does not make those decisions very professionally, because every four years a new president, with new advisors around him, takes over. The Soviets are presumably much better at these decisions, because the people who are involved in making them stay in office a much longer time. But leaders might be imagined who are insane, who want to destroy the world while appearing sane. [Consult Dror's *Crazy States*—Eds.] What is the probability of such an occurrence, of such a person's achieving a position of power and manipulating the levers and symbols to cause nuclear war? That is one possibility.

The other possibility is that of a leader who maintains—for fundamentalist religious reasons or because of blind hate—that it is better to rid the world of both nations than to allow the Soviet Union or the United States, as the case may be, to survive. This possibility concerns me. I would like to reduce the number of nuclear weapons to reduce somewhat the magnitude of this threat, but not their deterrent value. But I would like much more to have a system of collegial decision making that could be less subject to whims. During the Watergate affair there was some doubt that President Nixon would behave rationally and, according to James Schlesinger as secretary of defense, it was not clear during that period that any unusual orders from the president would have been obeyed.

A test of reason is always applied; however, the survival of the country and certainly the survival of individual careers are at stake. It is not clear that everyone would or should use individual initiative in a crisis. It is not obvious that political decision makers would behave rationally halfway through this chain of escalation, after many days without sleep, nuclear weapons having exploded all around them, and their families dead or their status uncertain. It is a terrible problem. As long as the ability to destroy exists, much more attention should be paid to command, control, and communications, which means to decision making.

This is especially true as political decision makers have a different scale of values. They work in the realm of the politically feasible, with a very short time horizon of a year or two years. If individuals had the same set of time discount rates, no one would ever bring up children or educate them, because, after all, childrearing is only going to pay off twenty or thirty years later. Political decision makers may have an inappropriate set of values; they do not understand that life and civilization are at stake.

C^3 is a very complicated question with high stakes; it should have much more work devoted to it. The United States should spend considerably more money on C^3 and proportionally less on the forces.

Some Positive Steps: Arms Control in the Context of Defense Management

My favorite approach to arms control is defense management. In the defense management approach, the United States would ask what weapons were needed and would not build any unnecessary ones. If there were a surplus, rather than looking for targets for them the United States would send them to cruise in the southern oceans, if they were submarines, or would cover them over with earth if they were ICBMs. (Not the other way around; you cannot send the ICBMs to cruise the southern oceans.)

If the United States continues to have arms control negotiations, we should recognize that negotiations are now captives of the individuals and interest groups who do not want arms control: the weapons developers. At present, proposed arms limitations must be structured to satisfy U.S. weapons developers so that arms control does not interfere with the development or deployment of any weapon that is planned. I think that is unacceptable. When a treaty is signed, these groups must be paid off so that they will support the treaty in the Congress. (Of course this is not a reference to paying people individually, although we probably should resume that practice—it would cost much less and would impair the national security less than does paying in very large weapons systems.) Then we pay again at the time of ratification if the treaty is not signed and ratified at the same time. I would agree with the implied criticism that the arms control approach as it has been practiced has lost effectiveness.

When SALT I was signed on May 26, 1972, SALT II was promised, preferably by the end of that year. But it was not until the end of 1974 that there was a memorandum of understanding at Vladivostok, and it was not until 1979 that SALT II was actually signed. [SALT II has not been ratified by the U.S. Senate, and the Reagan administration has apparently abandoned it—Eds.]

That sequence is too slow. It simply does not keep pace with the evolution of the threat. Thus, arms control negotiations should consist of short negotiations on particular points. If a draft treaty includes everything globally, it is too difficult to negotiate. No one will sign a treaty that is not in the interest of his side: the Soviet Union has to get something from a treaty or it will not sign; the United States has to get something from it, too. Incentives must exist on both sides.

The United States should set arms control limits and then should reduce the limits. But as long as the United States is building its forces, it is not reducing them. Instead we are providing arguments, many of them specious, why the existing U.S. forces are inadequate. The argument really becomes, "We need everything they have and more." However, no one suggests that the Soviets need everything that we have and more; they are not going to build a B-52 jet aircraft with cruise missiles because they cannot afford it. But U.S. analysts argue that the United States needs large missiles because the Soviet Union has large missiles. But at the time their ICBM force was constructed, the Soviet Union was unable to build small missiles. When there was no superpower limitations at all, the United States built small Minuteman missiles to replace the very large Atlas and Titan missiles. The United States built small missiles then because they were easier to house in relatively inexpensive silos; they suited U.S. needs. The United States does not need something different simply because the Soviet Union was unable to build small missiles. People do not consider whether a world in which both superpowers have silo-killing missiles is more dangerous than a world in which only one side has, which I think is the case.

Most U.S. security negotiations should be conducted unilaterally, through the way the United States manages its forces, without seeking bargaining chips, so that negotiations that currently do not progress at all could be settled more favorably. I also think that unilateral actions are easier than a unilateral nuclear nuclear freeze.

It is very difficult to know what to freeze when there are dual purpose weapons, and when there are people in the Pentagon who work on nuclear weapons, who work on paying the conventional forces, and who work on devising characteristics for new strategic and tactical systems. If it were only a matter of deciding that no one shows up for work tomorrow in the Pentagon, that freeze could be easy enough to define. But it is rather difficult to agree to freeze all work on strategic weapons, defensive or offensive, and only let some unspecified "good things" go on. For instance, under the terms of a nuclear freeze, does work on antisubmarine warfare continue? To the extent that ASW imperils Soviet strategic systems it is, from their point of view, destabilizing for deterrence and should be frozen. To the extent that ASW imperils Soviet hunter-killer submarines that threaten U.S. strategic systems, it is stabilizing from the U.S. perspective and should proceed. So it is extremely difficult to define the projects that should be frozen [at least in deterrence terms—Eds.].

If nuclear weapons are frozen, if there is a comprehensive test ban, if no more nuclear weapons are manufactured, if the stockpile of fissile material is declared—does that mean that nobody touches a nuclear weapon? How is remanufacture of nuclear weapons that are getting old or that need replaceable parts to be dealt with?

Despite these difficulties I could define a freeze. I could also define a comprehensive test ban. My comprehensive nuclear test ban would prohibit all nuclear explosions except those that can be conducted in permanently occupied buildings. There are small experimental nuclear reactions that could take years to define, so they might as well be defined by the environment rather than by permissible yield. The United States should make such proposals, with provisions for no more nuclear testing and for no new weapons, but with remanufacture allowed. To make a nuclear freeze verifiable would not be so easy. But in the United States if a nuclear freeze were published as an executive order, it would have the force of law and would create a better situation than the current one.

How long would such a unilateral freeze be in effect, and what would a reasonable response be if at the expiration of the freeze the Soviet Union had not put into effect a comparable freeze? Would there then be pressure to punish the Soviet Union by creating more self-defeating weapons systems? That prospect is my problem with defining a unilateral freeze. If the United States announces a nuclear freeze contingent for its continuation on the Soviets' doing likewise, what do we do at the end of it? Usually the United States would put in place a contingency program for the end of the freeze that would guarantee that the United States would be farther ahead of the Soviet Union than we would have been without the freeze, and give our representatives the incentive to make demands that are unacceptable on the Soviet side. Nevertheless, if someone gave me a mutual, verifiable nuclear freeze, I would sign it in an instant.

Some Positive Steps: A National Arms Control Institute

Another problem is that the United States does not do enough studying. The U.S. government does not look into arms limitation agreements with the Soviets until we actually enter into the negotiations. We should have institutes seriously conferring with the other side and asking what kinds of limitations, security arrangements, and protection against crazy people can be introduced.

Years ago there was an effort in the intellectual community to create an arms control institute for the U.S. Congress, the purpose of which would be to provide draft bills. The institute might be a conservative one, a radical one, or a liberal democratic institute; all shades of legislation would ensue. Institute staff would not just think about arms control problems but would provide draft action memos and draft legislation. I think that the United States should do much more in that regard. In that case one of the draft proposals could be picked up. Tens of millions of dollars a year would go into draft freezes that would be worked out with the other side.

But the last thing people want in Washington (or for that matter for the most part in universities or in any other organization) is options. They want to decide one way or another what is the right thing to do and to pretend that no other feasible course exists.

Notes

1. It may be argued that U.S. submarines do not attack Soviet silos, so they do not provoke attack in the same sense.
2. Garwin, Richard L., and Hans A. Bethe (1968). "Anti-ballistic Missile Systems," *Scientific American* 218:19:21-31 March.

References

Carter, Ashton B., and David N. Schwartz, eds. (1984). *Ballistic Missile Defense.* Washington DC: Brookings.
Dror, Yezekiel (1971). *Crazy States.* Lexington: D.C. Heath.
Garthoff, Raymond L. (1983). *Perspectives on the Strategic Balance.* Washington DC: Brookings.
Garwin, Richard (07/01/83). "Doctrines and Thinking on Nuclear War (Is there Wisdom Without Experience?)," a draft prepared for the Working Group on the Strategic Arms Race, 33rd Pugwash Conference, Venice, Italy (082683DTNW) [1].
———(06/00/83). "Who Proposes, Who Disposes, Who Pays?", *Bulletin of the Atomic Scientists* June-July. (060083WPWD) [2].
———(01/27/83). "Presentation to the Commission on Strategic Forces," (foils only) (012783PCSF) [3].
———(00/00/80). "Presidential Science Advising," *Science Advice to the President,* a special issue of *Technology in Society 2,* Pergamon Press Ltd.: 115-128. (000080.PSA).
———(10/00/77). "Reducing Dependence on Nuclear Weapons: A Second Nuclear Regime," in the 1980s Project/Council on Foreign Relations' Nuclear Weapons and World Politics. (100077RDNW).
Gray, Colin S., Keith B. Payne, and Associates (1984). *Missiles for the Nineties: ICBMs and Strategic Policy.* Boulder CO: Westview Press.
Jasani, Bhupendri, and Stockholm International Peace Research Institute, eds.

(1982). *Outer Space: A New Dimension of the Arms Race*. London: Taylor and Francis.

Sorrels, C. A. (1983). *U.S. Cruise Missiles Program: Development, Deployment, and Implications for the Military Balance*. Oxford, England: Brassey's, Pergamon. (Not for sale in the United States.)

Spinney, Franklin C., and James Clay Thompson (1984). *Defense Facts of Life: The Plans/Reality Mismatch*. Boulder CO: Westview Press.

Steinbruner, John D., and Leon V. Sigal, eds. (1983). *Alliance Security: NATO and the No-First-Use Question*. Washington DC: Brookings.

Herman Kahn

CENTRAL NUCLEAR WAR: COMMENTS, CONCEPTS, AND CONTEXTS

The late Herman Kahn was a specialist in public policy analysis, with a particular interest in deterrence issues. He directed the Hudson Institute's research programs on U.S. national security, arms control, foreign policy problems, economic and social development, and international business. Dr. Kahn's many books include the classic On Thermonuclear War, *and other notable contributions to the literature, such as* Thinking About the Unthinkable *and* The Year 2000.

In this summary, the eminent specialist considered several aspects of central nuclear war, including similarities and differences between central nuclear war and conventional war, current nuclear doctrine and strategies, scenarios of war origins, and issues for mobilization planning. He contributed to enlarging the academic debate on nuclear questions by specifying several possible consequences and ranges of policy alternatives in varying scenarios. Dr. Kahn has also advanced two telling forecasts here:

1. *that limited war is not, in principle, impossible; consequently, any doctrinal developments anticipating war-fighting should take into account this possibility;*
2. *that, although a mutual assured destruction (MAD) policy may provide a workable deterrent, once the deterrent fails, it is not a viable action policy and would not, in fact, be acted upon by a U.S. president.*

Instead of MAD, Dr. Kahn expressed a preference for NUTS (nuclear use theories), gnostic strategies, and LOUTish ("lucking out") policies. These are discussed below, in the context of the other material.

This is one of Dr. Kahn's last public commentaries, published here with the kind consent of the Hudson Institute and their gracious grant of copyright. This work is in some respects more circumspect than the classic Kahn theorizing.

Central Nuclear War: A Framework for Analysis

The topic of central nuclear war is a serious one best introduced by a joke, as is customary. Consider the slightly unfriendly joke about a tourist in Germany who asks for directions. When a German gives him directions, the tourist replies, "Thank you." The German then exclaims, "What do you mean, thank you? REPEAT them after me." That is the spirit in which my commentary should be taken.

My subject is the creation of a framework for analysis of central nuclear war (CNW) and of the problems associated with central nuclear war. This subject—war between the superpowers—is one to be taken seriously and to be discussed with professionals. Supporting documents can be obtained from the Hudson Institute.

This is an early treatment that is not definitive. At the same time it is well enough developed that five outlines comprise it, including:

1. How Is Central War Different?
2. Some Basic Comments on Current Nuclear Doctrines, Strategies, and Tactics
3. How Is Central War the Same?
4. Five Priority Canonical Hudson Central War "Requirements" Scenarios
5. Important Concepts and Issues for Mobilization Planning.

The first three of these outlines are concerned with the "revolution in warfare." This Russian phrase is quite useful. Soviet analysts use it to try to make clear to their own generals and students of military affairs that war in this era is different. Although the principles of war in one sense may not have changed, in another sense they have changed drastically since the advent of nuclear weapons.

The first outline explains how central nuclear war is different from other wars. The word "central" is used to indicate that the two superpowers' homelands are involved in the nuclear war. I use this terminology because the term "thermonuclear war" is occasionally confused with "theater nuclear war," but deterrence theorists use this terminology in two separate ways. Most historians and much of the public feel, I am sure, that history has to be thought of anew with the invention of thermonuclear weapons, and that there must be some policy or technique that will create peace for the rest of history. This oversimplifies the issues, of course, but war has been transformed; war is very different once thermonuclear weapons come into being. Thermonuclear weapons are not just a weapon like any other; thermonuclear weapons have a potential for evil that is extraordinarily large. It is important that the analyst and the reader both understand this difference, and that they know that each other understands it.

Many of the people I work with, even though they are often quite sophisticated, unconsciously fail to realize how dramatic a change nuclear weapons have caused, particularly thermonuclear weapons. The phrase central nuclear war is used to jog their mental processes, to make them understand that they must think in different ways, given the existence of thermonuclear weapons.

The second outline is called "Some Basic Comments on Current Nuclear Doctrines, Strategies, and Tactics." In it some serious but unorthodox remarks are made, concerning nuclear issues that I think of as very important. These are remarks that normally are not made; they just are not discussed. A similar omission of important problems in economics very often causes economists simply to miss the main trends. When the transnational corporation was building up, there were no articles by the U.S. Department of Commerce on it. When the Eurodollar market was building up, there were no articles by the Department of Commerce on it. In other words, momentous events often occur unnoticed and are only recorded after they have happened. I would like to keep that from happening in the case of current nuclear doctrines, strategies, and tactics.

The third outline summarizes "How Is Central Nuclear War the Same?" That is an important outline for the purposes of this chapter, because it is a revelation to most people that there are continuities as well as discontinuities in military policy since the creation of thermonuclear weapons; that there are some considerations that remain, if not eternal, at least very vital and important for the rest of history. This is the basic philosophical context of my summary here, which largely omits the central war requirements scenarios and the discussions of mobilization planning of interest mainly to professionals.

The professional outlines four and five are used to indicate to my colleagues that if they are not thinking at least at this level of complexity, with this richness and sophistication, they are not doing a good job of analysis. The whole CNW project is summarized by saying that the outlines provide a common language and context for discussing central nuclear war that is at the same time small enough to be manageable, precise enough to be efficient, and rich enough to cover most of the interesting issues.

If one works at the Hudson Institute, one has a touch of megalomania. About a third of the staff is there to fix the world, which is not normally a professional objective. In this expectation, we plan to use a version of this framework in a very useful way, not only to improve the level of discussion, but to make discussions among experts as well as laymen somewhat more realistic and more efficient.

How Is Central Nuclear War (CNW) Different?

I would like to convey an impossibly large amount of information here on the complexity and variety of analyses of CNW. Without discussing this systematically, I will make a number of points to create a common understanding of my position. I suspect there will be general agreement with these points.

Let us assume one wants to argue that one can survive a nuclear war; some argue that I argue that. Analyses of survivability are complex and uncertain, in at least ten issue areas. There is then a burden of proof on me, to make cases for each one of these ten issues and all of the subissues entailed by them appear persuasive, or perhaps more than persuasive.

Complexities and Uncertainties Relevant to Survivability

1. Various phased programs on both sides
2. The wartime operational performance of U.S. and Soviet forces
3. Immediate consequences of all relevant weapons effects (e.g., blast, nuclear and thermal radiation, electromagnetic pulse, dust, ground shock, debris)
4. Possibility of tactics designed to exploit or diminish these effects for narrow military purposes, for coercion, or for intrawar deterrence
5. Other effects of the size and shape of the war, including how war is terminated
6. Postattack problems of short-run survival and reorganization and, eventually, long-term economic and social recuperation
7. Impact of postwar economic, political, military, and social context—domestic and worldwide
8. Various health and genetic issues
9. Uncertain and potentially catastrophic environmental aftereffects often associated with nuclear war (such as a new Ice Age or destruction of the ozone layer)
10. Surprises (more likely and more significant with larger attacks and less restraint)

If one's country's life is to be bet on going into a thermonuclear war, a high level of proof may be desirable here. But a high level of proof cannot be furnished. What can be furnished is a convincing case for a "Scotch verdict" on the arguments against survivability. In Scotland, a criminal jury can come out with three verdicts: guilty, not guilty, and unproven. A Scotch verdict, a verdict of unproven, means that in the considered judgment of the jury the defendant is guilty, but the prosecution has not made a case beyond a reasonable doubt; hence, the defendant must be let go. But the jury thinks the world should know that in their opinion the defendant is guilty.

I will agree with the contention that there is a reasonable doubt of survivability on many of the CNW issues raised here. However, I will not agree that there is nothing in the idea when I command a Scotch verdict on survivability; if the public rejects the unproven verdict, I argue that the public should do more reading and research because it does not yet understand. We do not claim a Scotch verdict without high levels of documentation and understanding on these issues.

I do not claim a Scotch verdict that one could actually survive all the abovementioned ten effects of a large nuclear war, war in which 10,000 megatons or more are detonated. We simply do not have the data. There will be unexpected effects. I do argue that the picture of world annihilation following a medium nuclear war of approximately 5,000 megatons is almost certainly wrong. I have to conclude almost certainly; I cannot assert that it is certainly wrong because, again, the data simply do not exist. But there is no respectable study indicating that a rather large nuclear war would be the end of history.[1] It MAY be; the experiment has not been tried. But one cannot point to any respectable study that supports the apocalypse conclusion. Studies can be cited that argue that the ozone layer might be destroyed or a new Ice Age might be touched off; but these cataclysmic effects cannot be obtained either, using standard data. Assumptions off the mainstream must be used.

For example, it can be argued that if a given number of five-micron particles get out into the atmosphere, cut off a certain amount of solar radiation, and stay up a certain length of time, under some specified and unusual but not reasonable assumptions, this will touch off an Ice Age.

A much more probable calculation is that the ozone layer will be destroyed for some decades. That in itself does not kill human beings. People would dress the way Arabs dress in the desert, to protect themselves from the ultraviolet. But the absence of the ozone layer would change the vegetation and the animal life; it would make large-scale changes in the world. I am not going to take the position that man has always survived; therefore, he always has to survive at this point. Nuclear war is different. Probably men will survive. But for the first time in history, specialists such as myself who are trying to be sober have to say "as far as we know, people will survive."

The fact that I have to concede that, without liking it, shows that CNW is different. I would prefer to make a flat statement that human life cannot be destroyed; this fear is just a figment of the imagination. I think that one cannot, and I will bet a hundred to one that one will not, but I cannot say that I know. I can present too many calculations indicating that the prospects are very poor, and I know that there are many effects I do not know about. So I cannot endorse a statement of certain survivability.

It should be clear that I am not denying that a nuclear war would be a devastating event, and I am not a proponent of nuclear war. Is there anyone who is FOR cancer or FOR nuclear war? To the best of my knowledge, no one in the world advocates nuclear war. There may be some such people, but I have never met them and I meet all kinds of people. There are a few people who are fascinated by nuclear war, but even they would not be interested in seeing for themselves what it is actually like. So it can be assumed that the pro nuclear war case is empty. As far as I know, there is no one in the United States or the Soviet Union who is anxious to start a war, even for political reasons.

Later in this chapter I will make the point that there are no plausible scenarios for nuclear war. There are "not implausible" scenarios, or not completely implausible ones. On the other hand, I should also point out that the scenario that started World War I simply would not withstand intellectual scrutiny. It had too many anomalies in it. Plausible scenarios of the origins of World War I could definitely be written; before the war the international system was war-prone. But the specific scenario that actually occurred would not even be acceptable in a movie plot, and it certainly would not be acceptable in a contract study.

So the mere fact that plausible scenarios for the beginning of a nuclear war cannot be composed does not mean that the world is safe. I do not think that it is a better world because plausible scenarios cannot be written than it would if plausible scenarios could be developed. One would be very nervous, I suspect, in the latter case. Incidentally, I am not in the business of providing reassurance either, though I may be in the business of trying to provide reassurance about specific issues amenable to study. If you personally are worried about nuclear war, be my guest; I am, too.

In a short chapter it is inconceivable to make a good case for survival after CMW against a skeptic. It can be done in a more extensive paper, in which one can go through every single one of the effects listed above, suggesting failure modes and then pointing out why the failure mode does not in fact fail. That is an assertion and you can believe it or not. I would refer you to our studies of wars of different magnitudes for further information.

Reasons for Initiating CNW

Turning to the question of reasons for going to central nuclear war, there are four reasons of interest to any decision maker considering initiating central nuclear war:

1. None (i.e., inadvertent war)
2. Almost no emphasis on ambition or gains
3. Emphasis on averting disaster (e.g., consequences of not fighting may appear more disastrous than CNW)
4. Punishing a party for using nuclear weapons

The first possibility, which is the most important and most alarming, is that there might be no explicit reason for beginning CNW. War might begin accidentally because a switch was thrown; someone became excited; someone misunderstood something; someone played a game of "chicken" once too often. This, by the way, is World War I. None of the major European powers genuinely wanted a war in 1914. Some of the French bureaucrats did, but not the country as a whole and certainly not the president. Nonetheless the French entered a very large war without intending to, without wanting to. This unintentional involvement, or involvement precipitated by a vocal minority, could happen again. It might be harder than one would think, but certainly it is not impossible. And it might be easier than I think because I have not thought of all the possibilities. I have thought about a great many of them, but I am sure that I missed one or two.

There is no emphasis in the literature of the early 1980s on the second source of CNW listed above, ambition or a perceived gain as a reason to go to war. This is true both in the Soviet system and in the United States. Perhaps a handful of Americans could be found who think that the Soviets might actually go to war to exploit the so-called window of vulnerability. In one of my books I have mentioned the only three Americans with this outlook whom I could find.

This sentiment on war initiation for anticipated gain is quite isolated. An anecdote will give some sense of the small probability that expected gain could be a cause of CNW. Circa 1978, I was chairman of a strategic panel of the National Defense University. About twenty people participated, most of whom were hard-right conservatives, although Jeremy Stone, chairman of the American Federation of Scientists and a liberal, was there as well. In general these individuals considered themselves politically conservative and felt that they were also conservative in the judgment of the (American) general public. I asked these men to participate in a gedanken experiment. A gedanken experiment is a thought experiment much used in physics and philosophy and much employed by me in nuclear war issues. A gedanken experiment is not actually performed; it is unrealistic, or even counterfactual. But by going through the motions of thinking it through, one hopes that something can be learned. This was the very quick gedanken experiment:

Let us assume that around 1983, the so-called window of vulnerability opened up. And let us take an extreme case of the window of vulnerability, one which is a bit optimistic from the Soviet point of view and pessimistic in the American perspective, but not ridiculously so. In this hypothetical case, the Soviets presume that they can make a first strike on the United States. They further presume that if all goes well, they will probably win a clean victory with essentially no serious retaliation to their country. In this scenario, if events go badly, they will suffer fewer casualties than they did in World War II,[2] and under these circumstances they will be able to take over the world. Assume further that this window of vulnerability will disappear in the late '80s. Furthermore, if one surveys the Soviet Union today, it looks like a very bleak decade or two for them. During the next two decades, everything is going wrong. [This is evidently a reference to declining industrial and agricultural productivity in the USSR, as well as to projected labor shortages and unfavorable demographic trends—Eds.] By exploiting what I would consider their substantial superiority in the nuclear establishments, the Soviets could solve all their problems at once. What will they do?

For what it is worth, nineteen out of twenty participants thought that the Soviets would not resort to a nuclear strike under the circumstances of this gedanken experiment. The only panel participant who thought that the Soviets would preempt under these conditions was a physicist who was not a Soviet expert, and his judgment therefore was not particularly interesting to deterrence theorists.

I then made the point that at the plenary session of the panel I intended to report this position that almost all of the participants had taken. In fact, although most of us at that panel meeting felt that the window of vulnerability existed and that it is a window of danger, not merely an analytical problem, only one of us felt that the Soviets would plan to use the opportunity to preempt, or that it might cause a watershed change in history, at one stroke.

On the other hand, Henry Kissinger once wrote that there has never been a people in history who have spent as much on weapons as the Soviets have in the past one or two decades without using the weapons. And there is always a first time.[3] I am not criticizing Kissinger by giving his basic position here; I happen to think well of him. But this reasoning did not convince the panelists to change their judgment of the window of vulnerability rationale for a Soviet first strike.

No one on that panel thought it was sensible for the United States to rely on Soviet prudence and caution as protection for the United States. There were only two people in the room who were opposed to some kind of rearmament program to close the window of vulnerability, even though almost none of us thought that it represented a real danger in the sense of the Soviets' trying to exploit it, consciously and deliberately. Even so, we could still write scenarios in which the window of vulnerability would make a significant difference in history.

In both Soviet and U.S. analyses, the emphasis on going to a nuclear war is on averting disaster, the third reason listed. The Soviet analysis tends to proceed as follows: The capitalist world will crumble under the onslaughts of communism,[4] but philosophically, revolutionarily, not because of nuclear weapons. And then the capitalists, in a spasm of despair, will decide to attack the bastion of socialism.

Before N. S. Khrushchev,[5] war arising in this way between capitalist and socialist systems was said to be inevitable. It had to happen eventually because the capitalists would never give up without going to war. Khrushchev changed the ideological line, arguing that there are nuclear weapons in the world today that are quite different from old weaponry and, because of the difference caused by the new weaponry, the capitalists may well be deterred, even though they are being wiped off the stage of history. Therefore, the USSR might spend more money on consumer goods; the Soviets were not forced to allocate such a large percentage of their gross national product to military production.

The fatalistic inevitability of war doctrine was thrown out by Khrushchev, and a different opinion on superpower war was presented that still prevails. In this view, the USSR does not know whether the capitalists will attack or not in a spasm of despair. It may well be that the capitalists will be deterred; it may well be that they will not be deterred. Therefore, because war is not in principle impossible, the USSR must be prepared to fight and win a nuclear war, even though there is a good chance it will never have to be fought because the capitalists will be deterred.[6]

The standard Western scenarios for a Soviet attack on the West all assume that the Soviets are basically influenced by desperation. In other words, the emphasis is always on averting disaster; those who start the war feel that the consequences of not fighting may be more disastrous than those of fighting a nuclear war. That would mean that they had gone through those ten factors concerning the complexity and uncertainty of analyses of CNW mentioned above and have come to a conclusion that even given the multiple uncertainties of CNW, failure to go to war will yield consequences that are worse. There are multiple uncertainties in those ten items; there are uncertainties in the disaster that decision makers face when they contemplate CNW. They are balancing uncertainty against uncertainty, disaster against disaster. We believe, correctly or incorrectly, that under some circumstances a rational man might come up with a calculation that his country would be better off to strike than not to strike; his country would be better off to accept a lesser disaster.

A fourth reason for going to nuclear war, of which I personally approve, is to punish a nation that has used nuclear weapons first. I would be very pleased if nuclear weapons could be disinvented. I do not think this is possible. However, neither do I think that the defense of the West depends on nuclear weapons. In fact, I will argue the exact opposite: If nuclear weapons disappeared, the problem of defending the West would probably disappear, too. Western Europe can defend itself if it puts its mind to it. It does not need U.S. help. But the Western Europeans will not provide their own defense as long as there are nuclear weapons, because there is no point in building up conventional forces if an adversary can always use nuclear forces on your country.

Incidentally, I know of no Western European country willing to fight a nuclear war. They all take the same position taken by the West German peace groups, except that they do not espouse this position explicitly. The West German peace group argues as follows:

The Soviets do not wish to attack Western Europe. (That is certainly true under current conditions, in which both sides have nuclear weapons. It might even be true without nuclear weapons; we do not know.[7] But I do not know of any U.S. experts in whom I have much faith who think that the Soviets are very interested in attacking Western Europe.)

The second point the German peace groups make is that if the Soviets do attack and conquer Europe, they will be unable to digest it because Europeans have lived under a parliamentary system. Therefore, for example, it is not likely that West Germans would be as passive as the East Germans are. Western Europe simply could not be digested.

The third point the West German peace groups make is that (if point two is false and) if the Soviets do attack and digest Western Europe, it would be better to be a live East German than a dead West German. Life is just not that bad in the GDR.

I do not find fault with any of these three points, but I do find fault with the conclusion drawn from them, which is that if the choice is among Red, dead, or neutral, Western Europe prefers being neutral. That is clearly the Soviet objective for Western Europe—neutrality, not Red, not dead, but neutral, basically. German students and young people do not understand that being neutral in Central Europe will be very unpleasant, much more unpleasant than, for example, being neutral in Finland. Finland is a tough, hard country that knows how to deal with these situations. Finland maintains a great deal of self-discipline and in general is a highly independent country that is very careful not to irritate the Soviets. And occasionally the Finns do something the Soviets want, such as changing their president or their constitution.

My point is that the options really range over Red, dead, neutral, NATO, or some substitute for NATO.[8] From almost every point of view, particularly the Western European one, NATO or the substitute for NATO is demonstrably better than Red, dead, or neutral. Hence, why prejudge the question? Why limit the options? That is the basic position of Europe outside the peace groups. Europeans admit that the system would collapse if put under any severe strain. The basic defense posture of Continental Europe has always been preemptive surrender, or at least it has been from about 1972 on. If the Soviets attack and there is the risk of a nuclear war, many Europeans believe that although the United States and the Soviet Union could survive a nuclear war, no country in Europe could. Hence, perceiving the choice as Red or dead, they prefer Red.

One wonders how many people would disagree with their policy if the only choice really were the whole population Red or dead; not anyone as an individual, but every fellow citizen dead or Red. It is difficult to say how many would vote for the entire population to be Red, and how many would vote for the entire population to be dead. This is a very hard choice; it is too permanent.

So when I explain the European position on this, I am not criticizing the Europeans. I simply think that they have a more extensive range of choices than they realize. But, again, I do not blame them for feeling as they do.

Before Margaret Thatcher became prime minister, it used to be said that the British believed in preventive surrender—that they would not wait for the crisis; they would accommodate beforehand, making whatever compromise circumstances might require.

Why then do the Soviets pressure Western Europe? This is a serious question because the Soviets cannot make this choice without submitting to some dangers themselves. As a Western European would put it, the Soviets cannot be sure there would be no response. Someone might fire a weapon; the Americans might insist on firing them. (In West Germany, the United States, not the West Germans, has control of the nuclear weapons. There is a double-key arrangement, but the Americans have both keys, unlike the situation in England. The American key in the Thor missile used to say War/Peace. The British key was labeled Safe/Dangerous, which is a clue to what is going on.)

To repeat, the final reason that has been isolated for going to CNW is to punish another country for using nuclear weapons. My basic position is that the only purposes of nuclear weapons are to deter, to balance, or to correct for the possession and/or use of nuclear weapons by others. My article in the *New York Times Magazine*[9] argues in favor of a U.S. No-First-Use policy on nuclear weapons.[10] My position on No First Use goes back at least to 1963, when I wrote some articles for the *Yale Law School Journal* and the *Berkeley Law School Journal* on the reasons for No-First-Use policies. At that time, I thought that such a policy was bad for the United States but good for the world. The United States was a large, wealthy country and so it was not compelled to do everything for its own sake. I argued that such a country could make some sacrifices for world security. After all, the United States is part of the world. Even though the United States might lose a small amount as a nation, it is good for the world to gain for the world. I was speaking there of limiting potential risks such as nuclear proliferation and of the absolute importance of making the use of nuclear weapons as taboo as possible, so that if others used nuclear weapons the United States could argue that they had committed an "irreligious" act; thus, the United States could be angry and punish them correspondingly. Obviously, if one's own country is planning to use nuclear weapons itself, it cannot call someone else's use of nuclear weapons irreligious, or make such use taboo. I think it would be a good thing to make use of nuclear weapons a taboo.

My proposal in 1982 was in the national interest of the United States. It was a rearmament proposal, not a disarmament proposal. It was not like the proposal in *Foreign Affairs Quarterly*, which I would interpret as a disarmament proposal.[11] My proposal advanced the following line of reasoning:

It is important to have an adequate conventional defense in Western Europe. It is equally important, if the United States should promise No First Use, to make absolutely sure that the Russians will not use nuclear weapons first. The only way to guarantee that is for the United States to be prepared to fight a nuclear war, either to punish the Soviets or to negate the effects of their first use.

Whether a country punishes or negates depends very much on its capabilities compared to those of the other side. But the United States must make reasonably credible the proposition that any use of nuclear weapons by the Soviet Union will bring about some kind of punishment or balancing. And, I would argue, that cannot be accomplished very credibly with the U.S. nuclear establishment of 1982.

Another technical phrase that is important for CNW analysis entails the use of an apparent double negative. I have argued above that there are no plausible scenarios for nuclear war. But there are "not implausible" or "not completely implausible" scenarios, depending on the scenario's characteristics. That terminology does not include a double negative. If an event is defined as probable, that means the odds that the event will happen are greater than .5. If an event is defined as not probable, the odds that it will take place are less than .5. If I call an event, or a series of events, improbable, I mean that its probability is less than .1, or something in that neighborhood. If an event is defined as not improbable, then its probability is greater than .1, but it could still be less than .5. [Dr. Kahn refers to a range of those events that, while unlikely, are still more probable than the most extremely unlikely events—Eds.] So an event can be not improbable (probability not in the range $.0 < p. < .1$) without being probable ($p. > .5$) because it could fall in the range $.1 < p. < .5$; not incredible without being credible; not implausible without being plausible. This is an example of the use of an apparent double negative for precision. The literature written at the Hudson Institute is filled with these apparent double negatives.

Use of these designations is also a logical trick. If I hypothesize that an event is not implausible, an opponent must prove that it is implausible to contradict me,[12] which is difficult. One would really show it is not plausible (p. not greater than .5, so likely falling in the range $.0 < p. < .5$); but you cannot show that it is not implausible (p. not in the range .1 to .5). This particular debating trick reflects the reality that, in fact, the probability of nuclear war, as far as analysts can speculate, is very, very low. Nevertheless it is not so low that one should not be deeply concerned about it, should not worry about it, or should not be alarmed.

Furthermore, let us assume that a nuclear weapon was detonated by accident, again the first reason for going to CNW. There are probably about 5,000 missiles on alert around the world at any moment. If one exploded by accident and hit the United States, New York perhaps, it might touch off a war and it might not. But it is almost impossible to imagine explaining why one thought it was safe to live in a world with 5,000 missiles on alert after one of them had gone off by accident. One would face serious difficulties, of which the smallest might be that one would look foolish. Despite this, today even the people who claim to be most afraid of nuclear war in fact are normally perfectly quiet; their adrenalin does not pump with fear. Basically they trust the safety mechanisms of both superpowers. Otherwise these people would move out of the city or take other precautionary measures.

Current Nuclear Doctrines, Strategies, and Tactics

I have developed five basic positions with regard to current nuclear war doctrines, strategies, and tactics. I have omitted religious and philosophical pacifism in the latest form, which would comprise a sixth position. Except for this sixth position of religious or philosophical pacifism, there are no comfortable positions on this array. If anyone happens to hold one of these positions and feels perfectly self-righteous, comfortable, and unworried about it (and its consequences), he is either a fool or something worse.

1. Nuclear pacifism: more defensible and politically palatable in the age of social limits to growth and multi-megaton weapons, but with all the traditional problems and even fewer of the traditional virtues
2. MAD (Mutual Assured Destruction): simple, understandable, unaggressive, inexpensive, and relatively acceptable politically and emotionally, because it seems so practical and moral
3. NUTS (Nuclear Use Theories): relatively rational, logical, and academically defendable—but with some public relations problems
4. Gnostic (special knowledge or esoteric strategies and tactics): On the whole quite relevant and not unreasonable. Examples of gnostic strategies: multi-stable deterrence; use of "not incredible counterforce first strike" threats for extended deterrence; "tit for tat" nuclear exchanges, other limited strategic options (LSO), calculating war, some flexible (nuclear) response, other limited war
5. LOUTish (Lucking out) policies: rely on ambiguity and uncertainty, or psychological avoidance, to such an extent that they appear to many to be stupid or brutish. Nevertheless, they are often also hardheaded and realistic. Examples of loutish strategies: threatening nuclear escalation in the event NATO's conventional defenses fail; prevailing in protracted CNW after massive counter-city attacks; waging three-front (full-scale) wars with the Soviet Union without adequate mobilization

Once there are nuclear weapons in the world, particularly megaton weapons, the world is a bizarre place and all strategies for dealing with it are bizarre to a degree. Megaton weapons should not exist, but they do; let us not delude ourselves. I do not believe in world disarmament and I wish my government would drop statements advocating it, because they are deluding themselves. No one believes a totally disarmed world is possible, a world in which if someone hid 50 weapons he could probably take over. No one is really interested in a totally disarmed world. How many people are even interested in a world government?

World government entails a world legislature. I know of very few Americans who are interested in "one man, one vote" as a guiding principle for a world government, because that would mean a legislature dominated by India and China. I know of very few Americans who are interested in "one country, one vote," either, because that principle produces a legislature run by the Afro-Asian bloc. I happen to have a good solution to the problem: "one dollar, one vote." That principle reflects reality and yields a legislature run by the United States, Japan, West Germany, and the Soviet Union.[13] That is not such an undesirable outcome. But I am having some technical difficulties in selling the idea.

One might have world empire, but that would have to be imposed by force and would therefore involve all the problems that forceful imposition of rule entails. I have no great interest in that. I certainly do not want a world empire run by the Soviets, and I do not think the Americans could run a good world empire. So these are not options.

In my opinion the positions listed above are the only real options among current nuclear doctrines, strategies, and tactics. Consider nuclear pacifism. Its proponents do not care what the problems are; they refuse to be involved. This is dangerously close to the current position of the American Catholic bishops. They have taken the position, roughly, that the United States should follow a policy of deterrence for some time, but there must be real progress made in disarmament. I happen to think that disarmament really does not work, although I believe in arms control. I want to make the world safer; at some times that means increasing your arms and at other times that means decreasing arms. Anyone who thinks that decreasing arms always makes the world safer again has not thought about the problems. People who support implementation of a nuclear freeze simply believe in the usual amount of overkill. I, on the other hand, do not believe in any overkill except psychological overkill. Of course, if one can overkill by a factor of ten under all circumstances, the precise magnitude of overkill is unimportant: no one cares whether it is two or twenty. This is not an interesting question. However, there is an insurance issue here. There is also a diplomatic issue. Occasionally people can be impressed by the sheer size of the establishment. I would argue that neither of those issues is worth so much that I would be terribly interested in the degree of overkill. As far as I am concerned, it is not an interesting question: there is no overkill, I want to argue.

One may reply to this contention that there are ten tons of high explosive equivalent for every human being on the earth, which I think is roughly correct, although it might be five. But that figure has nothing to do with anything. During warfare there are hundreds of bullets for every soldier. As the systems get used, overkill does not come into being.[14] The only way any situation resembling overkill could be created in the superpower war case would be if the United States and the Soviets cooperated.

It is the case that by the Defense Department's own estimates the assured level of destruction of 35 percent of the Soviet population and 75 percent of their industry would actually be accomplished by only 400 equivalent megatons as deliverable from the U.S. strategic arsenal.[15] My earlier contention is that overkill cannot be determined only by counting weapons; a distributional question is assumed. One cannot simply count bullets to determine how many soldiers will be killed; similarly, one does not only count megatons to measure overkill. In a war, the opponent attempts to destroy one's fighting ability, and one tries to destroy his. The objective is not to destroy cities, particularly in the first part of the war. There is no clear reason for cities to be high priority targets in nuclear war. A country may evacuate the inhabitants of its cities (see below). But even if they evacuate, the buildings are very valuable. [However, presumably buildings are not time-urgent targets, except where some cities are also high-priority leadership targets—Eds.]

No one anticipates producing much war goods after a massive exchange of nuclear weapons. In the United States, for example, Boeing has approximately 80,000 contractors. No reasonable analysts think that these contractors will produce a great many B-1s post-CNW, after a massive exchange of nuclear weapons. To think otherwise would provide case of World War II thinking, but I argue that there are at least some discontinuities. Probably the most important single discontinuity is that one's adversary could hit cities, but he will not, because they are not military targets, except possibly for command and control.

I want to emphasize that city avoidance is only very possible; not all cities would be avoided. This is the most important first principle to learn if one is interested in the probable sequence of events during a nuclear war. I cannot say that cities will not be hit; that is a different statement. I do assert that there is no high priority reason for hitting cities in the first strike. There is probably no high priority reason for hitting them in the second strike, though there may be. If one is an American studying nuclear war, one will notice that the two biggest assets to the U.S. cause are Moscow and Leningrad. From the Soviet point of view, it is as though these cities were half their country. They do not rank Kiev and the lesser cities particularly highly. These two cities are the two greatest assets of the U.S. cause because by bargaining with them the United States can protect New York, Washington, Chicago, Los Angeles, and other U.S. cities. So is there any reason why a preemptor—the person who strikes first—should hit cities?[16] There may be. A countervalue attack may trigger some sequence of events such as a coup, or may disrupt decision making, or have some other consequence. But this would be a very strange calculation.

Some people think that the Soviets are evil, and so they will hit cities because they like to kill people in large masses. A number of people think that the United States is evil, and that Americans like to kill people in large masses. As far as I know, although one does not necessarily get the best quality of person on either the Soviet or the American side in key positions of responsibility, one does not get the worst either. These are not convincing arguments for a first strike on cities.

Returning to nuclear pacifism, there are people who maintain simply that they would not have anything to do with nuclear weapons.[17] In this connection, an anecdote may be relevant. I once saw a photograph taken at the end of World War II showing a Jewish man who had been in a concentration camp. He is shown with an American soldier. The caption to the photograph reads: " 'Are you Jewish?' I said, 'Yes.' He continued, 'You know, that's a good rifle. Out of that rifle comes peace and safety because it's an American rifle.' "

One may wish to make a comparable assertion for an U.S. 20-megaton bomb: "That is a good 20-megaton bomb; out of that bomb comes peace." But it is substantially harder to assert—one cannot have the same enthusiasm for it. Consequently, nuclear pacifism becomes very attractive. To me, it is also an evasion of responsibility. One has no right to take this position if one expects to exercise any influence over events. At the same time I am prepared to advocate nonpayment of war taxes for nuclear weapons. The juxtaposition of these opinions does not bother me.

MAD (mutual assured destruction) is another possible strategy, whether it is defined as some sort of a first strike or as retaliation if the adversary provokes the United States by attacking Europe. The individuals who believe in mutual assured destruction until recently have never objected to the acronym MAD. It is rather mad to be prepared to commit suicide every day of the week and every week of the year, every year of the century. That is the MAD foreign policy technique, to threaten that if one's adversary does something wrong, one is prepared to commit suicide; this would engulf both countries, making it mutual homicide. One of the Hudson Institute staff analysts has studied the prospects of nuclear-mined cities. He pointed out that it would be substantially cheaper and much safer if the United States were allowed to mine Soviet cities with nuclear weapons, and they could mine our cities with nuclear weapons. Then a very small number of nuclear devices would suffice [and no delivery vehicles are necessary—Eds.]. But that example shows how bizarre the concept of mutually assured destruction is.

Another option is to rely on NUTS—nuclear use theories. In this view, nuclear weapons might actually be used in a rational way, or at least semirationally, largely rationally, partly rationally [and not maximally irrationally.—Eds.]. Considering the multiple command and control problems and all of the political problems, the instrumental use of nuclear weapons is a somewhat nutty concept. I am a well-known NUT. I believe that it can happen; it can be done. I think that NUT is a superior policy when compared to MAD or to nuclear pacifism. But I understand that it is to a degree a nutty set of concepts. The public has no idea how difficult it is to conduct a nuclear war; there are command and control problems, even if the enemy does not interfere. And if he does interfere, C^4I (command, control, communications, countermeasures, and intelligence) becomes much more difficult. And that he will do; he will interfere.

Gnostic policies present a fourth choice, of religious, esoteric, or otherwise special knowledge. Many ideas that make a great deal of sense as far as I can determine remain difficult to explain, or gnostic. They may take ten to twenty minutes to explain. In ten to twenty minutes it is not difficult to explain a bridge move or a chess move, for example. Every chess player has ideas that take that long to explain. But in nuclear war, to a degree that is actually shocking, even the experts do not know these ideas that take ten to twenty minutes to explain.

My picture of nuclear war is roughly the following:

Imagine a group of quite bright and responsible people who study chess, but who never play a game or see a historical game. They just study moves. They study moves continuously, and they write papers about moves, and they play with moves, and they argue moves, and they talk about moves, and they give papers on moves, and they have sit-ins about moves, but they never play a game. Then a young person comes along with twenty games under his belt. Who would one think would win the first two or three games? But no one has experienced a nuclear war. There is not an experienced player among us.

This is a famous story we used to tell at the Rand Corporation. (People thought I was the hero of the story, but I was not.) A Strategic Air Command general asks a young defense analyst what makes him think that the analyst has the right or the ability to advise a general on how to fight a nuclear war, considering that the analyst is just a kid while the general has years of military experience. The defense analyst replies that studies indicate it takes about ten nuclear wars to get a sense of the range. (Ten, I think, is about right.) He asks the general: "How many have you fought?"

"Well, I haven't fought any."

"All right," the analyst replies, "why don't we two amateurs get together and see what we can do about this problem? You have more experience in command and control and morale. I have a lot more experience in physics than you have. But, you know, we are both amateurs."

Let us not delude ourselves. No one has hands-on experience in CNW, including Hiroshima and Nagasaki survivors, who are not relevant for the CNW case. And that is what it takes to understand anything completely.

But one can work out some rather interesting concepts, as indicated in the list of doctrines, strategies, and tactics given above. Some of the main strategies used are so-called LOUTish strategies. LOUT is for lucking out, LOUTish meaning stupid or brutish. I do make a concession here: very often these LOUTish strategies are also hardheaded and realistic. I can give you any number of examples of LOUTish strategies. LOUTish options may work, but such strategies cannot be called satisfactory.

This summarizes current U.S. nuclear doctrines, strategies, and tactics. I repeat, if a person stands in any one of these five positions—nuclear pacifism through LOUTish strategies—and claims to be in a comfortable position that is clearly right and from which all possible objections can be answered, he is just a fool. I want to emphasize that: he is just a fool. I happen to believe in two of these options, NUTS and Gnostic policies, and to a lesser extent in LOUTish strategies.

Further Exploration of a Gedanken Experiment

Gedanken experiments are potentially very misleading, but they are also most interesting and provide a sense of what is actually happening. I will illustrate two gedanken experiments to make some points by posing questions and suggesting answers that have currency today. Let me start with the simplest idea of all.

Gedanken Experiment I: Proportional Response to Limited Attack on the United States

Imagine that 30 seconds ago President Reagan was informed that a multi-megaton bomb had just landed on New York City and probably about 5,000,000 Americans were dead. What should the president do?

One option is to wait for ten minutes, because the report might have been erroneous. But I think President Reagan would not wait. Initially he would not believe the report. I think he would be right not to believe it and to request confirmation. The United States has a great variety of equipment that actually measures radiation, to supplement observers' reports. This incredibility and the request for confirmation are a kind of waiting, in other words.

If there is no question about the explosion over New York, the next step, prior to conferring with the Soviets on the Hot Line, is to determine whether the bomb was one of ours. There is that awful fear that someone putsched. The United States has a long record over the last twenty years of absolutely crazy putsches. Perhaps this hypothetical event represents another one, since the United States is to some extent a low-morale country now.

If the president is told that, as far as can be determined, the bomb is not one of ours, he would contact the Soviets on the Hot Line. A Soviet missile might have been launched by accident. The Soviets might not know what to do, so they might just be waiting for a U.S. response. Suppose that over the Hot Line the Soviet leader claims responsibility for the attack. Suppose further that the Soviets assert that the Soviet attack is meant to demonstrate to the world that the USSR cannot be pressured any further by the United

States. Suppose the Soviets claim, "The Chinese push us around, the Rumanians push us around, the Poles push us around, you push us around; everyone pushes us around, so we have just made a point that we ain't gonna take it anymore. We are not going to be pushed around again." The Soviet statement concludes that, as far as the Soviets are concerned, the matter is closed.

Obviously no one thinks the matter is closed. One reponse might be to fire a U.S. nuclear missile, perhaps targeted on the Soviet leadership. But they are probably hidden deep underground at this point. So, I do not think the United States would fire at the Soviet leaders, although that would certainly be a reasonable reaction.

It might also occur to the U.S. president to destroy Moscow, but that is a mistake. Suppose that one either thinks that it is a mistake to trade New York for Moscow, or one will destroy Moscow. I want the reader to vote: there are no nuclear pacifists at this moment; you are part of the crime. Many people would destroy Moscow, but many people think that is a mistake. If you think it is a mistake, what alternative response would you suggest?

One may consider taking Cuba, but if one did this the Soviets would be delighted. If one wants instead to destroy Moscow under these circumstances, one must let the Soviets know before the event that this is the U.S. plan. Cuba, on the other hand, is a real problem for them. It costs them about $3 billion a year. So the probable U.S. response would not be to hit Cuba. After all, in this scenario the Cubans had nothing to do with the attack on New York. However the United States does not want to convey to the Soviets the message that bombing New York was a good thing to do from their point of view.

Consider launching an attack that would destroy every Soviet city. I think in destroying the major Soviet cities, the United States would see communism thrown out. There would be a revolution; there would be no more communist state after that. But they then will destroy every U.S. city in return, as a result of which approximately 100 million Americans will be lost. This prospect might make one reconsider the commitment, but that is the commitment business.

If one fulfills this commitment, within ten years it might be possible for the United States to rebuild and still to have the largest gross national product in the world, but I do not care that this recovery might be possible. I am not going to see 100 million Americans killed, and I do not think Americans want to kill 150 million Russians either. This is a crazy gedanken experiment in that I do not think it will happen. But if it did happen, the proportional response is to hit Leningrad.

Confronted with the prospect of massive U.S. casualties, the United States is not extending its commitments any further, but remains faced with the accomplished fact that the Soviets hit New York. (One would be absolutely correct to believe that actually the Soviets will not do it, so the United States deters. But in this experiment the Soviets have hit New York, so one is faced with a choice.) If a prior commitment to destroy every Soviet city had been made, one would be perfectly correct, at least in theory, to fulfill it. But the president of the United States is not really going to fulfill this commitment; he certainly will not.

Suppose the president informs the Soviets that he will hold them under a nuclear threat until they surrender. They will not do it; they are not going to surrender.

Suppose instead that the president orders the Soviets to destroy an equivalent city, keeping in mind that Moscow would not be an equivalent of New York to the USSR. They will not destroy an equivalent city themselves. That is the other side's job. One equivalent city would be Leningrad. Moscow is more important to the Soviet Union than New York, Washington, and Chicago put together are to the United States. Suppose then that in retaliation the United States destroys Leningrad, which would be a proportional response, right or wrong. Out of curiosity, let us speculate on what happens next.

The Soviets will be very quiet and will pray to God that this nuclear confrontation is over. The first message they will convey to the Americans will be "Don't do anything more!" The Biblical advice is very interesting in this context: at least an eye for an eye, a tooth for a tooth to maintain the law. The law must be maintained. At most an eye for an eye, a tooth for a tooth, because escalation must be avoided. Biblical law is very clear on these requirements: It is an obligation to maintain the law, but there is no right to escalate. I happen to believe that that is not a bad theory for many situations.

If the United States hits Leningrad, consider what happens subsequently: Nothing. Nothing happens next. I say that with a high degree of confidence, because under those circumstances the Soviets will have expected Leningrad to be hit. They are no fools. If they bomb New York, although they will not destroy Leningrad themselves, they already will have written Leningrad off when the decision was made to attack New York. They are not dumb.

One may counter that inevitably a city-for-city exchange leads to escalation. There are risks of escalation. But I also know that if I follow that advice a great many cities will be destroyed. I would be sick that New York had been destroyed, and I would be sick that I would have to destroy Leningrad. I like Leningrad; it is a great city—beautiful museums, physicists everywhere. The best U.S. response in this case would be to disarm the Soviets and to punish the particular people concerned. But the United States cannot disarm them. If the United States were able to disarm the Soviets, that would be the best option. If you cannot disarm them, then this option is not available.

It might be expected that if the USSR were to bomb New York, the headquarters of the United Nations, there might be international repercussions. Although this is true, it does not bother the Soviets in the slightest and does not affect their decision. The Soviets would be very unpopular. And who cares?

Another objection to the structure of this gedanken experiment might be that the Soviet Union has a declared No-First-Use policy. But this objection raises further questions: Is it any more heinous for the USSR to hit New York if the USSR has promised No First Use than if they have not? Do they go to hell any longer? Do they burn any harder? Is it or is it not a question of intent? I think it may be a question of intent, to some extent. If one leaves intent aside in a gedanken experiment, if all theological considerations are eliminated and if one is only strictly speaking of a logical, physical, scientific world, one still does not return to normal political life after a nuclear exchange. One's own country will arm to the teeth; the adversary will arm to the teeth; in fact every country will arm to the teeth, because it is a lousy world in many ways. But I argue that there would be no other choice for the United States besides retaliation and consequent rapid rearmament in these circumstances, because the United States prefers a lousy world to no world.

A Variation on the Experiment

If the experiment progresses one step further and assumes that the United States chose to hit Moscow instead of Leningrad, consider how the USSR would respond in that case. I do not know what they would do; no one does. I do think their first response would be to ask whether Americans read their own literature. Retaliation targeting Moscow is American-type thinking, not Russian-type thinking. Because Moscow is more important to the USSR than New York, Washington, and Chicago put together are to the United States, retaliation against Moscow would make escalation likely. Would the Soviet Union then hit both Washington and Chicago in a return strike to even the score? If the United States attacks Moscow one will see exactly the escalation one would like to prevent: five for one, ten for one, twenty for one. On the other hand, even if the USSR prefers not to escalate, the Soviets cannot allow the United States an attack on Moscow without further action. I think they hit Philadelphia. And I think it stops there. That would be a typical pattern: tit, tat, tit.

In this experiment the Soviets made a preemptive attack on New York because, for one reason or another, they wanted to make clear to the world that they should not be pressured any further. Since they actually do not care that much whether they have been pushed around, they are not going to hit

New York. They could take some smaller action than that, but they still would not.

My point is that in Soviet judgment at that time in the gedanken experiment, the Soviets concluded that nobody would push them around in the future if they bombed New York; that is, that there would be real demonstration effects. There is some validity to that conclusion. But if the United States responds by destroying Moscow, the United States has escalated, because the cities are not of comparable value. Consequently, the USSR would strike Philadelphia to teach the United States that it cannot escalate with impunity.

This totally crazy analysis is presented here because, even as crazy as it is, it illustrates several points very starkly. These matters should be made very stark. Otherwise it is very difficult to illustrate the escalation process, because every city is complicated. If escalation is studied at a simpler level—assuming for example that the USSR destroyed a bridge and the United States responded by bombing another bridge—I do not know where escalation happens. I have to make the issues so stark that they swamp other considerations, such as who the president is and how he feels that morning; political considerations; the effect of UN; and demonstrations. The issues must be so stark that they even swamp attacking Cuba. I am attempting in these studies of escalation to make the case that a limited war is not impossible.

I do not know if the sequence of events described would really take place as I predict or not. But one cannot say that it is impossible. It might not work. But if it does, a limited war, a damnably big one, will have occurred. But it will have been limited, and it will have been terminated. If, in fact, this scenario does not work, I am wrong. But I am not wrong in principle. And I can present exactly the same set of circumstances at much lower levels of violence, although it is more complicated because there are more choices of target.

I mention that particular gedanken experiment to argue some points, I think correctly:

1. The usual picture of a Soviet–U.S. nuclear war, which assumes that the reaction of decision makers on both sides is to press every button in the house, is basically incorrect.
2. Both sides will be deeply concerned with the lives of their own people, if not with the other side's lives.
3. Because of this concern for life, if a country is provoked to an extreme degree and has no choice but mutual assured destruction, most likely it will not respond with mutual assured destruction, but with some variation of a limited tit-for-tat exchange.

If I had more space, I would review the history of tit-for-tat. Every single tribe has worked it out in some part of its history, almost without exception. The concept is peacekeeping, very much like U.N. peacekeeping. When the U.N. does peacekeeping, it does not attempt to determine who is right or wrong. The approach of the U.N. is to stop the violence. The primitive tribe has learned that it is very hard to stop the violence until the score has been evened. People tend to view tit-for-tat as escalation-breeding; the Hatfields and the McCoys come to mind. As a matter of actual record, at least at the village level, tit-for-tat exchanges have been used for thousands of years as a peacekeeping device and they have more or less worked in the absence of courts.

Popular Rejection of the Idea of Limited Nuclear War

Some of the public supports the view that escalation cannot be controlled, so that there is only one kind of nuclear war, an essentially unlimited nuclear war in which the earth will become a cinder and all life will become extinct. Those who take that view have accepted some hypotheses that are probably inaccurate in several respects. Thus, they are not thinking straight. They believe that every war has to blow up everything, all decision makers have to be dumb, and everyone has to press every button in the house. Additionally, they may think that this belief should be accepted even if it is not literally true, because the belief itself is a protection against nuclear war. I do not accept that. I believe this simplistic thinking represents a very great danger. This view is dangerous in a number of ways.

For one thing, it leads to developments such as the nuclear freeze movement, which is to say that it leads to a total disinterest in details. The nuclear freeze is the sort of thing one does if one really does not know what to do substantively, but wishes to get the government's attention. Even then the nuclear freeze is not a good first step, unless one believes that there is something good about the current strategic weapons balance, unless one believes that negotiating with the Soviets is undesirable, or unless one opposes a rearmament program. All three of these opinions are ill-advised. I may be wrong, too, but I have a group of arguments on my side suggesting that if I am wrong, I am not wrong in an obvious, simple way. I would be wrong because the arguments are very complicated.

The nuclear freeze might have prevented a great increase in the power of the U.S. ICBM force, but I do not believe that the fact that the United States has a counterforce capability is destabilizing. Nonetheless the freeze movement does make a point that I think is partially correct. That is that the United States may well achieve a fair counterforce capability in the next decade or so. The United States had an overwhelming counterforce capability from

1950 to 1965. The Soviets operated totally on alert. If the United States had wanted to attack them and destroy them, it was the easiest thing in the world then because the Soviets had absolutely zero alert capability. Neither the Soviets nor the Americans was worried about it. [The basis in the Soviet literature for this conclusion is unclear—Eds.] They were not worried about it; we were not worried about it. So in some sense, counterforce is not quite what you think it is. But one can never return to the situation of the 1950s and early 1960s.

The issues and evidence are themselves complicated. World War I was in part started by an armaments race. World War II was started by a nonarmaments race. The decision makers in Europe were not sufficiently concerned about German power. So disarmament is not always an answer to security problems. I happen to believe that the worst thing one can do in this particular field is to ignore the evidence and the arguments. It is a little evil. If one is satisfied with this ignorance, that is also a little immoral. I believe that, although I do not believe necessarily that the truth shall set you free on these issues.

One may think that the answer to this complicated problem is disarmament, but I do not support disarmament because any country with 50 or 100 weapons will take over in an otherwise disarmed world.

Further, I do not advocate disarmament because disarmament might be destabilizing in several ways. First and foremost, people begin to feel they can calculate the war and they feel they might take a risk because the price is so limited. If disarmament had reduced the numbers of missiles to fifty on a side, I would no longer assert that no one would resort to CNW for ambition. People might take the risk. If there are 500 or 1,000 on one side, the plans for a war of ambition alone cannot be made because it is too risky. Second, there are technical issues here. Basically, until about 1963 the United States was in essence keeping up with the Soviets and was substantially ahead of them. From 1963 on (for a number of reasons, mostly that Americans felt that the only fair strategic balance was rough equality), the United States really did not spend much money on weapons as a whole. If the operational expenses of the Vietnam War are subtracted out, in constant dollars the U.S. Defense Department budget was constant for the next seventeen years. The Soviet military budget went up by 4 to 5 percent a year.[18] That doubles in seventeen years, by the way. [President Reagan's January 1985 budget will have doubled total obligational spending authority for the U.S. military from 1980 to 1984, excluding military aid and the costs of nuclear weapons.—Eds.] At some point it had to come to a stop, and it came to a stop in President Carter's administration, though not because he wanted rearmament.

Some Common Attitudes Toward CNW: Denial and Unthinkability

There are a number of common attitudes toward CNW, and some strategies for dealing intellectually with CNW. I argue here that there is psychological or other rejection of the possibility of central nuclear war. CNW is literally unthinkable, because the survival of mankind is at stake. CNW would be the inevitable end of history, in this view; or at least it would be best to think that it would be, or at a minimum might be. The possibility that CNW might be the inevitable end of history is a very low-probability event, but I cannot ignore it. I will totally reject as being reasonable positions for any serious person to hold both the view that CNW would inevitably be the end of history and the view that it would be best to think so. I do not think it is desirable to think that CNW will be the end of history. It is a remarkably bad idea in itself and in my opinion it makes the world much more dangerous to believe that. This end-of-the-world hypothesis is not a new idea, by the way; it is an old idea and a bad one.

Simplistic Solutions to the Problems of CNW

Let me address some other questions to give a sense of what a fairly complete study would look like. A belief in simplistic solutions to the problems of central nuclear war is likely to persist. Of course, many now find simplistic solutions more attractive than ever, particularly people who support a position characterized by self-righteousness, moral indignation, and an almost complete ignorance of and indifference to nuances and details. This attitude is not new, though the tendency to be attracted to it may have increased recently.

The belief that the invention of nuclear weapons that might destroy all of life somehow improves people's safety, and the belief that this safety improves even more over time are at least problematical. Likewise, the belief that every nuclear weapon somehow detracts from people's safety should be examined. I might only point out some simple trends and possibilities such as the following: an interesting contemporary trend in the world is that an increase in the arms race may actually be stabilizing in some sense. Nevertheless this is counterintuitive; one does not want to believe it. One would prefer that this increase did not take place. The latest example of a stabilizing increase in the arms race was the growth in the number of missiles. I know of no arms control or disarmament advocates who thought that the replacement of bombers by missiles was desirable. Such people may exist, but I did not meet them, and neither did I read their papers. They all thought substitution of missiles for bombers would be dangerous; warning time would be only thirty minutes, and everything would be kept on alert. After the replacement occurred, most people thought the world was safer because missiles are more stable against accidents, war, or first strike than bombers are. So the evolution of intellectual positions was rather interesting. An enormous escalation in the arms race had concerned everyone who favored arms control or disarmament. They wished replacement could have been held back. After it happened, they argued that the world was safer.

I rather suspect that a similar event will occur in the early 21st century, and that is the emergence of a true multi-polar world. By the year 2000, there could be about eight powers with trillion-dollar gross national products. I suggest that the United State's GNP should be $4.5 trillion. In such a multi-polar world, the victor of any two-power confrontation could not hope to attain world domination. In fact, the victor would be weak compared to the other six or seven. Hence, any motivation one might have to go into a nuclear war for world dominance would be even further reduced by economic multi-polarity.

In addition, balance-of-power politics such as that which characterized Europe from 1815 to 1914 becomes possible in a multi-polar world. If there are only two major powers, a Cold War is difficult to avoid. Everything becomes a Cold War issue; El Salvador today is a Cold War. If there are three powers, two may ally against the third. In the case of four powers, two may ally against two. If there are five, one of the powers plays balance of power. If it is peace-loving, it aligns itself with the weaker powers or the more peace-loving powers. And six, seven and eight have similar effects.

In a true multi-polar world, such strategies as MAD and launch-on-warning, as well as freezes, become indefensible. I think that is good. Nonetheless, I would prefer to prevent the emergence of this true multi-polar world, even though my analysis indicates that it is much safer, because I do not trust my analysis, and I worry about any change. But if I had to bet on this proposition, I would argue that a multi-polar world would be a hell of a lot safer world than today's world. And I would probably win.

Five Priority Canonical Hudson CNW "Requirements" Scenarios

Let me present five scenarios on the origins of Central Nuclear War that will interest any professional analyst who is seriously looking at nuclear war.

   I. Surprise Attack Scenario, More or Less Out of the Blue.
      A. Deliberate Soviet attack: constrained, unmodified, or environmental
      B. Inadvertent war

This first scenario is a surprise attack out of the blue, which is not particularly probable but is included for completeness.

    II. Early Eruption from Intense Crisis Scenario
        A. Four typical "not implausible" crises in order of their relative plausibility (to the staff of the Hudson Institute)
            1. East European crisis (e.g., East German or Polish uprising or crisis in Yugoslavia)
            2. Persian Gulf disaster involving U.S. compound (horizontal) escalation or use of nuclear weapons
            3. Sino-Soviet war or crisis, U.S. intervention, and eventual escalation
            4. East Asian crisis involving escalation from PRC-ROK, PRC-Taiwan, North Korea-South Korea or some Vietnam confrontation
        B. Soviet strike
        C. More likely, Soviet evacuation. (There is almost no chance under current conditions of a U.S. preemption.)
        D. Very likely a U.S. evacuation
        E. Increased chance of inadvertent war: accident, irresponsible behavior, reciprocal fear of surprise attack, other action-reaction spiral
        F. Soviet or U.S. ultimatum and/or attack. (High probability that the attack will be constrained.)

In the second scenario a type of crisis is presumed in which people do not behave as though they were smart, or they take excessive chances, or they play the game of chicken. In part IIa above there are four typical "not implausible" crises. The crises taken most seriously at the Hudson Institute are those in Eastern Europe and those in the Persian Gulf, if the United States has dangerous policies that cause the escalation. A Sino-Soviet dispute is also a very important crisis type. Let me point out that England went to war in World War I not because England was attacked—the Germans had no intention of attacking England—but because Belgium was attacked. Let me also point out that France and England went to war in World War II because Poland was attacked. I am curious how simplistic proposals such as the nuclear freeze deal with the probability of nuclear war as the result of alliance or other commitment. The simple Pearl Harbor situation, in which the United States was directly attacked, may be expected to be relatively rare.

Allow me to clarify my assumptions. I am not assuming a nuclear war a priori. I argue that most of these crises would *not* cause nuclear war; they are not implausible. I argue that it is very difficult to write a plausible scenario for the origins of central nuclear war. Again, I invented the phrase "not implausible" to describe some of the relevant probabilities. I have argued that I can probably produce a "not implausible" scenario; if I cannot do that, I can at least produce a "not wildly implausible" one. So I am not assuming a nuclear war.

While I worry about many, many problems, I do not lose much sleep over the nuclear war problem. I support the current U.S. rearmament program because I think it is important to rearm, but if the United States did not rearm, I would not lose sleep about that either. I am compelled to think that the current rearmament program is complicating enormously the fight against inflation and the domestic economic recovery. At the same time the rearmament program is useful, because it is wrong for the United States to rely much on Soviet prudence and caution. Still, my judgment would be that it is a good bet for the United States to rely on Soviet prudence and caution.

I argue that the Soviets would not attack the United States even if they thought they might achieve a clean win. Very few specialists with whom I work think that nuclear war will happen, as they usually delimit it, "in the next two decades." We just do not. Nonetheless, analysts do think that it is important to keep doors closed on which the Soviets are not leaning, because once they lean on one, it is too late to close the door. If the reader thinks that this attitude is paranoid, that is his privilege. I do not think it is paranoia; I think it is reasonable caution.

The other CNW scenarios are not as fully detailed here:

III. Classic Type 2 Deterrence Scenario
   A. Soviet attack on Western Europe
   B. U.S. evacuation and perhaps ultimatum
   C. Eventually ultimatum, or careful U.S. attack accompanied by offer or ultimatum

IV. Protracted Crisis Scenario
   A. Inadvertent war, now relatively probable
   B. Scenario similar to II or III above
   C. Erosion of capability and/or treacherous relaxation of tension, then attack by enemy
   D. Limited war, including nuclear war at sea, followed by an escalation to central nuclear war
   E. Soviet provocation—initiation of U.S. mobilization—mobilization war, or declaration of war eventually followed by more or less "phony" war

V. Mobilization War Scenario

A. Mobilization war does not escalate, but there may be a limited war with conflicting requirements
B. Mobilization war does escalate to central nuclear war
  1. In one year: United States has, relatively speaking, a war-fighting posture, e.g., greatly improved C³I and civil defense
  2. In two years: United States has greatly improved war-fighting posture, e.g., huge expansion of existing forces and procurement of more or less on-the-shelf weapons systems
  3. In three years: Elaborate war-fighting posture, including initial development of new systems

At the Hudson Institute these five classes of CNW outbreak scenarios are thought of as providing a reasonable basis for planning U.S. central war posture and mobilization capabilities. They can also be used for educational and polemic purposes and somewhat less effectively as triggering scenarios—e.g., the 1950 Korean War triggered a relatively general U.S. and Allied mobilization that, if directed at anything, emphasized a Soviet attack on Western Europe. Thus the Joint Chiefs of Staff characterized the Korean War as the wrong war at the wrong place and the wrong time.

Editors' Notes

1. See Michael Levandowsky, Chapter 6 in this volume. Dr. Kahn's assessment of the literature predates the nuclear winter studies.

2. Soviet military casualties during the Second World War are estimated at over 20 million; at about 2 million for the Civil War and for the fighting against foreign armies attempting to oust the Bolshevik government. These figures omit delayed military casualties, civilian casualties from three famines and from epidemics, casualties of the forced collectivization and from the concentration camps in the 1930s. (See Feshbach 1982:6-7).

3. This reasoning creates at least two interesting consequences, depending on the choice of assumptions with which it is combined: 1. that the Soviets might provide the first occasion of such unused arsenals; or 2. that having built up weapons to specified levels, e.g., U.S.–Soviet parity, the Soviets might become less war-averse than they are argued to have been in the past. It is unclear whether the spending reference is to a relative or absolute comparison.

4. Or because of its own internal contradictions . . . .

5. Evidently Dr. Kahn referred in the first instance to Malenkov, though these statements were not far apart in time. See the general discussion in Ulam (1974), *Expansion and Coexistence: The History of Soviet Foreign Policy 1917-1973*, New York: Praeger. See also Rubenstein (1972), *The Foreign Policy of the Soviet Union*, New York: Random House.

6. There are repeated references to the possibility of a first strike on the Soviet Union in the Soviet professional military literature, although no credible reference has been found to the probability or inevitability of such a strike. For some sources

of Soviet thinking on nuclear war and arms control, see inter alia Kozlov and Milovidov (1972), *Philosophical Heritage of V. I. Lenin and Problems of Contemporary War,* Moscow: Izdat'elstvo Oboroni; G. Trofimenko (1980); *Changing Attitudes Toward Deterrence;* ACIS Working Paper No.25: July; M. Mil'shtein and Semeiko (1973), "Strategic Arms Limitation: Problems and Prospects," S.Sh.A.:12 (in Russian).

7. For an analysis that concurs with Dr. Kahn's parenthetical remark, see Jane Sharp (1984), "Arms Control Dilemmas," Papers on Rethinking National Security and Arms Control, Hubert H. Humphrey Institute of Public Affairs, University of Minnesota, Minneapolis: HHH Institute.

8. Or independent and not necessarily neutral as defined in the U.S.–Soviet context.

9. See inter alia Herman Kahn, (1982) "Thinking About Nuclear Morality," *New York Times Magazine* 13 June:42-44; Kahn interview with correspondent, "Build an Anti-missile System Now?", *U.S. News and World Report* 91, 21 September:53-54.

10. There are repeated No-First-Use statements in the Soviet press during 1978-79, of various character, including the NFU pledge in Leonid I. Brezhnev's 6 October 1979 speech in Berlin, reprinted in *Pravda* and in *Izvestia* (7 October 1979, p. 1 in both sources), and translated in the *Current Digest of the Soviet Press* 31:40 of 31 October 1979:2-4.

11. Bundy, McGeorge, George Kennan, Robert S. McNamara, and Gerard Smith (1982). "Nuclear Weapons and the Atlantic Alliance," *Foreign Affairs Quarterly* 60:753-768. Spring.

12. To continue the analogy, and omitting the cases of p. = any precise value, for simplicity, apparently Dr. Kahn would argue that a not implausible event would have a probability of .1 to .5, so a contradiction would be obtained if the real probability were less than .1. If our understanding is correct, a demonstration of plausibility (probability greater than .5) would also provide a contradiction. So the difficulty for the opponent is that the range of probabilities between 0 and .1 has no convenient name and might tend to be overlooked if the options have been falsely dichotomized.

13. And presumably selected OPEC states.

14. Here the reader is asked to make the determination that, at least in this respect, nuclear war is analogous to conventional war.

15. A somewhat dated estimate of U.S. total EMT is provided by Brown (1977) at 115,000-130,000 square miles exposed to 5 psi or approximately 2,000 EMT (1,916-2,166) if an equivalent megaton covers 60 square miles with 5 pounds per square inch overpressures. These calculations are based on the megatonnage available in 1975 on U.S. ICBMs and SLBMs. Note that estimates that 400 EMT could destroy either superpower as a functioning society have been attributed to former U.S. Secretary of Defense Robert McNamara.

16. Caveat preemptor.

17. This might also be called nuclear rejection or nuclear isolationism, as the pacifist position is more well-developed than is indicated here.

18. Other analysts report a 3 percent or a 4 percent annual increase in the Soviet military budget, over a lower base than in the United States; only some of this increment was devoted to Soviet strategic weapons. It should also be noted here that the Soviet defense budget is not a money allocation; it represents a budget of resources allocated to the military, with the potential problem of consequent shortfalls where shortages develop. There also appear to be significant differences in productivity of industry between the superpowers, complicating the interpretation of all of the a-

vailable sets of defense spending estimates.

References

Brodie, Bernard (1959). *Strategy in the Missile Age.* Princeton NJ: Princeton University Press.
Ermath, F. (1978). "How to Think About Soviet Military Doctrine." RAND paper P5939. Santa Monica CA: RAND. February.
Feshback, Murray (1982). "The Soviet Union: Population Trends and Dilemmas," *Population Bulletin* Vol. 37, No. 3. (Population Reference Bureau, Inc., Washington, D.C.)
Gallois, Pierre (1961). *The Balance of Terror: Strategy for the Nuclear Age.* [English edition of (1960) *Strategie de l'age Nucleaire.* Paris: Calmann-Levy.] Boston: Houghton Mifflin.
Garthoff, Raymond L. (1953). *Soviet Strategy in the Nuclear Age.* New York: Praeger.
Gray, Colin, and Keith Payne (1980). "Victory is Possible," *Foreign Policy* 39:Summer.
Kahn, Herman (1960). *On Thermonuclear War.* Princeton NJ: Princeton University Press.
——— (1962). *Thinking About the Unthinkable.* New York: Horizon Press.
——— (1965). *On Escalation: Metaphors and Scenarios.* New York: Praeger.
Lambeth, Benjamin (1976). *Selective Nuclear Options in American and Soviet Strategic Policy.* Santa Monica CA: RAND.
Morgan, Patrick (1977). *Deterrence: A Conceptual Analysis.* London: Sage.
Shulman, Marshall (1982). "U.S.–Soviet Relations and the Control of Nuclear Weapons," in Barry Blechman, ed., *Rethinking the U.S. Strategic Posture.* Cambridge MA: Ballinger.
Snyder, Glenn (1961). *Deterrence and Defense.* Princeton NJ: Princeton University Press.
Zavilov (1971). "Nuclear Weapons and War," *Survival* 13:3. March.

5

Judith Reppy

MILITARY SPENDING AND THE U.S. ECONOMY

Judith Reppy is an economist with degrees from Yale and Cornell. Since 1973 she has been associated with the Peace Studies Program at Cornell University, where she has specialized in the study of military research and development and the economic impact of defense spending. She is the coeditor, with F. A. Long, of The Genesis of New Weapons. *Dr. Reppy has published widely in economics journals.*

In this paper Dr. Reppy examines the macroeconomic, regional, and sectoral impact of military spending on the U.S. economy. She anticipates that because the military can outbid civilian enterprises, possible bottlenecks in supply of skilled labor may develop as the economic recovery subsides. She finds that a prolonged overemphasis on military concerns in U.S. research and development expenditures already may have begun to cause serious long-term handicaps for the United States in world markets. In particular, the international competitiveness of U.S.-made industrial machinery and electronic circuitry may have been diminished as one aspect of the long-term dynamic opportunity costs of military spending in the United States, and the civilian sector may have been deprived of technological innovations that it might otherwise have enjoyed.

Introduction

My topic is the impact of military spending on the U.S. economy. It should be noted that this is not the most important aspect of our military programs, even of the large military buildups that began in the Carter administration and have continued under President Reagan. Clearly the most important consequences of military spending are the weapons that are bought, the force structure that they support, and what we plan to do with them. The economic costs are secondary to these important aspects, but they are, nevertheless, a salient political issue, particularly because of the very large budget deficits that we are experiencing. The federal deficit for fiscal year 1983 was $195 billion; it is estimated at over $200 billion for fiscal year 1984. Given the current structure of the federal budget, it will be very difficult to reduce that deficit without reducing military spending, and yet we have an administration that insists that its military programs are sacrosanct. Thus, the impact of those very large spending programs on the economy is an issue that should be addressed.

Another way of looking at the costs of the military program is to recognize that the health of the economy is a constituent part of our national security. This has been formally recognized in National Security Council documents, at least since the Eisenhower administration. If the direct and indirect costs of our military programs are damaging the overall economy, national security is diminished. Whether this is a price we wish to pay is a question that can only be answered by reference to an estimate of what the costs to the economy are.

The late Senator Everett Dirksen once said, speaking of the defense budget, "A billion here, a billion there—pretty soon it adds up to real money." And we are talking about real money. Outlays for national defense have grown from $136 billion in fiscal year 1980 to an estimated $245 billion in fiscal year 1984. Defense spending is 28 percent of the federal budget and 7 percent of current gross national product. Both of these figures are higher now than they were during the past ten years.[1]

From the economist's point of view the most significant way to view the costs of defense spending is in terms of the opportunity costs incurred; that is, the true cost is measured by the value of what the resources could have been used for if they were not being used for military activities programs. In an economy with relatively free markets, such as that of the United States, dollar costs come close to measuring opportunity costs. In international comparison, however—particularly with the Soviet Union, where there is not a free market and prices are quite arbitrary—the monetary cost of military programs is not a true measure of their opportunity cost. And, as will be argued later, even in this country budgeted costs do not capture all of the opportunity costs of the military program.

The most commonly used measure of the burden of defense spending is the ratio of defense spending to the gross national product. It compares defense spending to a generally accepted measure of economic strength and has the advantage of being easily extended to international comparisons. But it is only a simple ratio, and it does not really tell very much about the capacity of an economy to sustain a given level of military spending. Taking a more analytical approach, there are at least three different levels that are relevant to evaluating the impact of military spending on the economy. In the short run we can ask about the macroeconomic and sectoral effects of defense spending, and in the longer run we are interested in the effects on the structure and performance of the U.S. economy.

Macroeconomic Effects

There is, of course, a great deal of interest among politicians in the short-term macroeconomic effects; that is, in the effects on economic aggregates such as levels of employment, the size of the deficit, rates of inflation, interest rates, and investment. It used to be that very little could be said about defense spending and the behavior of these indices of economic performance, in part because the economics profession as a whole has not been very interested in the subject and also for the more technical reason that econometric models of the economy did not include defense-specific equations. Defense spending was not distinguished from other categories of government spending, so that although you could ask the question, "If the government spends 100 million dollars more, what will be the effects?" you could not ask, "What will be the effects if 100 million dollars more are spent on defense?" and get an answer that differed from the answer to the more general question at either the macroeconomic or sectoral level.

In the last three years, however, that situation has changed, largely through the efforts of David Blond, an economist working in the Office of Program Analysis and Evaluation in the Department of Defense. Through his efforts and through contract work undertaken by major econometric firms, most notably Data Resources, Incorporated, a defense economic impact modeling system (DEIMS) has been developed.[2] It is now possible to estimate in some detail the short-term effects of changes in defense spending, subject, of course, to the usual caveats about economic forecasting models.

In general, the macroeconomic results of an increase in military spending are projected to be increases in gross national product, industrial output, employment, and increases in the federal deficit and rate of inflation.[3] These results are standard for any increase in government spending and are, it should be noted, quite sensitive to assumptions in the model about what is happening to the rest of the economy, particularly with respect to other government spending and tax policy.

In a recession the inflationary pressures from increased government spending are not likely to be a problem because of the large amount of slack in the economy. Even the special inflationary pressure from military spending, which is inherent in taking resources to produce a product that no one buys, are not a serious problem in a recession such as the one the United States experienced in the first years of the Carter-Reagan military buildup. The most serious concern about the large defense budgets has been that the government borrowing necessary to finance them will lead to higher interest rates and the crowding out of private investment in the capital markets. This potential discouragement of private investment forms a link between the short-term impacts of defense spending and longer-term effects. When an economy experiences low investment rates for years in a row, as the U.S. economy has, it is mortgaging its future economic productivity and growth.

Sectoral Effects

As was pointed out above, however, these aggregated effects on the economy are not uniquely associated with defense spending per se. In the Reagan administration, increases in government spending have been for defense, but the macroeconomic effects would occur from any source of high government spending and budget deficits. Thus, it is more interesting to look at the microeconomic effects in specific sectors and industries, because it is at this level that one finds effects that are definitely related to the fact that dollars are being spent for defense rather than for some other government activity. The DEIMS model provides a breakdown of the impact of defense spending on 400 different commodity-based sectors, which in turn are linked to a standard input-output model of the economy. Not surprisingly, the effects are strongest in a few industries, specifically ordinance and ammunition, shipbuilding, tank production, aircraft and missiles, and radio and TV communications. Most of the defense dollars are spent in these industries and, in turn, defense spending comprises a large fraction of their total sales. For instance, in 1982 military sales were over 50 percent of the sales in the aircraft industry and close to 70 percent in the shipbuilding industry.[4]

Thus, there is a concentration of spending in certain industries and for those industries defense dollars are important. There are also indirect impacts on other industries because of the demand of the defense sector for materials and other inputs. Some analysts have feared that increased military spending would lead to bottlenecks in these supplying industries, particularly because the number of firms selling to the defense contractors has decreased in the post-Vietnam period.[5] Shortages of goods that are also needed by civilian-based industries could generate ripples of inflation that in turn would spread to the rest of the economy.

These fears were greater at the beginning of the current military buildup because it was not foreseen how prolonged and deep the economic recession would be. The projected buildup was compared to the eroding defense industrial base and severe difficulties were forecast.[6] In their more extreme form these claims were surely exaggerated, as they allowed little scope for any flexibility in the economy, in particular for supplier response to higher military spending. Nor did they give sufficient weight to the fact that the growth in actual spending would be more gradual than the increases in budget authority for defense programs, thus allowing time for supply to adjust to the higher levels of demand. So far, because of the recession and the large amount of slack in the economy, there has not been any significant problem with bottlenecks. The rate of inflation in the defense sector has been falling as it has in the rest of the economy.

There may, however, be more cause for concern in the future, if all of the proposed military programs are funded and the civilian economy makes a strong recovery, although even in those circumstances the economy should prove resilient. One area in which bottlenecks may become important at an early date is in the supply of skilled labor. One of the ways in which defense spending differs from other federal government spending is that it draws on skilled labor, scientists, and engineers to a much greater extent than do other spending programs. Looking at the composition of the workforce by occupation, nondefense government spending has only 3 percent of its workers in the scientific and technical category, whereas defense spending has nearly 10 percent.[7] This suggests that in some occupations there may be shortages already, particularly in specialties such as electrical engineering and computing, and the military buildup may be straining an already tight labor market. Even with unemployment figures near 10 percent, there are some industries in which the military demand does make it more difficult for civilian-based firms to hire the skilled technical personnel that they want.

Regional Effects

Another aspect of the short-term impact of defense spending is the pattern of spending by regions. To a large extent the impact on regions is a product of the degree of concentration in industries described above, because the defense-related industries tend to be clustered in certain parts of the country. For obvious reasons, shipyards are located along the coasts. Aircraft production tends to be located largely on the West Coast, although there is still a substantial base in the Northeast with Grumman on Long Island and United Technologies in Connecticut.

In general, the Northeast has been a declining region for defense spending, and the major new installations of the Department of Defense have tended to be in the Sunbelt states. For example, although almost 4 percent of the national population is engaged in manufacturing, New Jersey has only 2 percent of the defense-related employment and about 2 percent of the Department of Defense (DOD) prime contracts. These figures have been declining since the Second World War, although in New Jersey they have not declined as sharply as in other states in the Northeast; twenty-five years ago New Jersey had 3 percent of the prime contracts and it now has a little over 2 percent. The probable reason for this relatively good performance compared to the rest of the region is that the major defense contractors in New Jersey are electronics contractors such as RCA, Inc., ITT, and Western Electric, so that the state has participated in the growth in defense spending for electronics even as it was losing in other categories of defense spending, e.g., through bases being closed.

The shift of the defense dollar from the Northeast and Midwest to the West and Southwest is a long-term trend, and one that is not likely to be reversed. There are real economies involved because of better weather and lower-cost labor and, once underway, the shift has been reinforced as clusters of parts manufacturers and other suppliers have relocated near the major contractors. Given a choice, most career military officers would rather live in Florida or Southern California than in Maine, so there is an incentive to locate bases and other facilities in the Sunbelt. A third factor, which may be the most important one, is that for many years control of Congressional committees was based on seniority rules, and in most cases that meant that they were controlled by Southern Democrats. Not surprisingly, over the years a large number of defense installations came to be located in the districts and states represented by these Congressional leaders.

The shift in location of defense-related economic activity has created a curious ambivalence in some legislators from the Northeast, who deplore the impact of the growing military budget on the funds available for social programs they support, but are very likely to turn around the next day to argue bitterly that the Department of Defense is not spending as much in their region as it should be. In fact, a major source of information about regional impact of defense spending is the research reports put out by the Coalition of Northeastern Governors and the Northeast-Midwest Research Institute, groups formed to lobby for increased federal spending in their regions.[8]

Long-Term Effects

The third aspect of the impact of military spending to be discussed is the long-term effect on the structure of the economy. Here again the emphasis is on sectoral effects: What parts of the economy are growing compared to other parts? Which technologies are changing rapidly? Which regions are prospering? These questions can be restated in terms of the concept of dynamic opportunity costs: What is the structure and performance of our economy today, compared to what it would have been if the large-scale military spending of the postwar period had not occurred and the resources had been allocated elsewhere?

This question only arises in the period since 1945. Over most of our history military spending was low, rising sharply with each war but falling just as precipitously at the end of the war. At first it seemed as if World War II would follow the same pattern. In 1940 defense spending stood at 1.6 percent of gross national product; it rose to 38.7 percent in 1944 and fell back to 5.2 percent by 1947 and 3.2 percent in 1948.[9] But this pattern was broken by the outset of the Cold War—particularly the Berlin crisis of 1948 and the outbreak of fighting in Korea—coupled with the new role for technology that had developed during the Second World War. The success of such innovations as radar, proximity fuses, and, overwhelmingly, the atomic bomb persuaded many that the country's military strength depended on its preeminence in technology. Once the idea that high technology has a real military utility was accepted, the obsolescence of existing military hardware inevitably became a constant pressure for new generations of weapons.

The political crises gave urgency to the push for rearmament, while the new role for technology ensured that development and procurement of ever more expensive weapons would be sustained even in the absence of actual war-fighting. The United States adopted a high level of military spending that, in real terms, has not varied from the levels of the mid-1950s, except for the Vietnam War period, until the current buildup in military spending began in 1979. The result of this sustained level of spending had been the institutionalization of a large defense industry in the private sector and of a large-scale program for military research and development. These activities are now woven into the fabric of our economy in a way that simply was not true before World War II.

There have been benefits, as well as costs, for the civilian economy from this expenditure of money and resources. The GI Bill provided educational opportunities for thousands of veterans; this was an investment in human capital that probably could have been funded only under the rubric of national security. The pattern of military spending described above, with its great emphasis on aircraft, electronics, and computers, has favored the growth of those sectors of the economy. The cost of this pattern is, of course, the areas that have been relatively neglected—for example, railroads—because they did not have a high military priority in the modern age.

Unfortunately there is no comprehensive methodology for evaluating these costs and benefits to reach a net assessment of the long-term economic impact of military spending. Aside from the difficulty of devising appropriate schemes of quantification, it is extraordinarily difficult to separate out influences of military spending from other secular influences on the economy over the decades.

With these caveats in mind, it is nevertheless interesting to analyze more closely the long-term impact of one category of military spending, namely, military spending for research and development (R & D). Spending for military R & D has constituted a very large fraction of total U.S. R & D in the postwar period, accounting for close to half of the total for the period as a whole and standing at about 30 percent in recent years, a figure that is rising again under the Reagan administration. Current spending is over $30 billion a year and is estimated at 70 percent of federal spending for R & D in fiscal year 1984.[10] As people tend to follow the dollars budgeted, it is safe to say that the distribution of scientists and engineers matches the pattern for R & D spending. Given the magnitude of these numbers, one would expect to see the mark of this large-scale military R & D activity (which has lasted now for over thirty years) in the flow of new technology and innovations and, ultimately, in the nation's economic performance and growth.

We have statistics that measure inputs of dollars and scientific manpower rather than outputs, and there are well-known difficulties in quantifying the outcomes of R & D activity. But at least two different kinds of effects on the economy of military R & D programs are possible, and, indeed, plausible. One is a net increase in the total level of innovation, with substantial support to the civilian economy. The argument here is that total R & D activity has been increased absolutely by the military programs, as equivalent resources would not have been made available for any purpose other than national security. The diffusion to the civilian sector from the accelerated developments in such areas as aircraft technology, electronics, and communications should then be seen as pure gain to the civilian economy.

But even though it is probably correct that, during most of the post-war period, the very high levels of spending for military R & D would not have been assigned to any other national goal, nevertheless there has been an opportunity cost to this spending, particularly if one looks at the margin where shifts in spending might have been possible. Moreover, whole areas of military technology have had very little relevance for the civilian economy, for example, programs in advanced nuclear weapons and submarine design. Even in those areas where military R & D has spurred technical changes that have had broad civilian applications, there is evidence that the line of technical development is different than it would have been if the needs of the civilian market had dominated the development. The military imprint has carried over into civilian products.

Case studies of military-related technologies support this proposition.[11] The early development of integrated circuits was significantly accelerated by the military interest in the technology, and the Department of Defense and NASA were the principle customers for the first devices that were manufactured. Eventually civilian uses for integrated circuits increased to the point that the military share of the market dropped to less than 10 percent. Throughout this period the applications in which the United States was most successful (as measured by our performance in international markets) were those in which a military interest had first shaped the technology, for example, in computers. Conversely, Japan, which had pursued mainly consumer-oriented applications, gained a dominant position in trade for products such as radios and televisions.[12] Current DOD programs for very high-speed integrated circuits are again emphasizing military needs, with the result that military requirements are shaping the technology under development. Hardening against radiation effects, for example, is a military requirement with little application to the civilian market, but one that requires definite changes in design and manufacturing processes. To the extent that requirements such as this influence the development of the technology, the U.S. industry may be somewhat handicapped in consumer applications.

A second revealing case is that of numerically controlled machine tools, a technology originally developed and introduced through an air force program. Commercial success in marketing these advanced machine tools, however, has been achieved by the Japanese, in part at least because the tools developed for air force requirements were too elaborate and costly for civilian applications.

In the current international business climate the United States faces serious competition from Japan and Western Europe in high-technology products. This was not the case in the immediate postwar period, when the United States was clearly the industrial and technological leader of the world. Under the new circumstances it may be that the allocation of the lion's share of our R&D resources to military programs entails significant handicaps to our competitiveness in world markets. These are the dynamic opportunity costs of large-scale military spending, costs that must be weighed against the economic benefits that have accrued from military R & D programs.

Summary

The costs of our very large military programs are not an insupportable burden; the United States is a wealthy country and can afford to defend itself. The economic costs do become an issue, however, if the programs are larger than necessary, as they surely are now, because in this case we bear the burden without receiving a commensurate good.

Military spending affects the performance of the economy both in the near term and in the long run. The immediate effects are played out largely through the impact of the defense budget on total government spending and the budget deficit. In the Reagan administration the large defense budgets have produced a Keynesian approach to the problems of recession and unemployment—despite the official rhetoric about supply side economics—and have not yet generated significant bottlenecks. In a period of economic recovery, however, continued high defense spending may generate inflationary pressures, particularly in those sectors of the economy in which military programs are concentrated.

In the long run the chief effects of military spending can be traced to the great emphasis that the United States has put on programs for military R&D. These programs have accelerated the development of some technologies, which in turn have benefited the civilian economy. But the concentration of scientific and technological resources in military programs has deprived other areas of technological progress and may have undermined the competitive position of the U.S. technological base in the world economy.

Notes

1. Department of Defense, Office of the Assistant Secretary of Defense (Comptroller) (1983). "National Defense Budget Estimates for FY 1984," Washington DC, March (mimeo):4,98.

2. David L. Blond (1982). "The Defense Economic Impact Modeling System," OSD, Washington DC, September (mimeo).

3. See, for example, George Brown (1982) "Defense and the Economy: An Analysis of the Reagan Administration's Programs," paper delivered at a conference on Improving National Security by Strengthening the Defense Industrial Base, May 10-12, Cambridge MA. The papers from the conference were printed in two parts as special editions 926 and 927 of *Current News,* Department of Defense, November 9, 10, 1982.

4. "Major Industrial Suppliers to Department of Defense Ranked by Defense Share of Production, 1984," DEIMS 7/14/83 (mimeo).

5. Jacques S. Gansler (1980). *The Defense Industry.* Cambridge MA: MIT Press, Chapter 6.

6. See, for example, the papers from the conference on Improving National Security by Strengthening the Defense Industrial Base.

7. David Blond (1983). "The Myth of the Vanishing Defense Resource," OSD/PAE mimeo; see also Table 1.8 in Robert DeGrasse, Jr. (1983). *Military Expansion, Economic Decline.* New York: Council of Economic Priorities:51.

8. See, for example, "A Case of Inequity: Regional Patterns in Defense Expenditures, 1950-1977," CONEG Policy Research Center, Inc., and the Northeast-Midwest Research Institute, August 1977.

9. Department of Defense, Office of the Assistant Secretary of Defense (Comptroller), "National Defense Budget Estimates for FY 1984":98.
10. National Science Foundation (1983). "Science Resources Studies' Highlights," NSF 83-323, October 14:3.
11. See Judith Reppy (1982). "Public Policy for New Technology: The VHSIC Program of the Department of Defense," Harvard Business School Case Records 9-382-760 (1982) and Reppy (1982). "The Role of the Air Force in the Development of Numerically Controlled Machine Tools," Harvard Business School Case Records 9-682-624 (1982). These case studies are now available directly from the author.
12. For example, in 1979 Japan's share of world exports in television receivers was 32 percent and in radio broadcast receivers was 55 percent, compared to the U.S. share of 7 percent and 2 percent, respectively. In computers, however, which were developed initially in response to military demand, the United States accounted for 39 percent of world exports. (United Nations. *1979 Yearbook of International Trade Statistics,* Vol. II.

References

Benoit, Emile (1973). *Defense and Economic Growth in Developing Countries.* Lexington MA: Lexington Books.
Berkowitz, M. (1970). *The Conversion of Military-Oriented Research and Development to Civilian Uses.* New York: Praeger.
Cusack, Thomas, and Michael Don Ward (1981). "Military Spending in the United States, Soviet Union, and China," *Journal of Conflict Resolution* 25:3:429-269.
Gansler, Jacques (1981). *The Defense Industry.* Cambridge MA: MIT Press.
Leontief, Wassily, and Faye Duchin (1983). *Military Spending: Facts and Figures, Worldwide Implications, and Future Outlook.* Oxford: Oxford University Press.
Nincic, Miroslav (1982). *The Arms Race: The Political Economy of Military Growth.* New York: Praeger.
Russett, Bruce M. (1979). *What Price Vigilance? The Burdens of National Defense.* New Haven CN: Yale University Press.
——— (1982). "Defense Expenditures and National Well-Being," *American Political Science Review* 76:4.
Thee, Marek (1983). "Military Research and Development: Its Impact on Society," in Kare Berg and Knut Erik Tranoy, eds. (1983), *Research Ethics.* New York: Alan R. Liss, Inc.
Thurow, L.C. (1981). "How to Wreck the Economy," *New York Review of Books* 28:8.
United Nations (undated). *Economic and Social Consequences of the Arms Race and of Military Expenditure: Report of the Secretary General.* New York: Unipub.

Michael Levandowsky

ENVIRONMENTAL CONSEQUENCES OF NUCLEAR WAR

Michael Levandowsky is a biologist and environmental scientist at the Haskins Laboratories of Pace University, and the secretary of Environmental Scientists Against the Arms Race, a group of ecologists, meteorologists, and other scientists. He has published many technical papers on population modeling, microbial conversion of wastes to energy sources, and the sensory biology of microorganisms, among other subjects.

In this essay Dr. Levandowsky discusses the historical use of scorched-earth tactics in war and observes that, as guerrilla wars have become more typical, military targets have become blurred. Entire geographic zones may be targeted, changing the nature of a war to an anticivilian and antienvironmental attack. A prospective nuclear strike is seen here as an extension of this indiscriminate use of firepower, with many lasting effects that cannot be confined to military targets. Professor Levandowsky discusses some of the possible second- and third-order ecological effects of nuclear war, including the possibility of "nuclear winter," that were overlooked until quite recently in most superpower war scenarios and that indicate the far-reaching interdependence of life on earth. His prognosis for life after nuclear war is substantially more pessimistic than that of Herman Kahn, who thought it possible that in the United States a GNP equivalent to that of prewar levels might be achieved within two decades. In this chapter, there is some indication that human survival itself could be the ultimate casualty of a nuclear war, even if targets were limited.

The Question of Expertise

I am not an expert on the environmental effects of nuclear war. Furthermore, no one else is either. That is a very curious aspect of this subject: there really are no experts on nuclear war. If anyone asserts that he or she is such an expert, that person is not telling the truth. This is an important point, because self-proclaimed experts have appeared in fair numbers recently. Two nuclear events have occurred in anger—Hiroshima and Nagasaki—but, beyond that, nowhere on earth has anyone experienced anything resembling a nuclear war; big, little, or medium-sized. Consequently, much of my assessment is speculative.

There are, however, some bedrock principles upon which we can rely to construct our arguments: if one believes a particular principle of meteorology, biology, ecology, or geology, then a particular conclusion may indeed follow. But even when these principles are applied, we are continually thinking of new possible effects and other events that might occur—scenarios, to use the trendy term. Really, no one can be certain of the effects of a nuclear exchange.

The Significance of the Natural Environment

Another odd aspect of this discussion about the consequences of nuclear war for civilization is that it has tended to ignore the natural environment. Well-known thinkers, such as the late Herman Kahn, analyze nuclear war in terms of human history, great political problems, economic problems, disasters befalling the human race, and peace and war. I am only discussing the environment. What is that? In the middle of a war, who will defend, for example, trees? It sounds almost silly. So I shall begin by addressing the issue of the military importance of the environment specifically and explicitly.

The ordinary civilian views war as a duel in which one side wins and the other loses. Warriors are killed, but civilians generally survive, unless they unluckily happen to live in a battlefield. The environment is never explicitly mentioned, ordinarily, but is assumed to be constant. Sometimes it is, in fact, an escape. A quotation by Dietrich Bonhoeffer, writing from prison in Nazi Germany in 1943, illustrates this use of the environment. That was a period of great stress, and it certainly was a period of great human conflict. Bonhoeffer, imprisoned because he was involved in a plot to assassinate Hitler, eventually paid with his life. But in 1943, during a period of imprisonment, he wrote to his parents, quoting from Theodore Storm, a German romantic poet:

> Und geht es draussen noch so toll,
> unchristlich oder christlich,

ist doch die Welt, die schoene Welt
so gaenzlich unverwuestlich.

In the context of World War II the poem says that, however crazy, Christian, or unchristian the society of Germany or of Europe might have been at that time, this beautiful world was quite indestructible. Bonhoeffer was referring to a prison garden that was beautiful in spring, even though he knew that terrible events were taking place outside. He considered that garden a given, above the human conflict. This may not be a reasonable assumption in nuclear war scenarios.

Historical Sketch of Environmental War

Actually the history of conventional warfare shows that the environment has entered into war plans very explicitly and classically. Arthur Westing is one of the few people who has addressed the issue of hostile use of the environment in any depth, and much of the following derives from his writings (SIPRI, 1980).

In the history of warfare, the scorched-earth policy appears very early. During the war between the Scythians and the Persians in 512 B.C., for example, the Scythians simply retreated before the Persians, destroying all the crops, cattle, and sheep they could find and poisoning or filling up the wells. This was a scorched-earth policy in 512 B.C. Many other examples can be found, including that of the Mongols under Genghis Kahn and later under Tamerlane. Mesopotamian society, which had developed in a very rich agricultural region, was essentially destroyed from 1213 A.D. to about 1224 by Tamerlane. Mounds of skulls were piled up, civilians were slaughtered, and the intricate irrigation system was destroyed or fell into disuse because of the destruction of the society. From historical accounts it is not clear whether this was sheer wantonness or whether there was some scorched-earth policy as a military strategy, but the effects are clear: since then Mesopotamia has not been the Fertile Crescent. It is now mostly a desert. In such a case there can be irreversible ecological or geographical changes. Once irrigation ceases, crops and other plants no longer grow there and the land dries out. Organic material washes out if it does rain after this process has begun; erosion occurs because plants do not hold the soil and organic material is not replenished. There may be dust storms. In the end there is only sand and gravel. Sand has a very low heat capacity. Because in this rather coarse material there is little that will absorb water, the climate changes. The land has less buffering capacity against the extremes of temperature of night and day.

Wars through thousands of years of history have produced these effects. The reverse of this process can be seen in Israel recently, where desert or near-desert has been planted and irrigated. As the organic material is built up, the Israelis actually have changed the climate. The land is now buffering the temperature regime, and the amount of rainfall has increased.

Some low spots in our own era could be cited. In the Thirty Years War of the middle 1600s, several armies overran what is now Czechoslovakia, wiping out the crops for several years running, so that people were reduced to cannibalism. A large proportion of the population died of starvation-related diseases and some directly of starvation. These casualties were probably only side effects of the war; it is not clear that there was an explicit scorched-earth policy. Later in the same century, the Dutch opened a dike and flooded a large part of Holland to keep the French out, an explicit use of the environment in warfare. In the 19th century, Napoleon was defeated by a scorched-earth policy in Russia. The retreating enemy destroyed all possible sources of food or shelter.

During 1850-64, the Taiping Rebellion in China was put down very brutally. Crops were destroyed in large areas. It is estimated that, as a result, roughly 20 to 40 million people died, some 7 percent of the population.

During the American Revolution, General George Washington, through Deputy Major General John Sullivan, planned and executed a very thorough (for those days) search-and-destroy campaign against the Iroquois Indians, allies of the British. Washington earned himself the lasting nickname of "Destroyer" among the Iroquois, by destroying crops and villages wherever he found them. The strategy was to get rid of the crops, because this would eliminate the Iroquois people as a military force.

Environmental War: The "Humane" Total War

The use of environmental war became explicit in our country during the Civil War. Philip Sheridan, in the Shenandoah Valley, and William Sherman, in Georgia, developed a "total war" philosophy, as it was called. Sheridan expressed the opinion that most people conceive of death in battle as the worst part of a war. They think of war itself as a kind of duel between two armies. The older people who stay at home pressure the younger people to enlist to continue this duel, and it is expected that the side that kills the most will win the war. But Sheridan disagreed:

> Death is popularly considered the maximum punishment in war, but it is not. Reduction to poverty brings prayers for peace more surely and more quickly than does the destruction of human life, as the selfishness

of man has demonstrated in more than one great conflict. (SIPRI, 1980)

Sheridan's point was that war is ended not necessarily by fighting the other army, but by bringing the war home to the people behind the army. Explicitly, Sherman, Sheridan, and others believed that this was a humane approach to war. They adopted it deliberately as a policy likely to bring the war to an end more quickly. The Civil War ended. But these and other generals from the Civil War continued to use such tactics in fighting the Native Americans in the West. In fact, in our whole history with regard to the Native Americans, antienvironmental and antipersonnel strategy is a leitmotif: destroy the crops, destroy the agriculture, destroy the villages. One very clear example occurs during the Navajo Wars, 1849-1861, in which that society was essentially wrecked as a unit by this method. The U.S. forces destroyed crops and animals, and that is how they won the war. They considered this a humane method.

In the Second Boer War in 1899, the Boers destroyed large areas of the veldt to deny the British food for their animals, which were strategic necessities. The U.S. war in the Philippines at the turn of the century was similar in that it was an anticivilian, antipersonnel war and crop destruction was a part of the military strategy.

In this century, similar tactics have been used. In 1938, the Chinese destroyed a dike in the Yellow River to slow down the invading Japanese army. Ensuing floods led to incredible destruction. The Yellow River, when it gets out of control, is famous in China. In this case, the river was not brought under control again until 1947, so for ten years it destroyed crops and topsoil in three provinces, ruining millions of hectares of farmland. Eleven cities and perhaps 4,000 villages were wiped out. I am not sure whether it slowed down the Japanese.

During World War II, the Germans again opened the dikes in Holland and flooded 17 percent of the land there. They also followed a scorched-earth policy in Norway to slow down a hypothetical Russian invasion. At the same time, the Americans and perhaps the British were trying to use incendiary bombing against the German wheat fields, with only moderate success.

We see that scorched-earth policies are old in history, and they have become established as a deliberate choice among military tactics for the United States and other countries. Curiously enough, in the Second World War the proposal to drop chemical agents on crops in Japan was vetoed. One of the important people in that case, Admiral William Leahy, advised President Franklin Roosevelt that chemical crop destruction would violate every Christian ethic and all the known laws of war. So, in fact, chemical war on Japanese crops was not used, but it had been proposed.

On the other hand, of course, not so much later the United States did drop two atomic bombs in Japan. The justification for the use of nuclear weapons was similar to that used for the scorched-earth policy, although this was not exactly a scorched-earth policy, but rather the destruction of a large civilian population in two cities that were not high priority industrial targets, although there were industries there. The argument was that the use of nuclear weapons would end the war promptly, and although the weapons would kill many people, fewer people would die overall—in particular, fewer of our own soldiers. The logic was similar to that of General Sheridan a century before.

Unfocused Targets Expand

About that time, perhaps at that very moment, something new entered into our view of war in this country and probably elsewhere in the First World: our targets became entire zones, rather than individuals. As Westing points out, this can be seen by looking at a few numbers from World War II, Korea, and Vietnam. There were many more military casualties in World War II than in the other two wars, because the former was a larger war. For these three wars, from earliest to most recent, the ratio was 15:2:1 U.S. military fatalities [using U.S. casualties in Vietnam as a denominator—Eds.]. If the number of military casualties is divided by the number of members of the armed forces to normalize those ratios, the same decreasing order is still obtained, but a smaller number appears for World War II: 3:2:1. So, per member of the armed forces, three times as many U.S. military personnel died in World War II as in Vietnam. If the amounts of munitions used in those three wars are examined, the opposite results are obtained. There are various ways to make this comparison. Since the technology was changing, it is difficult to compare munitions precisely, but the bottom line—the expenditures—can always be compared, taking inflation into account. Deflated figures show U.S. expenditures for munitions in the Second World War, Korea, and Vietnam in the ratio of 1:5:7. But if expenditures are divided by the number of enemy soldiers killed—to determine how much, on average, it cost to kill an enemy soldier—the ratios become 1:6:18. Controlling for inflation and other economic effects, it was much more expensive to kill an enemy soldier in Vietnam than it was in World War II, using U.S. munitions.

These figures illustrate the change in the nature of targets for which munitions were used. In Korea, to some extent, and then much more in Vietnam, targets became less well-defined, broader. All sorts of jargon crept in. As part of a process called "interdiction" certain zones were designated as enemy zones, essentially free-fire zones into which many bombs were dropped and many shells were fired. People in these zones were presumed to be enemies because they were there. In theory, the civilian population had been warned to leave the area by various means, such as dropping leaflets or sometimes playing tapes from megaphones suspended from planes. There were also informal methods to mark the free-fire zone, such as, in some places, hanging the ace of spades on a tree, which was supposed to be recognized as a sign of death. Perhaps it was to some extent. After this purported notification, civilians still in the zone were considered enemies. If they happened to be seen, they were shot.

But, in general, people were not targets; whole areas were. There was much less personal combat or duel. Soldiers did not go in with bayonets, but instead pressed buttons or called up air strikes from rather far away—a high-technology war, which cost a great deal more per enemy soldier killed. I do not know whether a similar trend exists now in Afghanistan, but that is the impression one gets from reports filtering out.

General War on the Environment

Thus, a new philosophy of war, on entire zones of the environment, has arisen. In Vietnam, the environment was seen explicitly as part of the enemy. There was a scorched-earth policy, not just to deny nourishment to the enemy, but also to destroy hiding places such as mangrove swamps or forests. Destroying the vegetation became the objective; the vegetation became the enemy. At least it did not move; it was there and herbicides could be dropped on it.

This attitude has not withered away since then, and the people who adopted it in practice for over a decade are still with us. Many of them are senior officers in the Pentagon, so the "war against the environment and against civilians" attitude is something to ponder.

Nuclear Explosions

We come finally to atomic bombs, which are certainly high-technology weaponry. A brief description of the immediate effects of atomic explosions will be given, followed by a discussion of some possible long-term environmental effects.

First of all, something must be said about magnitudes. It is customary to refer to nuclear weapons in terms of their equivalent explosive power in TNT. The Hiroshima bomb was equivalent to about twelve thousand tons of TNT. I once worked with TNT, and I was very impressed with what a few pounds of it would do in a mine. It is hard for me to imagine the force of a whole ton of it, and Hiroshima had an explosion that released the equivalent of about 12,000 tons. Yet that was a very crude, primitive bomb. The bomb dropped on Nagasaki is estimated to have yielded about 22,000 tons of TNT equivalent, or 22 kilotons. That was the beginning stage. Now there are bombs smaller than a kiloton. These may be used as tactical (battlefield) weapons in Europe, in case the United States or the Soviet Union decides to have a small nuclear war there. But most of the bombs, especially the strategic nuclear weapons that would be targeted on the East Coast of the United States, would presumably be more than a kiloton and perhaps a good deal more. The United States now has many bombs with yields of a megaton—the equivalent of a million tons of TNT—although an explosion of this order of magnitude is hard to imagine. Furthermore, there are 10-megaton bombs and even a few 50-megaton specimens. We have hit the big time.

Let us consider the overall effect of a nuclear detonation. There are multiple initial effects. A very significant one is the thermal radiation. A relatively small object suddenly generates immense heat—comparable to the temperature on the surface of the sun, literally an unearthly heat. When matter is heated, it radiates electromagnetic radiation, the so-called black-body radiation. This heats up the immediately surrounding air. That air and the substances that encase the bomb become so hot that they in turn radiate at a very high frequency. In fact, they radiate soft X-ray radiation, which means that the explosion releases an incredible amount of energy. This soft X-ray radiation goes out from the bomb a few meters until it is reabsorbed by the atmosphere, which then emits radiation at lower frequencies, in the ultraviolet and then in the visible light range. Depending on the power of the bomb, spreading out hundreds or thousands of meters from the explosion center the air is so hot that it glows with visible light. This is the famous fireball. [See the illustration given by Frank von Hippel in Chapter 2—Eds.] Heat causes the air to glow, which I emphasize because air must be extremely hot to glow. In addition to that visible radiation, there is a large quantity of infrared or thermal radiation, extending (depending on the size of the bomb) for a number of kilometers on all sides. This thermal radiation can start fires. Within a certain lethal range, organisms are burned to death. Beyond that lies an ignition range, within which fires may start spontaneously. In an urban area this would of course involve houses or factories, but the same effects could also start forest fires. So thermal radiation—intense heat—is one effect.

The fireball itself also has a long-range significance, which depends on the altitude of the detonation. If the explosion occurs sufficiently high in the air, the fireball occurs above the ground. On the other hand, if the bomb is near the surface when it goes off, the fireball includes the ground. If the fireball hits the ground, in that extremely hot zone the soil and other material will vaporize. A few seconds later winds will rush in as a reaction to the blast wave (which I will discuss below). These winds will push up the vaporized debris, which has been cooked by the fireball in contact with the soil. The material will be carried up into the fireball as the hot air expands and rises to great heights. Depending on the power of the bomb, the vaporized debris will condense into particles, which may stay in the lower atmosphere (the troposphere) or may even go on up into the stratosphere, the upper atmosphere. Thus the atmosphere will be full of particulate matter from the soil and elsewhere, to which finer particles of radioactive materials from the bomb can attach. This, in the long run, becomes radioactive fallout. On the other hand, if the bomb detonates sufficiently high up that the fireball does not hit the ground, there are other effects (such as the lofting of large amounts of water vapor), but the condensation of particulate matter does not occur; consequently, there is less fallout. So high altitude detonations produce a very different situation. Low explosions over water result in a radioactive fog.

There are slight differences in sequence in the account here, compared with the real event, but there is no attempt here to get all the effects necessarily in the right time sequence. Another more or less simultaneous effect is the blast wave, which is a mechanical force. This force will crush buildings and knock down trees and people within a certain radius. The blast wave moves out from the center of the explosion, with mechanical effects on the environment. I was curious to find out whether there was any possibility that this blast wave might interact with instabilities in the crust of the earth to cause some kind of seismic event. Geologists with whom I spoke shrugged their shoulders and indicated that it was a very hard question to answer. New York, for example, lies in a relatively stable geographical area, but parts of California do not. [The central Mississippi Valley in the United States and the entire Pacific perimeter are also frequently cited as geologically unstable — Eds.] In any case, a tremendous mechanical force is also produced.

There are also several kinds of radiation occurring almost simultaneously, depending on the type of bomb. Neutrons and gamma rays are produced, which are lethal in sufficient dosage. As neutrons are absorbed very rapidly in the atmosphere, the radius of lethality for this effect for medium and large bombs is less than the radius of lethality for other kinds of radiation.[1] (If you are on ground zero of a nuclear explosion, you will die by about five different processes more or less simultaneously; as you move out from the center the effects fall away one after another.) Gamma rays travel a bit farther than neutrons.

Another effect, observed in early bomb tests but only recently explained, is a large pulse of radio waves. This electromagnetic pulse tends to destroy electronic equipment over wide areas.

Then there is fallout, and that is complex. Some aspects of it have already been mentioned. Approximately 300 species of radionuclides are produced in a fission bomb. Some of these have a very short half-life; some have a very long half-life. Some of them are biologically very dangerous because they may enter the food chain, e.g., the strontium and cesium isotopes. Strontium is very similar chemically to calcium; it tends to be picked up by cells as though it were calcium. In the body, strontium enters into the orthodox biochemistry of the cells and may be stored in long-range, slowly-turning-over depots such as the bones or the teeth, remaining radioactive for a very long time. Some strontium isotopes, such as strontium-90, have a reasonably long half-life, so their radiation could last. The same is true for some of the cesium isotopes that mimic potassium. [The half-life of strontium-90—the amount of time required for half of its atoms to disintegrate, not the amount of time before it becomes "harmless"—is 28 years. The half-life of cesium-137 is 27 years.—Eds.]

All of the radionuclides produced as the bomb explodes will spread out into the atmosphere. If the detonation is sufficiently high, they may form very tiny particles that may travel fairly high into either the troposphere or the stratosphere, and they may stay up there for years, gradually falling as global, long-range, delayed fallout. On the other hand, if they are absorbed onto the larger particles carried up from the soil, they may come down fairly rapidly. In fact, they may precipitate in the form of rain or snow. In Hiroshima, there was the famous black rain, which was essentially fallout. Hot, particulate-containing air rises; as it rises it expands and then cools. Meteorologists call this adiabatic cooling. As it cools, atmospheric water vapor condenses and rain forms. But the rain comes down with most of the particulate fallout. In Hiroshima, the fallout came down promptly as a rain; in other cases it would perhaps come down more slowly as dust. Where and in what form the fallout came down to earth would depend very much on the pattern of the winds and on the general meteorological situation. For a one-megaton bomb, there might be a zone of very high level radioactive fallout extending perhaps several hundred kilometers downwind.

Those are the major immediate effects of detonation of nuclear weapons. A few rough calculations of the consequences—not just for people or industries, but for organisms in general—can also be made. Again, this is highly speculative and entails many assumptions. One should try to make conservative assumptions.

If either the United States or the Soviet Union sends a nuclear weapon thousands of miles, probably it will be a fairly large weapon, so that if it does not strike precisely, the explosion still will wipe out the target. The thermal radiation alone from a one-megaton bomb would generate a zone of about

100 square miles of 50 percent death. A toxicologist would call that the LD50 zone. Half of the mammals in that area would die from the effects of thermal radiation alone. The plants would burn. The total effect would depend also on the kind of plants and on the season of the year. But, in general, in a zone of about 85 square miles the plants would ignite from the heat. In New Jersey, for example, forests and other large plant communities would be affected. Rather large forest fires could be expected to start in such a region, even in winter.

The mechanical effects of trees being knocked down would occur in a zone of about 55 square miles, according to this calculation. Death of most vertebrates from the mechanical force of the blast alone would prevail in approximately two square miles. So radiation and blast effects have different impact ranges.

LD50 zones for immediate radiation must be calculated separately for each species because organisms vary in sensitivity to radiation. There has been some experimental work on this question. Of course, the experimental work involves convenient radiation sources such as gamma radiation from cobalt, which does not necessarily simulate the events in an actual explosion. But for trees, which are relatively sensitive, a one-megaton explosion would create a lethal zone of about 50 square miles. For other vegetation, the lethal zone would be about 11 square miles, and for vertebrates it would be about 144 square miles, just from the initial radiation. This does not take into account the long-range fallout effects, which are more complex and harder to predict.

Potential Short-term Ecological Effects of Nuclear War: The Prognosis for New Jersey

To focus the discussion, let us examine, as a concrete example, a small state on the East Coast of the United States. New Jersey has roughly three parts:

1. Northern New Jersey is relatively less populated and consists of very rich farmland; some wild areas, culminating in High Point State Forest; and some residential areas. There are few obvious military targets in this region; on the other hand, it is downwind of and not far away from Bethlehem and Pittsburgh, Pennsylvania, which are certainly important industrial targets.

2. Much of the middle part of New Jersey is a low, flat plain, with a tremendous amount of industry and also some military targets, such as Picatinny Arsenal and Long Branch Navy Depot. There is an air force base and an army base. There is a great deal of petrochemical industry and a very fine harbor. Certain industries—for example, the pharmaceutical industry—are concentrated here, or essential aspects of the enterprises are carried on here. A nu-

clear strike on central New Jersey would nearly destroy the U.S. pharmaceutical industry, with the exception of one or two companies elsewhere. So if one thinks in terms of a scorched-earth policy, or simply of interdicting in some sense the supply line of the enemy, leaving aside the actual military targets, central New Jersey is certainly a prime strategic target and would receive quite a few bombs in any reasonable scenario.

3. Southern New Jersey is a little different. It is a large open area with a very small population. The Pine Barrens are interesting to the ecologist, but not highly populated. There is little heavy industry; however, there are two nuclear power plants on the southern coast that might be considered quite strategic. Also, southern New Jersey is downwind of the whole industrial area of Wilmington, Delaware, and Philadelphia, Pennsylvania, where important ports, industries, and military targets are located. The fallout from these presumably targeted sites might be expected to cover most of the southern part of New Jersey.

I would say, then, that the central part of New Jersey would be essentially sterilized in a nuclear exchange in which megaton weapons were used. The lethal zones of the bombs of a kiloton up to a megaton that might be expected to fall on the reasonable targets in central New Jersey overlap a great deal, not to mention the effects of bombs hitting nearby New York City.

As for northern and southern New Jersey, perhaps there are not so many targets, but there would still be fallout. The northern part is an agricultural region, a rich truck-farming area, but it would be highly contaminated.

Long-term Ecological Effects: The Nuclear Winter

We turn now to the longer-range effects of nuclear war. Because of the smoke from all the urban and forest fires, and because of the dust and debris that would be injected into the atmosphere, there have recently been some well-publicized speculations about meteorological repercussions. There have been cases in which forest fires—in places such as Alberta, upper Michigan, California, and various western states in the United States—have altered the climate downwind significantly, at least for short periods. Once particulate material is carried into the atmosphere, if it rises into the stratosphere it may remain there for some time. It may also travel long distances. (For example, dust from the Sahara can be trapped in Florida; acid rain in Bermuda originates in New Jersey.) So the climate-changing effects of particulate matter might be almost global. In a nuclear exchange, meteorologists interested in these questions think that probably there would ensue a period of time during which the earth, particularly the northern hemisphere, would be deeply shaded. Of course, forests and plants in general [including the ocean-borne algae that manufacture much of the earth's oxygen—Eds.] would suffer from this shading, but that might be less significant than the effect on climate itself.

To understand the potential for climatic change, two fundamental principles must be grasped. First, the temperature of the earth's surface is controlled by both an internal heat source—natural radioactive decay of unstable elements within the earth—and an external source—solar radiation. The internal source remains constant, but the external source varies: in winter less solar radiation reaches the northern latitudes and it gets colder. Some solar energy is absorbed as it passes through the atmosphere, but most of it reaches and is absorbed by the earth's surface. Thus, under normal conditions it is mainly the surface that is heated and that in turn warms the atmosphere. That is why the atmosphere is warmer near the ground, and becomes colder at high altitudes. The instability caused by warm, buoyant air underneath cold, dense air leads to atmospheric turbulence and convection currents that cause the weather.

The second fundamental principle to understand is that a sufficiently dense layer of fine soot and smoke particles at a high altitude will intercept most of the solar heat.

When these two principles are put together, one can see that such a layer of particles would lead to cooling of the earth's surface and hence to cooling of the nearby lower atmosphere. The obvious question to ask then is, "What is the magnitude of this effect?" This question was addressed in 1983 in computer simulation models that predicted the nuclear winter. Since that tentative climatic result was obtained and its plausible ecological consequences were published (Ehrlich et al., 1984), several groups have conducted further research on this question, and the assumptions of the original model have received a good deal of scrutiny.

Even considering the imprecision of meteorology and the relative lack of sophistication of some simulations, it seems quite clear that there is great cause for concern. The most recent, extensive work on nuclear winter (by Carrier and his colleagues at Harvard) indicates a strong likelihood of severe and sudden climatic effects from even a limited nuclear exchange. Subfreezing temperatures on land would occur within days, even if it were summer, and this effect would very likely spread to areas that were not directly involved in the war. The consequences of such drastic climatic change on biota, especially if it occurred in the summer, would be severe indeed: wholesale destruction of ecosystems would probably take place, in some cases irreversibly, with massive extinction of entire species. The nuclear winter effect would probably spread to the tropics, where it would be particularly devastating to the cold-intolerant communities there.

In addition to these specific concerns about the potential effects of a nuclear exchange on global temperatures, there is a more general, but less defined, fear that the presence of large amounts of smoke, soot, and dust in the upper reaches of the troposphere and possibly the stratosphere would change the thermal stratification of the atmosphere, leading to far-reaching, unpredictable changes in climate. As mentioned earlier, the fact that air is at present warmest at the bottom of the lower atmosphere, or troposphere, leads to convective instabilities that are the cause of winds and weather. In the upper atmosphere, or stratosphere, on the contrary, the air temperature increases with altitude, and this leads to a very stable, unchanging climate—there is very little "weather" in the usual sense in the stratosphere. That is why dust and other material injected into the stratosphere tend to remain there almost indefinitely. This structure, based ultimately on the solar warming of the earth's land and water surface, might well be changed in unanticipated ways if most of the solar warming occurred instead in the upper troposphere, because of absorption by soot or other particles. This might have very drastic effects on climate that are not anticipated even by nuclear winter model simulations.

Additional Environmental Effects

There are some other possible effects of nuclear war on the environment. The severe heat of the bombs would cause a chemical reaction between nitrogen and oxygen in the air to form various nitrous oxides. These are highly reactive compounds that have a complex history after they are formed. They react chemically in the presence of light. If the nitrous oxides travel high enough into the stratosphere, quite a few experts suggest that the chemical reactions that would occur might well degrade the protective ozone layer. That is the layer that protects us from much of the ultraviolet radiation of the sun. Thus, as a consequence of nuclear explosions, incursion of larger amounts of ultraviolet down to the earth's surface might be expected, which would be highly damaging to all terrestrial living things, although aquatic life forms would be somewhat shielded by the water. This effect would persist long after the shading effect of soot, smoke, and other material had passed.

If there were only smaller detonations or relatively small nuclear exchanges, the nitrous oxides might not reach the stratosphere. Instead they would rise into the troposphere, our lower atmosphere, where they would paradoxically have the opposite effect of producing more ozone and other toxic materials, including some phytotoxins (plant poisons) of fairly complex structure that would be expected to produce extra stress on agriculture and on wild vegetation.

Meanwhile, the vegetation would be dying from radiation, or from shading, or from freezing, or from these phytotoxins in the air. Where vegetation dies, soil erosion begins. Large areas in, for example, northern and southern New Jersey—particularly northern New Jersey, where the soil is rich—would tend to lose that soil from erosion, both water erosion (floods) and wind erosion (dust storms). This erosion in turn would strip some of the remaining vegetation, producing depleted soil, not only because of the loss of nutrients in the vanishing topsoil, but also because of losses from so-called nutrient dumping; that is, from the loss of nutrients locked up in plants when they died. It seems quite possible to a number of ecologists that such a process might be irreversible. The standard ecological succession expected when a forest is cut down—the famous "old field" succession studied extensively by ecologists—might not occur at all, because the postwar soil would be drastically changed. It is not even clear where propagules—that is, the seeds and other reproductive bodies—would come from if there were general destruction. Quite a different vegetation might eventually emerge.

Long-term radiation in the form of biologically active radionuclides such as strontium and cesium isotopes might accumulate in tissues and add to this stress on the plants. Conjectures about what would eventually survive are very speculative. But we do know that some forms of plant life are more resilient than others. Grasses, for example, tend to be more resistant than trees, so perhaps some grasses might survive. Many insects, interestingly, turn out to be dramatically more resistant to radiation than vertebrates. It could be that with the death of the vertebrates and other predators, some insects would survive and flourish. A period in which there were large numbers of herbivorous insects helping to wipe out much of the residual plant population could be imagined.

In this view, bare areas would emerge, dust storms would occur, and perhaps a different climate would evolve because of irreversible environmental and meteorological changes. These changes in the soil and vegetation could develop as in the model of Iraq (Mesopotamia) mentioned at the beginning of this chapter, although in a different temperature range. There would be a rather desolate landscape: very few species living there, large bare areas, large amounts of silt in the fresh water. This would have a pronounced adverse effect on aquatic communities. Along the seashore, for example, there are shellfish; a potentially major human food source, especially if agriculture failed. But it is not clear that this would be available, because of damage from the tremendous siltation caused by erosion into the water carried into the estuaries, usually a natural nursery for the major fisheries of the world and certainly for the shellfisheries.

This bare ecological background, a remnant of the normal, natural environment, does not fit the Storm poem cited by Bonhoeffer. It is not clear whether human populations surviving a nuclear war would be able to survive in the postattack period in such an environment.

Note

1. For smaller-yield weapons or enhanced radiation weapons, effects might vary. The term "neutron bomb" for enhanced radiation weapons refers to the early stages of radiation emerging, not to later fallout. But the mix of gamma rays and neutrons can be modified by various methods, including modifying the casing of the bomb (because some casings will tend to absorb neutrons and some will tend to absorb gamma rays) and by other methods. In a small bomb—a tactical weapon—the lethal zone of radiation can be appreciable compared with the zones of destruction of blast or thermal radiation. The zone of blast destruction would be smaller than the lethal zone due to radiation, which is itself a relatively small zone because neutrons are absorbed by the atmosphere. And, if the explosion is designed so that the neutrons are predominant, then indeed there would be a certain killing by neutrons.

The blast wave of enhanced radiation weapons is relatively small. It does not knock down that many structures, especially if its yield is less than a kiloton. Of course, near the explosion's center, it does collapse buildings.

There may be appreciable fallout effects because neutron bombs will have a fireball, no matter how small, and there may be surface explosions. In a battleground situation, a captain or perhaps a first lieutenant may have to decide where to aim a neutron bomb. In the midst of battle, is he really going to worry much about whether it will hit the surface or whether it will explode in the air? He may, but I suspect there would be surface detonations.

It would make sense in a cost-benefit calculation not to have too sophisticated a guidance system or a fuse for a very small bomb that is only going to travel a few hundred miles at the most. There might well be weapons that detonate on contact and produce surface explosions. Surface explosions will lead, even with small bombs, to large quantities of fallout. Thus, it is not clear that neutron bombs could be used on the Continent without destroying European culture.

It would also appear that even a "surgical" air strike on, for example, U.S. missile bases would have widespread effects, including ecological ones. We can assume that large-yield nuclear weapons would be used, and these would tend to destroy the ozone layer that protects us from solar ultraviolet radiation, as discussed in the text.

References

Ehrlich, Paul; Carl Sagan; Donald Kennedy; and Walter Orr Roberts (1984). *The Cold and the Dark*. New York: W. W. Norton.
Harwell, Mark (1984). *Nuclear Winter*. New York and Heidelberg: Springer-Verlag.
SIPRI (Arthur Westing) (1980). *Warfare in a Fragile World—Military Impact on the Human Environment*. Stockholm International Peace Research Institute. New York: Crane, Russak.

Turco, R. P.; O. B. Toon; T. P. Ackerman; J. B. Pollack; and Carl Sagan (1983). "Nuclear Winter: Global Consequences of Multiple Nuclear Explosions," *Science,* 222, 23 December: 1283.

Westing, Arthur (1984). *Environmental Warfare: A Technical, Legal, and Policy Appraisal.* Philadelphia PA: Taylor and Francis for SIPRI.

——— (1984). *Herbicides in War: The Long-Term Ecological and Human Consequences.* Philadelphia PA: Taylor and Francis for SIPRI.

H. Jack Geiger

7

MEDICAL CONSEQUENCES OF NUCLEAR WAR

H. Jack Geiger, M.D., is a nationally prominent expert on the medical consequences of nuclear war. He is Arthur C. Logan Professor of Community Medicine at the School of Biomedical Education of City College, City University of New York. He was also one of the original founders of Physicians for Social Responsibility (PSR) in 1961 and is currently president of PSR. Dr. Geiger is a member of International Physicians for the Prevention of Nuclear War and serves on its board of directors.

Dr. Geiger details the types of injuries caused by nuclear blast, shock, thermal radiation, and ionizing radiation. He points out that even a limited nuclear strike could pose insuperable problems for health care delivery systems in the United States, due, among other effects, to the number of burn cases, greatly exceeding the supply of hospital beds for patients thus afflicted. Even where facilities might be adequate, triage cannot be done for victims of ionizing radiation, as the symptoms on presentation may be indistinguishable regardless of the radiation dose received. Dr. Geiger explains that the interactive effects of radiation, trauma, malnutrition, and infection would increase casualties manyfold over the usual figures in which tolls from each of these causes have been estimated separately. As a further demographic consequence, there are long-term genetic effects that may actually become more severe over time rather than becoming attenuated, as has been hypothesized earlier.

In contrast with Herman Kahn's views, Dr. Geiger argues that limited nuclear war is not possible, and that scenarios envisioning a superpower nuclear war that does not escalate to all-out war are based on erroneous assumptions. Dr. Geiger also takes issue with the views of the current U.S. administration, that the Soviet Union has a margin of strategic superiority and that U.S. strategic forces have essentially "stood still" with respect to the Soviet Union during the 1970s.

Introduction: A Problem of Magnitude

Some percentage of the American public has seen a film called "The Last Epidemic." I appear in one segment of this film, discussing the effects of a one-megaton nuclear weapon dropped on San Francisco. There is quite graphic footage of San Francisco intercut with footage of Hiroshima and Nagasaki. Because "The Last Epidemic" has had considerable television exposure, I sometimes think that I have become a nuclear Dracula—every night on some television screen somewhere in America, after midnight, I am dropping a one-megaton bomb on San Francisco.

In this chapter I will discuss the effects of a one-megaton weapon and will discuss why one megaton is the unit of measure. Then I will comment on the political and social contexts of nuclear issues, touching on matters also discussed by Herman Kahn, by Frank von Hippel, and by other contributors to this volume.

First, it makes no sense to discuss "medical" consequences of a nuclear attack or "medical" consequences of nuclear war. This is a peculiar, perverted use of the word medical, to describe a degree and kind of injury, suffering, death, and devastation literally beyond human capacity to comprehend. It makes no sense to talk of victims and survivors because there will be very little functional distinction between them in the circumstances under consideration. There are problems in simply attempting to comprehend a scale of destruction that is in itself so great that differences become qualitative.

It is odd that everyone knows nuclear war, even the explosion of a single thermonuclear weapon, would be dreadful, yet almost everyone turns away from the details and does not want to examine how dreadful it would be. In one sense that is understandable, because denial is psychologically necessary. On the other hand, I think that people are not stimulated to an adequate perception of the danger until they look at those details and begin to multiply one megaton times the amount of megatonnage that is in fact available. There are important qualitative differences. Even a small thermonuclear explosion begins at a temperature of 130 million degrees and at a pressure of 100 million atmospheres. A thermonuclear explosion is like a small sun on the surface of the earth, not ninety-three million miles away.

One megaton is used as a unit of measure for thermonuclear weapons simply because it is convenient. A megaton represents one million tons of TNT-equivalent explosive force, which is not a very manageable concept. To imagine the destructive power of one megaton, one is required to imagine eighty Hiroshima bombs exploding simultaneously in the same place. Twenty megatons represents the power of 1,600 Hiroshima weapons exploding simultaneously in the same place. One megaton, for example, could be represented by a freight train 300 miles long—roughly from New York to Portland, Maine—filled with TNT. If one were standing still watching the train passing at fifty miles per hour, one would have to stand there for six hours until it had gone by. That amount of explosive power is now available in a weapon the size of a small refrigerator, and a one-megaton bomb is a modest weapon in today's arsenals.

The United States and the Soviet Union in 1985 count fifteen thousand megatons between them; not warheads, megatons. It is difficult to comprehend the power of fifteen thousand megatons. If fifteen thousand megatons were divided into Hiroshima-sized weapons, and if one such Hiroshima-sized weapon were exploded every minute—sixty an hour, 1,440 a day—eight months and two weeks would have to elapse before fifteen thousand megatons had been used up.

World arms expenditures—the total being spent by the United States, the Soviet Union, and other nations on their own weapons development and on the manufacture and sale of weapons to other nations—came to approximately 1.4 billion dollars a day, a million dollars a minute, in 1982. It is more now. And the United States, to pick a figure from my own field, in all of 1981 spent a little over 50 billion dollars on every aspect of health care. That amounted to about twelve days of the arms race. In one day of 1982, the world spent 1.4 billion dollars on arms, including nuclear arms. Yet all of this discussion is only an attempt to make comprehensible a concept that escapes us.

Physicists know all about what happens in the first 69 billionth of a second of a thermonuclear explosion. The events that follow are all well known, and yet a megaton is unfathomable because it is unprecedented. Hiroshima and Nagasaki as experiences were not precedents, not merely because of the difference in size (those weapons were firecrackers in terms of what is available now), but because those cases fit an intuitive picture of disaster: they were not completely unlike a fire, an earthquake, an explosion, a tidal wave, or a hurricane. The effects of these hazards are dreadful, but they are decremental with time; they wear off gradually. This is not the situation one would be confronted with in any significant nuclear exchange.

The effects of nuclear weapons are extremely long-lasting. They are in some ways incremental rather than decremental with time. Above all, there will be no outside world on which anyone can safely rely for help, because every other place that might have been a resource will in all probability have been subject to attack and will have been destroyed. One megaton (and that is only one warhead, one way of delivering it) could be only one out of about fifty thousand warheads in the mutual possession of the United States and the Soviet Union. [The Stockholm International Place Research Institute *World Armaments and Disarmament Yearbook* gives a figure of forty thousand for the United States and a global total of one hundred thousand active and war reserve nuclear warheads as early as 1978 (SIPRI 1978: 323).—Eds.] This discussion concerns only one megaton when, in any significant population-targeted exchange, the targeting rule of thumb is one megaton for every five hundred thousand people, or even for every two hundred thousand. So the New York metropolitan area, for example, would receive thirty-two megatons by that formula, not one.

Of course one does not have to detonate one megaton to get a megaton's-worth of damage. The effect of MIRVing (using multiple independently targetable re-entry vehicles for several separate bomblets) on a single warhead is to make it much more efficient. So much of the energy in a single one-megaton explosion is "wasted" in overkill in the inner circles around ground zero—simply making the rubble bounce—that one can achieve the same tolls of death, devastation, and desolation at about one-third of the megatonnage. Four 80-kiloton weapons, or eight 40-kiloton weapons (the type carried on many U.S. delivery vehicles now), total only 320 kilotons or about a third of a megaton. Yet, because of their dispersal, they capitalize on the otherwise overlapping effects in concentric circles, to kill about as many people and destroy about as much area as the explosion of a single one-megaton device with approximately three times their combined yield. Of course, damage can be increased by increasing megatonnage and by increasing accuracy, as well as by dispersal. If the megatonnage is doubled, the increase in lethality may vary from a two- to fourfold increase in the capacity to kill people. And if the accuracy of a warhead-delivering missile is doubled, the lethality of the warhead increases tenfold. That is one of the reasons for the great concentration of effort on accuracy of strategic weapons delivery vehicles in the last decade or so.

Finally, another artifice of using one megaton as an example is that it fits an unrealistic picture of attack that implies that the war is over in three minutes of a single strike. In all probability, in any industrial area (such as the eastern seaboard of the United States) or any urban area, a realistic scenario, as Dr. Kahn indicated in Chapter 4, might include one strike of a megaton or so at ten o'clock in the morning, another at four in the afternoon, another perhaps at midnight and one three days later. Given the number of warheads on submarines that may surface as much as two weeks after the event, to participate, a fifth strike two or three weeks later must be contemplated. Thus, five or more strikes and their effects must be anticipated, rather than a single effect. And one megaton, finally, is only one megaton out of current estimates in civil defense and Department of Defense scenarios for the United States, which forecast the use of a total of roughly 6,600 megatons on the United States in the event of thermonuclear war.

Effects of Nuclear Weapons

The effects of these weapons are varied, although fallout comes to mind first. But 50 percent of the energy of thermonuclear weapons is released as blast, about 35 percent as heat, and only about 15 percent as immediate and delayed radioactivity. The ideal real-world sequence, as Jonathan Schell envisioned in *The Fate of the Earth,* is somehow to observe all of this and not to suffer its effects. The first effect anyone within thirty-five miles of a thermonuclear explosion would be aware of would be a blinding flash of light. At fifty miles it would be brighter than the noonday sun. This flash would be followed almost immediately by the appearance of the fireball and by an enormous thermal pulse, which is heat radiating from that fireball for two or three seconds, traveling at just under the speed of light. After that is the blast wave. Let us consider blast first.

The blast effects of thermonuclear weapons, or of any nuclear weapons, represent such an increase in scale that they are qualitatively different from the blast effects of conventional weapons. These effects include two kinds of overpressure, or pressure above atmospheric pressure. The first is static overpressure. That is the great crushing force of this released energy. It is as if the sky were to come down like an anvil and crush flat—or almost flat—everything beneath it, with greatest intensity at ground zero and at lesser intensities, according to formulas that are easy to calculate, radiating out from ground zero. The second form of overpressure is dynamic overpressure, or wind. Winds with enormous velocity are associated with this release of energy and with these kinds of explosions.

The first force, the static overpressure, is the collapsing and crushing force. Human beings are extraordinarily resilient in the face of static overpressure: they have to suffer up to thirty pounds per square inch (psi) or so before lungs begin to rupture and before there are profound effects on the circulatory and respiratory systems. But everyone close enough to be subject to this static overpressure would be killed by two or three other combinations of forces. Nonetheless, that static overpressure would be a great killer because it would knock down most of the buildings on the inhabitants, leaving at best steel-reinforced skyscrapers' skeletons standing empty. Second, dynamic overpressure would create flying missiles out of all of the material that was not vaporized, that was crushed, pounded, and reduced to rubble in the first mile and a half to two and three miles out from ground zero in a one-megaton airburst. If there were a one-megaton airburst over the Empire State Building, the Empire State Building would be approximately uniformly distributed over seven square miles. A small, rock-sized piece of debris (concrete, steel, wood, a piece of a car or building structure) at thirteen miles from the explosion would be traveling at a velocity sufficient to give a 50 percent probability of skull fracture if it happened to land on someone's head. Flying people must also be considered. Winds of even 180 miles per hour (and in this example there would be winds initially at 500 to 700 miles an hour) at distances of five and six miles from ground zero would be more than sufficient to pick up a 180-pound adult and throw him or her a considerable distance against any debris, standing wall, or any other object at a force several times the force of gravity. That, in physical terms applied to humans, is a brief summary of blast effects.

Heat, about five miles or six miles further out from ground zero, becomes the major killer as blast effects become attenuated. There are two kinds of effects of heat on human beings: direct effects and indirect effects. Direct effects would be direct burns, flash burns, second- and third-degree burns from the thermal pulse, which would literally char and broil human flesh at very substantial distances, due to direct exposure to the heat. How many people would be so affected is one of the great variables of any thermonuclear attack. It would depend in part on the weather, on how much moisture was in the air, and on whether it was clear or cloudy. It would depend, in addition, on whether there were still buildings standing and whether potential victims were in the shadow of one of those buildings in relation to the fireball, because the thermal pulse precedes blast. And it would depend on the time of year, because many more people are outside with light clothing on during the summer months than in the dead of winter. In all cases there would be direct burns, and for much greater distances than the direct effects there would be indirect burns. Indirect burns are flame burns, caused by the spontaneous ignition of clothing and, simply put, from the spontaneous ignition of the environment inside and outside. Again, this spontaneous ignition would occur at substantial distances—six, seven, or even eleven miles from ground zero, depending on other conditions. If one were eleven miles away from an airburst on a clear day, everything flammable inside buildings would catch fire—all of the cushions, all of the wood, the carpeting, any drapes, and the normal furnishings of homes and offices. Enormous numbers of secondary burns would be created by the heat effect. In Detroit—to give one example of the order of magnitude of nuclear war consequences rather carefully calculated by the Office of Technology Assessment in its study of the effects of thermonuclear weapons—with four million people in the metropolitan area, depending on conditions, among the people still alive after the blast effect (so only initial survivors are included), there would be a minimum of two thousand and a maximum of one hundred ninety thousand people with third-degree burns over 25 percent or more of their body surfaces. In the New York metropolitan area, with sixty million people, the comparable figures would be a minimum of eight thousand third-degree burns of that severity and a maximum of seven hundred sixty thousand. I do not know how one imagines three-quarters of a million people in one place with third-degree burns over 25 percent or more of their body surfaces. In all of the United States there are only two thousand burn beds, beds in the special wards and facilities required for the treatment of third-degree burns. While money is hardly the point, the treatment of the average extensive third-degree burn costs roughly a quarter of a million dollars or more, and it requires surgeons as well as complex facilities of all kinds, none of which are likely to exist after thermonuclear attack.

There are two other effects that would increase remarkably the number of burns as well as the number of total deaths. Those are two kinds of fires: conflagration and firestorm. Conflagration is analogous to a huge brushfire, blowing in whatever direction the prevailing wind blows, consuming everything flammable in its path until it reaches a major firebreak, such as the Hudson River in the case of New York. Conflagrations are very destructive; they would kill many people trapped in blast rubble or too injured to run quickly. But conflagrations are probably not as destructive as the firestorm. A firestorm is the coalescence of all the thousands of individual fires created by a thermonuclear weapon. All of those blast-induced fires—exploding gasoline stations, ruptured natural gas lines, downed power lines, exploding boilers in buildings, and more—would coalesce into a single self-sustaining fire. Stationary, it would cover a very large area and burn at extremely high temperatures, perhaps exceeding 800 degrees centigrade, creating large amounts of toxic gases such as carbon monoxide and sucking in oxygen from the outside with centrifugal winds of 200 miles per hour or more. There was such a firestorm at Hiroshima but not at Nagasaki,[1] and in consequence of conventional bombing at Hamburg and Dresden during World War II. Something is known about it.

One of the lessons of the bombing of those cities is that the survivors were generally those who fled their bomb shelters, because conventional shelters in a firestorm simply become crematoria in which people are simultaneously dry-roasted by the temperature and asphyxiated by the toxic gases. Thus, if one is faced with the prospect of firestorm, which is likely after nuclear detonations, one must be equipped not only with a blast-proof shelter, but with a deep shelter that is thermally insulated and has both an independent oxygen supply and a method for venting toxic gases. When the civil defense case is presented, it would be worth asking if such shelters are included in the U.S. civil defense plans for all of us. They are included for the people who will be rushed to the hollowed-out mountains in Virginia and Denver, but they are not going to be available, obviously, for the population at large.

And last, beyond blast and heat, there is radiation. This is the most complex of the effects to calculate because the effects in terms of human beings depend on the total amount of radiation exposure; on the type of radiation (alpha radiation, beta and gamma rays, neutrons); on the rate at which it is delivered; on the duration of the exposure; on whether it is whole-body exposure or partial exposure; on the source (that is, whether it is outside or something you can swallow or inhale); and on the individual's state of health. Of course anywhere in the circle at ground zero, radiation really does not matter. It has been calculated that one could be protected against 1,100 rads by about 24 inches of concrete shielding, but, obviously, the problem with this method of protection is that the 24 inches of concrete (and a great deal more) would, in the event of a nuclear explosion, be lying on top of any survivors rather than shielding them. There presumably would be 100 percent mortality in that first circle. In general, the dose of radiation that will kill a healthy adult is 450 rems.[2] An ordinary chest x-ray is a tiny fraction of one rem. The dose that will kill a healthy infant is 225 rems. The dose that will kill a chronically ill person, an elderly person, or anyone other than a healthy adult is considerably less than 450 rems.

These are lethal doses when combined injuries are not considered. But there would be injuries from nuclear blast and from heat that would be combined with severe radiation injury. Blast injuries would include skull fractures and crushing injuries of the chest and pelvis, as well as broken arms and legs. Blast injuries also would include paralyzing lesions and fractures of the spinal cord, profound laceration, hemorrhage, and shock. All of these would occur, in combination with second- and third-degree burns, as combined injuries. Combined injuries—two sublethal injuries—greatly increase the risk of death, e.g., a very moderate dose of radiation to a standard burn increases the mortality from that burn about eightfold.

And finally, there are medium-term effects of radiation that must be taken into account when civil defense is considered. Large areas of land would be made uninhabitable for significant periods of time because of residual radioactivity, so that fallout shelters would have to be suitable for human habitation for a minimum of two weeks. In many areas shelters would have to do for four weeks or longer or survivors would risk significant exposure to radioactivity.[3]

In any case, there would also be long-term effects, including striking increases in the incidence of cancer and leukemia. The unquantifiable genetic effects on subsequent generations[4] can only be estimated.

The Medical Dilemma

In the absurd postattack scenario in which medical care is still possible, there would be no way for a physician or any other health worker, in the absence of radiation monitors and precise histories, to distinguish among the people who had received moderate amounts of radiation exposure who would survive with no help, those exposed to greater amounts of radiation who would survive only if they received intensive medical care, and those exposed to the greatest amounts of radiation who would die irrespective of the kind or intensity of medical care given them. All of the early symptoms are the same. Moderate doses and lethal doses of radiation produce symptoms that look alike initially, and adult psychogenic symptoms also are indistinguishable. Many people would throw up in the aftermath of a nuclear explosion, but diarrhea and vomiting are also symptoms of radiation sickness. And of course neither physicians nor victims would have radiation monitors or precise medical histories at hand. As all of the symptoms of radiation on early examination appear the same, there would be no way to do triage.

Yet there would be severe short-term medical problems. Radiation exposure damages the bone marrow. For example, one of the effects on the bone marrow (aside from reducing the white cell count in particular, so that people become extraordinarily susceptible to infection) is that radiation destroys platelets that are responsible for blood clotting. Consequently, people hemorrhage, into the skin, among other ways. A cross-section of the lining of the gastrointestinal tract under normal circumstances, compared with the same lining after a moderate to severe dose of radiation, would illustrate the fact that radiation causes almost all rapidly dividing tissues, including bone marrow and the gastrointestinal tract, to bleed. Not only is there great possibility of infection, there is great loss of body fluids. One does not need to know anything about the central nervous system to know that for it, too, whatever remains following exposure to high levels of ionizing radiation would be dead. These would be neutron bomb effects, perhaps.

Research has also shown some of the long-term effects of radiation, such as the increased incidence of cancer, genetic damage, and injury to the rest of the environment. For example, food sources—both plants and animals—would be covered with particulate fallout and might take up and concentrate some radioactive isotopes, increasing the length and intensity of survivors' exposure to radiation. [See the discussion of environmental effects in Chapter 6, and the histories of the Marshall Islanders in U.S. government documents, and for example, Donald McHenry, *Micronesia: Trust Betrayed* (Carnegie Endowment for International Peace: New York and Washington, 1975).—Eds.]

It is also known that oxides of nitrogen, which are both released and formed by thermonuclear explosions, would be very likely to reach the upper levels of the atmosphere, where the ozone layer is all of three-quarters of a centimeter thick. The ozone layer is solely responsible for shielding the earth from penetrating or "hard" ultraviolet radiation. This layer would be significantly damaged in a nuclear war. One cannot tell the probability, but, according to the National Academy of Sciences, there is a significant risk that penetrating ultraviolet radiation would be admitted to the environment for six or seven years, predominantly in the northern hemisphere, although there would also be about 30 percent of the effect in the southern hemisphere.

The Postattack Periods: Shelter and Survival

For New York on a weekday during working hours, in clear weather with a firestorm, a single explosion of a one-megaton warhead would kill rather more than 2 million people outright and would profoundly injure approximately another 3.4 million immediately. After the immediate casualties, the "shelter period" would begin, which is the two to four weeks during which all survivors should remain in shelters. The "survival period"—from thirty days to sixty days on—would follow this shelter period.

Life in those shelters during the shelter period would be thirty days with inadequate food; with inadequate water, if any at all; with inadequate preparation and provisions for sanitation; with, in all probability, largely or totally inadequate radiation protection; with people suffering from trauma; with overcrowding; with victims of radiation sickness—nausea, vomiting, and diarrhea; with people whose resistance to infection has been reduced because of that radiation; with people who have walked in carrying the viruses and bacteria of gastrointestinal disease, respiratory disease, or hepatitis. One of the effects of significant radiation dose is to convert inactive tuberculosis to an active state. Overall, one could not invent a better scenario for the epidemic spread of disease than to put this kind of population into shelters for thirty days in the postattack period.

In the survival period, when some people would emerge (in addition to all the human corpses left from this devastation that have not been conveniently consumed by fire) there would be trillions of insects. Literally there would be trillions, because insects are extraordinarily radiation-resistant compared to humans and other mammals, and all of their predators—the birds in particular—would have been killed off by radiation and heat. Trillions of insects provide another scenario for epidemic waves of plague, typhus, rabies, and gastrointestinal disease. There would ensue severe shortages of food, compounding the medical problems.

Malnutrition and infection are synergistic with each other, one making the other worse. Most of the remaining uncontaminated food in the United

States would be where the population was not: in the upper Midwest in silos. There would be a very limited amount of fuel left, because most of the petroleum industry would have been destroyed. The surviving population would have the difficult choice of determining whether to use the fuel to haul the remaining food to the remaining population, thereby depriving itself of the fuel it would need to plant the following year's crop on which everyone's long-term survival would depend, or allowing massive starvation in the short term. Of course, the prospects for food production would be poor, because of the penetrating ultraviolet effects on plants and on the ecosystem generally, on the flora and fauna, which Dr. Levandowsky and others discuss. Most of the diurnal animals simply would be blinded, with all of the consequent effects on the ecostructure.

The long-term survival of a postattack population in any significant number is indeed in doubt. A very good case in fact can be made that the nation would be best off that had the lowest number of survivors after a thermonuclear exchange. It would have fewer survivors in relation to limited remaining resources compared to the nation that had more survivors with the same limited resources. (This entire discussion ignores the ordinary ongoing incidence of illness and normal mortality, which would of course be compounded by the effects mentioned.)

It should be obvious that hospitals would be destroyed. Because they are concentrated in targeted areas, physicians would be killed in greater ratios than would the rest of the population. The social fabric of communication, cooperation, and organization would be ruptured in ways that not only would make medical care impossible, but also would disrupt normal methods of finding food, maintaining the family structure, or finding shelter and housing. The simplest social activities would falter.

The meaning of survival for human beings is social. But survival in a nuclear war is not what the civil defense documents would have one believe: it is not some mere biological body count; it is not still being physically active, only slightly injured, or uninjured at some point after a thermonuclear attack. It is being alive in some kind of social fabric capable of sustaining life.

The Role of Public Opinion

The appropriate response to this information may be depression today, but anger tomorrow. The most inappropriate feeling is helplessness.

One anecdote will make it clear that public pressure can reduce these risks. In 1960 concerned scientists and physicians began to look at and record data on radioactivity. We published a case study of radioactivity in Boston in 1962, which made a very substantial impact. During the 1950s Governor Nelson Rockefeller and President Dwight D. Eisenhower had been reassuring the public that all that was necessary was to build fallout shelters in the front yard or the back yard. [See the "With Enough Shovels" remark of T. K. Jones in Strobe Talbott, *Deadly Gambits* (New York: Knopf, 1984), p. 287, and Scheer, *With Enough Shovels*.—Eds.] Edward Teller was suggesting that a little radiation was good for people; it stirred up the genes. The publication of our data on projected effects of nuclear war had some effect, but it did not produce much policy change. Then some of our colleagues began to be worried about strontium-90 as a consequence of atmospheric testing of nuclear weapons. They were convinced that it had entered the food chain. To prove their hypothesis, they had the bright idea of collecting baby teeth as they were shed. (Strontium resembles calcium chemically, and it accumulates in bones and teeth.) Over a considerable period of months, thousands of baby teeth in St. Louis were collected and analyzed. Analysis demonstrated that there was a significant amount of strontium-90 in the teeth of babies in St. Louis. From the time the data were published, it took only three months for the United States to sign a treaty that is still in effect: the Partial Test Ban Treaty of 1963, prohibiting all tests in the atmosphere [as well as underwater and in space—Eds.]. A test ban was not what the government wanted to do; it was not a preference of either the Department of Defense or of the administration. But the mothers and fathers of America made it clear that atmospheric testing could not continue because of its effects on the children. Public opposition was so strong that the government had to listen. This example shows that well-informed people who speak out can have an effect.

It is a shame that having accomplished the Partial Test Ban Treaty we went on to other issues. The public and to some extent the scientific community gave up on the Comprehensive Test Ban (draft treaty) at that time because we thought we had solved the environmental contamination problems posed by nuclear weapons. [Comprehensive Test Ban talks had a brief revival in the 1970s: A Swedish CTB working paper was submitted to the Conference of the Committee on Disarmament in 1971; a Soviet draft treaty was transmitted to the UN General Assembly in 1975; and the United States and the Soviet Union appeared, with the UN, to have made progress toward agreement by late 1977, with the United States, the Soviet Union, and Britain working out the details of on-site inspection and the installation in each signatory country of a seismic detection network. There was some indication that this treaty might substitute for the Peaceful Nuclear Explosions (PNE) and Threshold Test Ban (TTB) treaties. The late Senator Frank Church apparently expected terms of the CTB Treaty to have been settled by late 1978 or early 1979,[5] although this had not been announced by February 1980, when the Swedish representative to the Committee on Disarmament requested that the "elements of the treaty" finally be published. The 1983 edition of the

U.S. Department of State Arms Control and Disarmament Agency (ACDA) Documents on Disarmament reports that the CTBT has been "seriously delayed" by the world political situation.—Eds.]

Of course the fact was that no one stopped building weapons; no one stopped building weapons systems, and no one stopped improving them. The great hypothetical case that we used in Boston in 1962 was a national attack of 1,600 megatons. The model attack on the United States in the mid-eighties is 6,600 megatons, or more than four times the 1962 level. That is what more than twenty additional years of relying on nuclear weapons to increase our security has accomplished for us.

We are still, by the way, measuring and suffering the effects of fallout from that atmospheric testing twenty years ago. We know that testing increased the rates of cancer and leukemia in children in southwestern Utah (which was the highest fallout area) by 2.4 times between 1951 and 1958. Indeed, it could be said that the only credible definition of a limited nuclear war is the assault carried out on the children of southwest Utah by the Atomic Energy Commission and the Department of Defense from 1951 to 1958. Strontium-90 from these tests is still drifting down today, although the rate is decreasing. Approximately 92,000 curies of strontium-90 fell to earth in 1975, the last time it was measured. (A curie is a measure of radioactivity equal to 3.7×10^{10} disintegrations per second.) This is not a great deal until it is picked up in the food chain through the grass, is ingested by cows, and is concentrated in their milk and laid down in concentrated amounts in human bones and teeth.

The Arms Race Continues

The major arguments that provide the context to justify continuing the nuclear arms race and building even more warheads can be summarized very briefly.

1. Americans are told that they are faced with a margin of Soviet superiority. However, a quote from the secretary of defense's annual *Report to Congress* for Fiscal Year 1982 plainly states, "The United States and the Soviet Union are roughly equal in strategic nuclear power."[6] Despite this assessment in 1982, Americans have been warned that we are faced with the consequences of a huge buildup by the Soviet Union. In the 1970s, according to the Reagan administration, the Soviets built up their arsenal relentlessly while the United States stood still, which purportedly explains why the United States is behind. It is indeed quite true that from 1970 to 1980 the Soviet arsenal grew from roughly 1,800 warheads to 6,000, and between 1980 to 1982 it grew to about 8,000. [Part of this growth is in the European

theatre, where the number of weapons increased while megatonnage decreased.—Eds.] Between 1970 and 1980 the United States' arsenal expanded from 4,000 warheads to 10,000. Not only is the United States ahead in total number of warheads, the U.S. increase hardly meets a definition of standing still. It is also noteworthy that the Soviet buildup follows that of the United States. If the nuclear weapons systems and warheads of the two countries are graphed, the United States generally increases the number of weapons first, and that increase is inevitably followed by a Soviet buildup. We then leapfrog. They then leapfrog.

There is a proposal of the current administration, included in the budget of 1,700,000,000,000 (one trillion, 700 billion) dollars of American tax money over 1982-87, for the addition of 17,000 more nuclear warheads to our arsenal.

2. Americans are told that the Soviet Union has first-strike capability and can safely use its first strike. First strike means, of course, that one side can destroy the other's weapons before they can be launched, not leaving enough of the other's for effective retaliation.

This is transparent nonsense, not to be denied by any of the convoluted arguments offered by Department of Defense apologists or others, who are usually attempting to confuse people totally with arcane figures. They imply that unless one can divide the square root of the throw weight by the diameter of the ocean and circular error probable, one cannot understand any of this. All one must really understand is, first, that more than two-thirds of U.S. nuclear weapons are on submarines, which are effectively invulnerable. [Other estimates are about 70 percent of U.S. deployed strategic weapons.—Eds.] Only 25 percent of Soviet weapons are on submarines; the majority are on the more vulnerable ICBMs. U.S. submarines are faster. They are equipped with more warheads. They can stay out on patrol longer, and the United States has more submarines on patrol at any one time than does the Soviet Union. The warheads on one U.S. submarine can destroy every Russian city of over one hundred thousand people. The warheads on two U.S. strategic submarines (and there are about thirty-two) can destroy all Russian cities. President Reagan has asked for fifteen more of these submarines. Thus, the second thing one really needs to know is that there is no moment, now or in the foreseeable future, and there is no conceivable scenario in which the Soviet Union could attack the United States without being destroyed in retaliation, even if the United States lost every land-based missile in the Triad. The public needs to know that.

The public also needs to know that the effective destruction of either the United States or the Soviet Union as an intact and functioning society would require at most about 400 megatons. So the two superpowers "need" about 800 megatons to ensure mutual destruction. Yet, as I pointed out at the beginning of this chapter, the two superpowers have, between us, close to fifteen thousand megatons.

3. The third pernicious argument is that nuclear war can be limited or, as Secretary of Defense Caspar Weinberger sometimes likes to say, "protracted." It should be clear to everyone that this is a perverse use of the word "limited." Even a one-megaton bomb explosion would be a bigger explosion than has ever occurred. The public should know that there never yet has been produced a credible scenario for limited nuclear war; that is, one in which not all of the missiles are used, but only parts of the arsenals, and only some of the destruction is done. [See *On Thermonuclear War,* Kahn, 1960, and other sources for opposing views.—Eds.] This argument presumes that at some point one side can communicate with the other to request a ceasefire. The argument overlooks the fact that the acknowledged first target of each side is what is called C^3: the communication, command, and control structure. Assuming that the phones still work, it assumes further that there will be someone on the other end to answer, and it assumes that somebody on the other end will have some mechanism for turning off the attack. Precisely the point of first strike or the first wave of attack is to make that kind of control impossible on both sides. The argument hypothesizes further that a nation such as the United States, Great Britain, or the Soviet Union, which already has suffered millions of deaths and still has thousands of unused nuclear weapons in its arsenal, will stop. Limited nuclear war calculations are based on the most gross kind of error.

The continuing public debate on arms control should be informed by a skeptical attitude toward these limits. The public also should recall that its opinions have been influential. The vote on the nuclear freeze resolution in the House of Representatives was quite close, 204 to 202. A one- or two-vote change would have resulted in passage of the freeze. Instead, it was defeated at nine o'clock, on the evening of August 5, 1982. Media commentators noted that the failure of the freeze occurred on the eve of the anniversary of the bombing of Hiroshima. With a peculiarly American ethnocentrism, no one in the media realized that nine o'clock in the evening on August 5th in Washington, D.C., is eleven o'clock in the morning on August 6th in Hiroshima. So the moment at which the U.S. House of Representatives voted down the freeze was the thirty-seventh anniversary of the moment survivors were clustered on the bridges on the outskirts of Hiroshima, trying to get out of the destroyed city.

A classic photograph has been taken of the traces of some soul vaporized at Hiroshima—a sort of negative shadow burned into a pair of concrete steps. This photograph indicates that the problem we now face is different from all problems ever confronted before. Thirty-seven years later, the divided vote in the U.S. House of Representatives expressed a contested U.S.

commitment to continue making many more nuclear weapons.

Notes

1. *The Effects of Nuclear Weapons* (1962, rev. 1964) notes (p. 350:7.75) somewhat more ambiguously, "... no definite firestorm occurred at Nagasaki...."
2. Rad and rem measures are very similar measures of energy absorbed. One rad is equal to the energy absorption of 100 ergs per gram of irradiated material. A rem (roentgen equivalent man) is a unit dose of ionizing radiation yielding the same biological effect as one roentgen of X-rays, or an amount that will produce ions carrying one electrostatic unit of electricity (+ or −) in 1 cc. of dry air, or 2.1×10^9 ion pairs in 1 cc. of air. According to Alexander (1957:37-38), if 34 electron volts of energy are transferred to the gas every time an ion pair is formed, exposure of tissue to 1 roentgen results in an uptake of "almost" 100 ergs per gram of tissue irradiated. Thus a rem equals "almost" a rad.
3. The effects of weapons vary depending on several factors including whether they are detonated as groundbursts or airbursts. With the airburst the only effect of major concern outside the first circle is delayed fallout, radioactive particles that drift over a considerable period of time and land relatively far away. Delayed fallout gives off a relatively small dose of ionizing radiation to a very large number of people. Groundbursts are the "dirty" ones because they dig huge craters in the ground, creating gigantic overpressures that turn everything into rubble. But the circles of consequent destruction have smaller radii. The blast effect is not as widespread but it is much more intense. Millions of tons of pulverized and vaporized rocks, steel, buildings, and people are sucked up into the mushroom cloud. There they form nuclei on which radioactive isotopes condense, and within ten, twenty, or thirty minutes they start coming down, the heavier particles first as immediate fallout. Where they land depends on which way and how hard the wind is blowing.
4. Some researchers suggest that these effects on the gene pool may also be incremental rather than decremental with time.
5. See the censored report "Strategic Arms Limitations and the Comprehensive Test Ban Negotiations," especially pages 11 and 13; and Representative Inga Thorsson's statement to the Committee on Disarmament, cited in the U.S. Arms Control and Disarmament Agency's *Documents on Disarmament* (1980:45).
6. Brown, Harold (1981). *Report of Secretary of Defense Harold Brown to the Congress on the Fiscal Year 1982 Budget, Fiscal Year 1983 Authorization Request and Fiscal Years 1982-1986 Defense Programs.* Washington DC: U.S. Government Printing Office. In this source there is an implicit reference to parity on 37; and a definition, a discussion, and an assertion of superpower parity on pages 43 and 44.

References

Alexander, Peter (1957). *Atomic Radiation and Life.* London: Penguin.
Arms Control and Disarmament Agency (1983). *Documents on Disarmament 1980.*
    "Statement of Swedish Representative Thorsson to the Committee on Disarmament, 12 February 1980." Washington DC: U.S. Government Printing Office.

Church, Frank (made public in 1978). "Strategic Arms Limitations and the Comprehensive Test Ban Negotiations." Washington DC: U.S. Government Printing Office.

Glasstone, Samuel, ed. (1957 and 1964). *The Effects of Nuclear Weapons,* U.S. Department of Defense and U.S. AEC (1962). Washington DC: U.S. Government Printing Office.

Office of Technology Assessment of the Congress of the United States (1979). *The Effects of Nuclear War.* Washington DC: U.S. Government Printing Office.

Scheer, Robert (1982). *With Enough Shovels: Reagan, Bush and Nuclear War.* New York: Random House.

UN Report of the Secretary-General and Consultative Group (1968). *Effects of the Possible Use of Nuclear Weapons and the Security and Economic Implications for States of the Acquisition and Further Development of These Weapons.* New York: U.N. Publications.

George Rathjens

A CRITICAL ANALYSIS OF THE ARMS CONTROL RECORD

George Rathjens has worked in Washington, D.C., in the Office of the Secretary of Defense and in the Office of the Special Assistant to the President for Science and Technology. Dr. Rathjens has held several positions with the U.S. Arms Control and Disarmament Agency, as well as with the Institute for Defense Analysis. In 1979 and 1980, he served as the Deputy U.S. Representative for Nonproliferation of Nuclear Weapons in the Department of State. In the following assessment of the accomplishments of arms control, Dr. Rathjens argues that the arms control process between the superpowers may have become counterproductive. Notwithstanding some significant positive achievements, such as the reduction in nuclear contamination brought about by the Partial Test Ban Treaty, Dr. Rathjens observes that the requirements for U.S. Senate advice and consent on arms control measures (in combination with other political pressures) present serious obstacles to meaningful agreements. As the length of time required for negotiations—when ongoing—to produce a draft treaty grows, the probability increases that new weapons systems will be deployed before agreement can be reached. Likewise, as negotiations are broken up and resumed, new weapons systems—not otherwise justified and ostensibly to be used as bargaining chips in future negotiations—will be developed.

Introduction

Some twenty years ago the U.S. academic community began to think seriously about negotiating limits on strategic arms. It was a seminal period, and out of that, by consensus, a codification of the objectives of arms control negotiations emerged. There were three objectives:

1. It was hoped, first and foremost, that through negotiations the risk of war could be reduced;
2. that the damage that would likely result should war occur could be reduced; and
3. that the cost of maintaining the defense establishment could be limited.

I assert that we have failed miserably on all counts. We have failed to the point that people hardly ever even think of these original objectives when thinking about SALT, START, or any other arms control negotiations. It is difficult to persuade people to measure such agreements or proposals against those original criteria, although I think it should be done.

In this chapter some of the problems in negotiations will be discussed, and an assessment of several of the major arms control efforts we have been through will be presented.

First consider the SALT II negotiations, as an illustration of the difficulties of negotiations. These negotiations took seven years, 1972-79. A treaty was written but the United States has not ratified it. During that period, the interim agreement limiting offensive forces and the Antiballistic Missile Treaty previously negotiated at SALT I (1972) were in force, and they were observed. Notwithstanding the observance of SALT I limitations and the ABM Treaty, during those seven years the number of missile warheads the Soviet Union could deliver against the United States was doubled. The number the United States could deliver against the Soviet Union also increased dramatically. This suggests that something is wrong. Clearly, the SALT I Interim Agreement did not enact limits that would mean much of a reduction in damage to either of these countries, should a war occur. And I would submit that nothing has happened as a result of either SALT I or SALT II that had the slightest bearing on the likelihood that the superpowers would go to war. Also, both countries spent enormous amounts of money on new weapons during those years. Moreover, President Reagan proposed during 1981-82 to increase expenditures on strategic weapons by about thirty billion dollars a year over the succeeding six years, notwithstanding the declaratory policy intent of the United States to observe the terms of these major agreements that it has negotiated. So it is difficult to argue that the SALT efforts have saved the United States much money, and there is very little prospect of saving much during the next few years.

I do not think that any particularly important weapons programs have been stopped during this period, with some very minor exceptions. The defense program is rather like a gigantic balloon: when it is squeezed in one place, it pops out somewhere else. It seems to me that this analogy describes the recent history of arms control fairly well, by and large. The SALT I Interim Agreement limiting offensive missiles and the SALT II Treaty (draft) provide examples. These agreements imposed limits on the numbers of ballistic missiles that each side could build. Subsequently the United States, and later the Soviet Union, built cruise missiles instead. Thus, there is no reason to think that there is, as a result of the history of limitations on ballistic missiles, any diminution in the number of weapons that could be delivered, nor any diminution in the amount of money being spent. A different means of getting warheads to their targets has been developed instead.

There are other examples of this phenomenon. One that most people probably do not know about concerns not a formal treaty but an informal understanding in 1958. In a way, the development of multiple warheads can be traced to that event. The United States and the Soviet Union had halted testing of nuclear weapons for about two years (1958-60). At the time, the U.S. Navy wanted a new warhead for its submarine-launched missile program. An air force warhead that had been tested might have been used, but the air force warhead was not acceptable; and with a moratorium on testing, the navy was driven to using three small, already-tested warheads on a single missile. Thus the moratorium did not stop the United States from building all of the missiles wanted by the armed services and warheads for them. The armed services simply adapted to the constraints.

These displacement effects suggest that it is really rather difficult to turn the arms control process around in a major way, although at one point—and I think it has only been once in the thirty years of my involvement—the United States has really seriously tried. This unique serious attempt occurred in 1977, when President Jimmy Carter sent Cyrus Vance to Moscow with some new proposals that could have made a difference. The Vance proposals suggested actually cutting numbers significantly and severely limiting the testing of missiles. Had the latter happened, it would have been very difficult to develop new ICBMs or to demonstrate improvements in accuracy to the point that the military would have been confident of them. But that particular proposal got nowhere, evidently because the administration presented it in a way that was almost designed to elicit a negative response.

The prospects for progress in achieving any of the three objectives of arms control—reducing the risk of war, reducing the damage that would result should war occur, or reducing the costs of maintaining military capability—are dim. Arms control advocates in the United States are reduced to selling each arms control agreement on the grounds that the next one will be significant in achieving one of these objectives, or, more generally, on the grounds that the process is worthwhile, specific accomplishments aside.

Is the Arms Control Process Worthwhile?

I want to consider at some length whether the arms control process is worthwhile. I think an objective assessment requires a negative view; a rather depressing, pessimistic view. There are very severe problems, which I want to highlight, involved in any negotiations process. At the same time, there are some advantages.

At the beginning of the Kennedy administration, before the United States began significant negotiations on strategic weapons, Robert McNamara was secretary of defense, and he was perhaps as responsible as anyone in the United States for our having gotten into strategic arms negotiations. The United States observed that even if no agreements at all were obtained, negotiations would be worthwhile because, simply by talking with the Russians, Americans would obtain a better understanding of their concerns; the Russians would gain a better understanding of American concerns; and this would enable the superpowers to live together more comfortably, with reduced tensions. The process would be worthwhile in its own right, even if there were no concrete agreements. There is something to be said for this, but not a great deal. There is one other advantage in negotiations, the outcome aside: in the United States, negotiations that might lead to a treaty do lead to an involvement of key parts of the bureaucracy and the Congress that would otherwise be less likely. For example, members of the Senate Foreign Relations Committee feel a special responsibility to be informed about weapons that might be affected by a prospective treaty.

Despite these positive aspects, if one is going to negotiate effectively, one must have something to put on the table, something about which to talk to the other fellow, as a price for his giving up something or for his doing whatever one wants. This, the bargaining chip argument, is usually adduced as the most powerful argument against arms control negotiations. I think there is a great deal in the bargaining chip argument as a case against arms control. U.S. participation in these negotiations provides a great opportunity for those who favor a particular weapons program to argue that it must be supported so that the United States can bargain effectively with the other fellow. This appeal for bargaining chips would not be too disadvantageous for arms control if negotiations lasted about a week, considering that the weapons development and procurement process takes several years. But the negotiations do not last only a week. SALT I negotiations lasted three years, and, again, SALT II negotiations lasted seven years. At this rate, there is every reason to extrapolate. Even if negotiations pick up speed, a dozen years could well elapse before a START agreement is reached, and a great deal can happen in periods that long. In particular, once a weapons program is well underway it develops a constituency, and it may become impossible to stop.

As my friend Raymond Garthoff has said, one man's bargaining chip becomes another man's vital interest.

This has happened over and over again with weapons systems that the United States really did not want very much. An instance from the SALT I negotiations is illustrative, although it does not quite fit my case. In the late sixties, there was a major debate about whether the United States should deploy a ballistic missile defense system, a system to defend the United States against the other fellow's missiles. Many in government and academic circles thought a BMD/ABM was a bad idea. Some did not want the system components in their backyards; others thought that it would not work; still others thought that if the United States built it, it would induce the Soviets to build more warheads so that both countries would be worse off than before the United States started to build its ballistic missile defense system.

It was a technically inadequate system for the job that it was to have done and, by 1969-70, it appeared that ABM deployment could not be supported in the Senate. So the advocates of the system claimed the ABM was needed so that the United States could bargain effectively with the Soviet Union, and that was the position taken by the administration. This claim made it possible to sell the ABM system. A critical number of senators were unwilling to be tarred with sabotaging the most important arms control negotiations in prospect by voting against the only good bargaining chip the administration had. Consequently, the bargaining chip argument turned votes around in the case of the ABM. The negotiations continued, money was appropriated for the ABM system, and the United States bought it. This case does not quite fit the pattern described earlier, inasmuch as this was one of the rare instances in which the bargaining chip was cashed: the United States actually stopped building the system and achieved a treaty that limited ABM deployment. All it cost the United States was $5.7 billion. Nevertheless, the ABM provides the first good example, at least in my involvement in this business, of a case in which a major arms control negotiation was used to justify a system that otherwise could not possibly have withstood serious scrutiny. There are other examples.

In 1972 the United States was proceeding with the Trident program, which involved both a large new missile and a large strategic submarine (the first of which has now been launched) that carries twenty-four missiles. Why the United States needs a submarine of that size is another issue. It is another scandal. In any case, in 1972 members of Congress, which had been quite willing to supply money to support research and development (R&D) for this program, began to have doubts about proceeding as rapidly as the administration wanted. Some did not think that the United States had progressed sufficiently in the R&D process to provide all of the money for procurement requested by the administration. When the issue came up in the

Senate, it looked as though the administration request would be rejected. To stave off this rejection, the administration argued, in effect, that since SALT II was coming up, the United States needed the Trident program to negotiate effectively with the Soviet Union, which had new offensive missile programs while the United States had none.

In fact, I believe that, to enhance the U.S. bargaining position, the president went to the secretary of defense simply to request that more money be spent on strategic systems, without much regard for what might be bought. Trident was the only program capable of absorbing more money at the time. The result of the president's request was to switch a vote in the Armed Services Committee in Congress so that the request for funds survived there, eight to eight. Had it not been for the argument that Trident was necessary for SALT II, the program would have proceeded at the usual rate. Instead, it was accelerated, ostensibly so that the United States could negotiate effectively for a treaty that remains unratified.

There are other cases. The whole cruise missile program was alleged, at least by Henry Kissinger, to be a bargaining chip that got out of hand. Dr. Kissinger argued that, with the ballistic missile programs constrained, the U.S. cruise missile program was speeded up so that the United States could bargain effectively in SALT. And then, contrary to his expectations, as he put it, the military fell in love with cruise missiles, so now the United States has a massive cruise missile program. The United States intends to put three thousand of them on bombers, and an additional 464 already are being deployed on the ground in Europe. This program probably would not have been invented—probably would not have gotten anywhere—but for the fact that the United States needed cruise missiles "to bargain effectively." There had been no great interest in this program in the U.S. military services, but once its funding increased a constituency developed. There is not a chance that it could now be turned off.

Further examples of cases in which arms control efforts have been used to justify military programs that could not possibly have been justified on other grounds involve tactical force programs. These examples are overwhelmingly powerful and must be brought up.

There was once a period of some disenchantment in the United States about maintaining military forces in Europe. Senator Mike Mansfield, the majority leader in the Senate, proposed their withdrawal, and it looked as though his position was going to carry. If one's administration encounters this problem the answer is to prepare for arms control negotiations that will require the United States to leave troops in Europe so that the United States can bargain effectively. And, of course, that is what the United States did by entering into negotiations with the Soviet Union on mutual balanced force reductions many years ago, in October 1973. These negotiations still continue, having gotten nowhere. But they have been highly successful from the point of view of the Executive branch. With the negotiations, talk of unilaterally withdrawing the U.S. forces stopped, and Senator Mansfield went on to other things.

A very similar series of events took place after the U.S. two-track NATO decision of 1979. There has been a controversy among our European allies—particularly the Dutch, the Belgians, and the Germans—about our putting 464 new cruise missiles and 108 new ballistic missiles (Pershing II missiles) in Europe.

I question whether these missiles will ever be deployed in Holland, as the opposition to them is so great there. But Germany was the key country. To keep the Germans aboard, again, the United States entered into an arms control negotiation—the intermediate-range nuclear force (INF) talks in Geneva—and argued that, if the negotiations were to have any chance of success, deployment must proceed. [These talks began on October 17, 1982, and were broken off after deployment began, as in the Soviet view these missiles destroyed the basis for negotiations. Apparently this was one of several topics covered in the March 1985 arms control discussions, and INF may be subsumed in the substantive strategic talks.—Eds.] The Reagan administration entered into INF negotiations, obviously, because they offered the only possibility of salvaging the deployment decision. But for the talks, German public opinion would almost certainly have forced rejection of cruise missile and Pershing II deployment, and there would be no hope of going ahead. It is the most unambiguous and cynical example ever seen of arms control's being used to justify a weapons program that would otherwise not survive.

Perhaps enough has been said about bargaining chips. There are other problems in negotiations.

At least in the U.S. system—it is probably a lot truer in the West than in the East—the hardest bargaining may be the internal bargaining. Every time the United States enters into arms negotiations, be it in Geneva, Vienna, or Helsinki, much of the tough bargaining has taken place in Washington. It goes on within and among the armed services, the Congress, the executive branch, and others. If the military establishment is to be persuaded to go along with a treaty about which it has some doubts, one that may limit some of the options it might prefer to have, it can be promised alternative programs, to ensure that the chairman of the Joint Chiefs of Staff will go up on the Hill to testify before the Armed Services Committee and the Foreign Relations Committee that the treaty is wonderful, or at least acceptable.

The U.S. system is particularly vulnerable to this pressure, more so than any other in the world, because of the structure of the U.S. Constitution. It takes two-thirds of the Senate to ratify a treaty; this means that a one-third minority in the Senate, plus one, can block a treaty. A president who really wants to get a treaty sold will cater to that one-third every time. It is conceivable that a one-third minority would vote for a treaty if funds for programs not covered by the treaty were cut off. But that has not happened. On the contrary, the Senate minority agrees to vote for the treaty under discussion if the administration agrees to buy other systems not covered by the treaty. So, in effect, the treaty-making process in the United States permits a minority to have an almost ironclad way to get military programs that perhaps the majority of the Congress and the executive branch would not want through the Congress and out of the administration.

Some examples of the manner in which the military, including the Joint Chiefs of Staff and others in the Department of Defense, work with their supporters in Congress to get the president to support programs that he might otherwise reject can be provided. The Limited Test Ban Treaty of 1963, which prohibits testing nuclear weapons in every environment except underground, is a case in point. President John F. Kennedy was worried about getting enough support for the Partial Test Ban Treaty in the Senate—needlessly worried, considering that, when the vote came, there was a large majority. But in his nervousness about it, he acceded to the so-called safeguards that were dictated by the Joint Chiefs of Staff as their conditions for going along with the treaty. One of these conditions was a vigorous underground testing program. The result of Kennedy's concession was that, after the treaty, the United States accelerated its rate of nuclear testing. That was a consequential concession to get the chiefs, and with them the congressional committees, to accede to the treaty. The other requirements were, in this case, innocuous and one, perhaps two, were probably even desirable:

1. The administration promised to keep the weapons laboratories alive with large appropriations. Thus, there have been vigorous research and development programs at the Los Alamos and Lawrence Livermore national laboratories.
2. The administration promised to maintain a task force in readiness so that the United States could go out to the South Pacific to resume atmospheric testing quickly if the Soviet Union should break the treaty. U.S. Joint Task Force Eight was put together, providing one more job for a three-star general or an admiral. The task force stayed in business for a few years, but it was phased out eventually.
3. Finally, there was another promise. The president promised to enact a vigorous verification program to ensure that the Soviets were complying with the treaty.

Similar events took place in SALT I. Again, the Joint Chiefs dictated conditions, this time called assurances, for their support. One of these assurances is especially noteworthy: "to maximize strategic capabilities within the constraints of the agreements." If this assurance is interpreted literally, it means that the president is to support buying every conceivable system not specifically ruled out by agreement! This assurance never has been interpreted in quite that way, but that was what the Joint Chiefs were after.

Another "safeguard" in SALT I was that the United States would have such a vigorous research and development program relating to nuclear weapons that the United States could be sure of maintaining technological superiority over the Soviet Union. If that is not a prescription for an arms race, I never have heard one. Assume the Soviet generals could impose the same requirements on the Politburo, and consider the consequences.

Those are the most serious problems that come up in arms control negotiations, and they become increasingly serious the longer the negotiations go on. There are other, less serious, problems with the negotiations process that also should be highlighted.

Anyone who has been in this business for any significant length of time and is looking for what is possible, and for what the difficulties are, will appreciate the fact that it is very difficult to negotiate except from a position of near symmetry. [This may be true both with respect to hardware and to doctrine. Symmetry is rough parity in weapons systems-level comparisons.— Eds.] It is almost impossible to negotiate agreements permitting one side to do something that the other side cannot do. This limitation greatly constrains what can be accomplished. If one side is significantly ahead in one area, one might as well kiss that area off; there is no hope of limiting it by agreement. A good example of the futility of negotiations in areas of pronounced asymmetry or inequality lies in the rather desultory efforts to try to prevent the development of capabilities to deliver warheads, each to a different target, with a single missile (MIRVing). Many thought that the development of MIRVs was very unfortunate, that MIRV'd missiles would perhaps make nuclear war more likely and would certainly accelerate the arms race. And so there was some slight effort in SALT I to negotiate an end to MIRV development and deployment, but it was destined to go nowhere. The prevailing view in the U.S. bureaucracy was that the United States should not give up or bring to a halt work in an area in which the United States had a substantial technological lead. And if one spoke with the Russians, as I did, their attitude was that they should not agree to a treaty that would freeze them into a position of technological inferiority.

But in a sense the prospects for agreement may not be quite as poor as I have suggested. If the positions of the two sides are not almost symmetric, one may still be able to get a deal, provided it permits one to make them symmetric. One does this by allowing the weaker side to build up to the level of the stronger side. That is called arms control! The best example of that leveling up appears in SALT I in the ABM case. The United States was interested in building a defense, not of its cities, but of its missile sites. The Soviet Union had a half-baked defense of Moscow that we expected would not work. So one can imagine how the treaty finally worked out. Each side was allowed the construction of both kinds of defense: defense of one missile base and of one city. In that way we achieved system-level parity, or symmetry, instead of closing off the whole ABM option. [As Dr. Rathjens points out below, the 1974 Protocol to the ABM Treaty reduces the number of ABM sites to one, with an option to reverse the choice of site.—Eds.]

There are other examples. When President Ford went to Vladivostok, so that he and the late General Secretary Leonid Brezhnev could begin negotiating the outlines of what could have been SALT II had Ford won a second term, a critical question was setting a limit on the number of missiles each side would be allowed to have. One can guess where the limit was set. At the time, the Soviet Union had more missiles than did the United States, so the limit was set at the Soviet level. The president maintained that, having agreed to that limit, the United States should build up to it. Until that time, neither the Joint Chiefs of Staff nor anyone else had seriously argued for a buildup to those missile levels and, fortunately, the United States has not followed through on President Ford's suggestion.

Finally, there is the issue of verification. It is virtually a graven-in-stone proposition that the United States will not enter into an arms control treaty unless it can verify whether or not the Soviet Union is complying. As an example, it might have been preferable to have had a Comprehensive Test Ban Treaty rather than the Partial Test Ban, but the United States could not—or at least felt it could not—agree to a comprehensive accord at the time. This reluctance followed from a verification problem. For nuclear weapons tested underground, the main method of detection is to pick up the seismic shock, but distinguishing the seismic shock patterns of nuclear weapons from the shock generated by earthquakes was problematical. By 1984 the United States had developed techniques that allow these patterns to be distinguished well enough that there is not much of a problem. The United States could sign a Comprehensive Test Ban Treaty tomorrow, and could be fairly certain that it was being complied with. My own view is that we should have one, not because it is important to the U.S.–Soviet arms competition; it is scarcely relevant to that at all, as both U.S. and Soviet nuclear weapons technology is so mature that it would not make much difference whether one side continued testing or not. But a Comprehensive Test Ban Treaty to which other nations would subscribe could be important in reducing the likelihood of the spread of nuclear weapons. (The present U.S. administration has taken a totally different view on the CTB, and has announced that it will not even pursue the CTB negotiations, although a draft ready for signature apparently existed when SALT II was ready for ratification.) U.S. seismic stations outside the Soviet Union do give the United States a means of knowing whether or not the Soviet Union is testing weapons underground; further, the United States can get some measure of the yield of any tests the Soviets conduct. So seismic detection, an example of national technical means, has improved to the point that verification is no longer an obstacle to nuclear test agreements. [Further, there is treaty language for positioning of on-site seismic detection equipment in both superpowers.—Eds.]

The United States has entered into agreements, some of which are mentioned below, for which U.S. verification capabilities are very poor, but set these atypical agreements aside for the moment. By and large, the United States has taken a very tough line on verification; that is one of the fundamental areas of difference between the United States and the Soviet Union. Generally the United States has insisted that a verification capability be in place first and then the United States will implement the agreement. The Soviet position has been just the reverse: the arms control or disarmament agreement comes first, and whatever verification capability is required will be put into place afterwards. The U.S. preoccupation with verification is reflected in the fact that, during SALT I, the principal policy-formulating body was the Verification Panel. Apparently, no one thought of organizing any other interagency policy committee, but they did think of the need for a verification panel; when other issues arose that required resolution, they were handled by the Verification Panel. Thus, the Verification Panel dealt with policy for every aspect of the negotiations; in effect, it became the tail that wags the dog.

This emphasis on verification may or may not be undesirable. It is perhaps understandable (although remarkable in a way) that, when the issue is a treaty or an agreement, the United States demands a very much higher standard of surveillance evidence from the Soviet Union than is required of the CIA and of the other intelligence agencies in the absence of a treaty. It suddenly becomes ever so much more important to know exactly how many missiles the Soviet Union has, or exactly how many warheads, or exactly how much plutonium they are producing; whereas without the treaty the United States is quite prepared to live with wider margins of error. The verification issue becomes an excuse for some who are opposed to a treaty not to go along with it. They will argue that it cannot be verified. I am sure that any person who engaged in discussions on the nuclear freeze heard that verification argument from the opposition. So verification becomes important, and imposing very high standards greatly limits what can be done. Treaties cannot be obtained in some areas important to us, areas in which intelligence capability otherwise is judged adequate, because the United

States has a double standard: there is one standard if the United States is interested in a treaty and another for day-to-day business when the issues are not treaty-related.

There are exceptional instances in which the United States has been willing to conclude treaties even though U.S. capabilities for verifying compliance were poor. One example is the agreement proscribing the placement of weapons of mass destruction in space, the 1967 Outer Space Treaty. I was involved in the backup work on that one. We decided that the United States could not verify it very well, but we did not care, because it would not make any difference if the Soviet Union put weapons of mass destruction in space in any case. What good would it do them? The United States would not worry about it, so we might just as well have the treaty, especially as political leaders benefit at times by having a treaty; for example, before an election.

In view of the difficulties of negotiations, unilateral actions (such as the moratorium) and informal agreements (such as the decision to cut defense spending by both superpowers) may be effective. I should perhaps elaborate on the mutual example idea. Following Brezhnev's October 1979 speech in Berlin, the Soviets pulled some tanks and troops out of Eastern Europe and announced to the United States that they were doing it—in effect, inviting some reciprocation. The Soviet Union did not say that reciprocation would require our pulling troops and tanks out; in fact, there was an explicit statement that these reductions were not contingent on a reciprocal or proportional response. Perhaps the United States could have taken some action that would have sent a signal to the Soviet Union indicating interest in arms control. But that Soviet move did not work. Although the Europeans took it rather seriously, the Carter administration did not. The Carter administration interpreted the Soviet move as an insignificant one, made for propaganda effect, and it did not react. [The size of the troop withdrawal was quite close to the discrepancy between agreed counts of NATO and WTO forces in the Vienna Mutual Balanced Force Reductions (MBFR) negotiations. The Soviets seem to have hoped that this unilateral withdrawal would break the MBFR deadlock and perhaps revive interest in SALT II.—Eds.]

In any case, unilateralism is a very unpopular idea, and there are problems in trying to make progress on arms control and disarmament through unilateral moves taken in the hope or expectation of reciprocation. One of the problems is that the decision-making processes, particularly in the Soviet Union, are very cumbersome and take an enormous amount of time. One side may expect a response from the other in what is an unrealistically short time and may draw a negative inference when it is not forthcoming. [Or a response may actually precede the events that caused it, where decision makers publicly anticipate future developments, further clouding the waters.—Eds.]

A Critical Assessment of Major Arms Control Efforts

Although evidence justifies a very negative view of the major arms control efforts in the post–World War II period, and of the arms control process itself, there are positive comments to be made. In a somewhat differentiated view, it can be seen that some of the agreements reached have been worthwhile, some highly worthwhile, and others not worth much at all.

Agreements covering the whole range of issues related to testing of nuclear weapons have been positive. In 1958 there was a moratorium on atmospheric testing, which is described above. Under this moratorium, for two and a half years the United States and the Soviet Union refrained from nuclear weapons testing. During that time, the superpowers attempted to negotiate a comprehensive treaty that would prohibit all such tests. This attempt failed because a higher standard of verification was required for a treaty than was accepted for the moratorium. The United States insisted on the right to conduct up to seven inspections of suspicious events per year inside the Soviet Union and, because the Soviet Union would not accede to our demand, the Comprehensive Test Ban failed. I do not know any person in the United States who believes that the Soviet Union cheated during that moratorium. They did not test, nor did the United States, for those two and a half years. There were people who raised doubts and questions about the moratorium, but it worked; yet a comprehensive treaty proved to be beyond reach because of the verification question.

However, the Partial Test Ban Treaty still in force, which proscribes nuclear testing except underground and was the next best thing to a CTB, was achieved. It has been of some importance in reducing the understanding of weapons effects, because underground it is difficult to measure all of the effects of nuclear weapons that can be observed in testing above the earth's surface. But the major effect of the Partial Test Ban has been as an environmental measure. [See Levandowsky, Chapter 6.- –Eds.] At the time of this treaty, parents in the United States were deeply distressed about the possibility of their children's getting cancer from strontium-90, which was being produced in weapons tests and finding its way into the milk supply through the food chain. [See Geiger, Chapter 7.—Eds.] That concern was the reason the United States helped achieve this treaty, which has almost stopped atmospheric testing. The Chinese [and reportedly the French, after a moratorium of their own,—Eds.] are still contaminating the biosphere with radioactivity as they continue testing, but the Russians and the Americans are not. Several thousand people per year are probably still being killed by fallout from those tests before 1963, but, except for the Chinese, such testing is not continuing, and the numbers of fatalities per year is not growing. Thus, as an environmental protection measure, the Limited (Partial) Test Ban Treaty rates an A in my book, although it deserves no more than a C as an arms control agreement.

Another treaty on the books, the Threshold Test Ban Treaty, signed in July 1974, proscribes underground testing of weapons with yields above 150 kilotons, but the United States has not ratified that one because of the administration's reluctance to bring it before the Senate. The debate that would follow would be too embarrassing. Some people would ask for a justification of the 150-kiloton threshold and would ask why all nuclear testing, or at least all tests down to a much lower threshold, should not be stopped, inasmuch as verification would probably be adequate down to around 10 or 20 kilotons. The answer would have to be that the threshold was set at 150 kilotons simply because both sides wanted to test up to that level.

This drives home the point most forcefully that, if one puts aside the resolution of the Cuban missile crisis, neither the United States nor the Soviet Union ever has entered into an agreement that would prevent either from doing anything it really wanted to do. This may be the most important argument made in this chapter. The superpowers may make mistakes. It is conceivable that the United States or the Soviet Union could enter into an agreement and later realize that it was a mistake (the ABM Treaty could prove to be an example if at some point the United States decides it really wants to defend ICBMs) but, by and large, the superpowers have known what they are about. The record with respect to the Threshold Test Ban Treaty is even worse than has been indicated. Implementation was actually delayed by agreement, so that each side could sneak in a few more tests above the 150-kiloton level before the treaty would have been brought into force had it been ratified. Both sides apparently accelerated their testing programs to do so. The treaty was such an evident exercise in hypocrisy that it hardly deserves more than an F on any count.

The ABM Treaty of 1972 (which is part of SALT I and is still in force) permitted each superpower to have two defense sites, but it later developed that neither side wanted two, so a protocol was negotiated subsequently in 1974 to reduce the number of defense sites permitted in each country from two to one. This reduction made it possible for people in both the White House and the Kremlin to get some brownie points for progress on arms control when they needed them. Despite these ulterior motives, that treaty is of some importance. I do not think it has reduced the risk of war. It has not had very much effect on military expenditures in my view, although there are people who would argue otherwise. They would say that if the ABM Treaty did not exist, most likely both sides would be spending a great deal on ballistic missile defense [as may yet be the case—Eds.], and probably the United States and the Soviet Union would then spend much more on offensive systems to counter the other fellow's defenses. My own view is that the United

States would not be doing very much because there are no technically attractive options for either side. The fact of technical infeasibility, however, has not stopped either superpower from spending money in all cases, so it is conceivable that the ABM Treaty has been a big money-saver for a time, and the High Frontier proposal, also known as Star Wars or the Strategic Defense Initiative, may provide a counterexample. But the main accomplishment of the treaty, now or in the future, is the reduction in uncertainty in American minds about what the Soviet Union might do. They could still abrogate the treaty; the United States could too. But somehow the United States is inclined to think that it is less likely that the Soviet Union will build a ballistic missile defense under the ABM Treaty than it would be if that treaty did not exist, and so the United States is more relaxed. That being so, I give the ABM Treaty about a B+.

There was also another agreement on offensive weapons that was a product of SALT I, the Interim Agreement on the Limitation of Strategic Offensive Arms (1972). It permitted the Soviet Union substantially larger force levels than it did the United States. Such inequalities make agreement unlikely. The agreement was approved by the Congress but—not surprisingly—not without several objections, including a resolution (the Jackson Amendment) that carried overwhelmingly in the Senate instructing the president thereafter to negotiate only agreements that permit numerically equal limits.

The SALT I agreement was defended with great vigor on the grounds that it would not prevent the United States from doing anything that it wanted to do anyway! Although we cannot be certain, it is difficult to believe that this agreement prevented the Soviets from doing anything they wanted either. Moreover, its negotiation delayed the conclusion of the ABM Treaty considerably and, as noted, it caused great dissension because of its unequal limits. A grade of C- may be generous.

On the positive side, one of the most important consequences of SALT was the U.S.–Soviet agreement that neither side would interfere with the other's national technical means to verify treaty compliance. That means that the superpowers have agreed that the United States will not destroy Soviet satellites observing the United States, and the Soviet Union will not destroy U.S. surveillance satellites. We will not try to knock out other instrumentation each superpower uses for surveillance. That is a very important aspect of these agreements.

The national technical means of verification include the familiar satellites. Reconnaissance satellites date from 1960, and they are of great importance. In the election campaign of 1960, John F. Kennedy charged the Eisenhower administration with allowing a missile gap to develop, alleging that the Russians were getting ahead in the missile business. Those of us who had access to intelligence information knew by the end of 1960 that the missile gap was a phony issue. From the photographs first taken with the U-2, and then from those taken with satellites, it became known that there was not any Russian ICBM deployment at all, to speak of. The president chose to keep this intelligence secret. But in 1959—in contrast to 1960—insiders, myself included, *were* worried about a missile gap, because at that time we did not have good intelligence. We did not know what the Russians were doing about ICBM deployment; we did not know what they were going to do. And, in planning what the United States should do, people naturally tend to fear the worst. They project the worst that the other fellow could do and then plan everything on that worst-case assumption. If the United States had not had reasonably accurate satellite reconnaissance from 1960 on, my guess is that the United States would have had expenditures at least three or four times as large over the ensuing years on strategic arms programs as we have had.

From the comments made by government spokesmen, and from the agreements that are negotiated, it is clear that the United States can rely on national technical means to count Soviet submarines, aircraft, and missile-launching silos. Further, U.S. national technical means can distinguish among different missiles and among kinds of silos from which missiles can be launched. This provides some indication of the precision of satellite surveillance.

Satellites also can pick up telemetry. The United States used to have facilities in Turkey and Iran that operated very powerful radars to look at Soviet test ranges, when the Soviet Union was testing its missiles. Having picked up telemetry from a test, the United States could estimate the specifications of the new missile—how big it was, what the payload was likely to be, what kind of propulsion it had, and other information of that kind. So agreement on tolerating national technical means of verification, including seismic detection, is an important accomplishment of the SALT process.

SALT II was a much more complicated negotiation, which led to a complicated treaty. During seven years of negotiations the United States paid a price, for the reasons cited above, in impetus for unnecessary weapons programs, including cruise missile programs, probably more rapid movement with Trident than would otherwise have taken place, and who knows how many programs on the other side. All things considered, my view is that SALT II may have been a mistake from the start, and I would not rate it higher than a C. Still, having gotten a treaty, I would have voted for it, had I been in the Senate. The country had already paid the price during the negotiations, so the United States might just as well have gotten the small benefits of ratifying the treaty. (Actually, some of those benefits were realized, such as they are, for even without ratification the terms of the treaty largely were observed, at least in the early 1980s.)

I have been in favor of the nuclear freeze as an expression of public concern—as an objective; but other advocates and critics clearly have a more formal, operative understanding in mind, particularly as they discuss a mutual, verifiable freeze. The freeze proposals of 1982 and later are not the first versions. President Lyndon Johnson proposed a freeze in 1964. Unfortunately, the United States did not get one then because the Soviet Union would not agree to a freeze at that time. One can imagine what would have happened if there had been a nuclear freeze in 1964. President Reagan would not be worried about windows of vulnerability; the Soviet Union would not have SS-18 missiles; neither side would have MIRVs. The United States would have saved billions of dollars and would be at least as secure.

I thought *Call for a Freeze,* written in 1979 by one of my students, Randall Forsberg [director of the Institute for Defense and Disarmament Studies, Brookline Massachusetts—Eds.], made sense, as did the original resolution of Senators Kennedy and Hatfield that called for a cessation of construction, deployment, and testing of nuclear systems. However, to get a few more votes on the Senate floor, these senators changed the wording of their resolution so that the United States would not "stop," but would "begin exploration" with the Soviet Union about how and when to implement a freeze. This wording in a freeze resolution was a prescription for never-ending negotiation. If the Reagan staff had had their wits about them, they would have jumped on that bandwagon in a minute and agreed to a freeze; they would have expressed a desire to start talks with the Soviet Union as soon as possible on how and when to implement the freeze; and they would have claimed that to negotiate it effectively the United States would have to build the B-1, the MX, and every other system one can imagine. Luckily, they did not have their wits about them, and they are now so committed to opposition to the freeze that I do not think they can soon reverse themselves. But whether in this administration's second term or in the next administration, if the United States ever attempts to conclude a formal treaty of agreement as comprehensive as the freeze, the negotiations will be prolonged, and therefore there will be plenty of opportunity for the pernicious effects of the negotiating process to manifest themselves.

References

Brauch, Hans G., and Duncan L. Clarke, eds. (1983). *Decisionmaking for Arms Limitation in the 1980's: Assessments and Prospects.* Cambridge MA: Ballinger.
Bundy, McGeorge, George F. Kennan, Robert McNamara, and Gerard Smith (1982). "Nuclear Weapons and the Atlantic Alliance," *Foreign Affairs* 60:4:761.
Chayes, Abram, and Jerome Weisner, eds (1969). *ABM: An Evaluation of the Decision*

to Deploy an Anti-Ballistic Missile System. New York: Harper and Row.

Clarke, Duncan L. (1979). *The Politics of Arms Control: The Role and Effectiveness of the U.S. Arms Control and Disarmament Agency.* New York: Free Press.

Huisken, Ron (1980). *The Cruise Missile and Arms Control.* Canberra: Australian National University Press.

Inozemtsev, N. N. (1980). *Peace and Disarmament.* Moscow: Progress Publishers.

Long, Frederic A., and George W. Rathjens, eds. (1975). *Arms, Defense Policy and Arms Control.* New York: Norton.

Nitze, Paul H., et al. (1979). *The Fateful Ends and Shades of SALT: Past . . . Present . . . and Yet to Come.* New York: Crane Russak.

Potter, William C., ed. (1980). *Verification and SALT.* Boulder CO: Westview Press.

Rathjens, George W. (1969). "The Dynamics of the Arms Race," *Scientific American,* April.

———, Abram Chayes, and Jack Ruina. (1974). *Nuclear Arms Control Agreements: Process and Impact.* Washington DC: Carnegie Endowment.

Russett, Bruce (1983). *Prisoners of Insecurity: Nuclear Deterrence, the Arms Race, and Arms Control.* New York: W. H. Freeman.

Smith, Gerard (1980). *Doubletalk: The Story of the First Strategic Arms Limitation Talks.* New York: Doubleday.

Stockholm International Peace Research Institute (1982). *Agreements for Arms Control: A Critical Survey.* London: Taylor and Francis.

——— *The Arms Race and Arms Control.* London: Taylor and Francis.

Talbott, Strobe (1979). *End Game: The Inside Story of SALT II.* New York: Harper and Row.

——— (1984). *Deadly Gambits: The Reagan Administration and the Stalemate in Nuclear Arms Control.* New York: Alfred A. Knopf.

Yefremov, A. Y. (1979). *Nuclear Disarmament.* Moscow: Progress Publishers.

SELECTED PROVISIONS OF SUPERPOWER ARMS CONTROL ACCORDS

I. Selected Treaty Language on Arms Control, Ending the Arms Race, and General and Complete Disarmament

Many of the statements supporting the goals of arms control—an end to the arms race, and eventual general and complete disarmament—appear in the preambles of the relevant treaties and have been argued to be without legal effect. However, Article VI of the Nonproliferation Treaty (NPT) is a strong commitment in the body of the treaty. It represents an undertaking of the NPT and cannot be interpreted as a pious-hopes-and-good-wishes statement of the preamble, without legal effect. If the analogy to U.S. contract law applies, even statements in support of stopping the arms race and working toward general and complete disarmament that appear only in the preambles of selected treaties would be interpreted as admissions of fact. Thus, the arguments that commitments to negotiations for general complete disarmament (GCD) do not have the force of law can be countered on two grounds, though arguments questioning the sincerity of these commitments may be more difficult to refute. (Herman Kahn advised against making these commitments because of the potential damage to U.S. credibility in treaty making.) The general commitment made in Article VI of the NPT on ending or limiting the arms race is cited again in the text of the SALT I Treaty, the SALT Interim Agreement (1972), and the 1979 draft of SALT II. President Reagan also repeated the U.S. commitment to the "complete elimination of nuclear weapons" in his press conference of 9 January 1985, on the probably spurious grounds that complete nuclear disarmament is easier to verify than are reductions.

Treaty Banning Nuclear Weapons Tests in the Atmosphere, in Outer Space and Under Water
Partial Test Ban Treaty
U.S. signed and ratified 1963, in force 1963

Preamble, Paragraph 2. "Proclaiming as their principal aim the speediest possible achievement of an agreement on general and complete disarmament under strict international control in accordance with the objectives of the United Nations which would put an end to the armaments race and eliminate the incentive to the production and testing of all kinds of weapons, including nuclear weapons...."(ACDA 1982:41)

Treaty for the Prohibition of Nuclear Weapons in Latin America
Treaty of Tlatelolco
U.S. signed 1967; in force 1968

Preamble, Paragraphs 2-4. "Desiring to contribute, so far as lies in their power, towards ending the armaments race, especially in the field of nuclear weapons, and towards strengthening a world at peace....

"Recalling that the United Nations General Assembly, in its Resolution 808 (IX), adopted unanimously as one of the three points of a coordinated programme of disarmament 'the total prohibition of the use and manufacture of nuclear weapons'....

"Recalling that militarily denuclearized zones are not an end in themselves but rather a means for achieving general and complete disarmament at a later stage...." (ACDA 1982:64)

[Language repeated in Additional Protocol I, U.S. signed 1977, ratified 1981; Additional Protocol II, U.S. signed 1968, ratified 1971. (ACDA 1982:76)]

Treaty on the Nonproliferation of Nuclear Weapons
Nonproliferation Treaty
U.S. signed 1968, ratified 1969; in force 1970

Preamble, Paragraphs 2, 9-12. "Considering the devastation that would be visited upon all mankind by a nuclear war and the consequent need to make every effort to avert the danger of such a war....

"Declaring their intention to achieve at the earliest possible date the cessation of the nuclear arms race and to undertake effective measures in the direction of nuclear disarmament,

"Urging the cooperation of all states in the attainment of this objective,

"Recalling the determination expressed by the Parties to the 1963 Treaty banning nuclear weapon tests in the atmosphere, in outer space and under water in its Preamble to seek to achieve the discontinuance of all test explosions of nuclear weapons for all time and to continue negotiations to this end,

"Desiring to further the easing of international tension... to facilitate the cessation of the manufacture of nuclear weapons, the liquidation of all their existing stockpiles, and the elimination from national arsenals of nuclear weapons and the means of their delivery pursuant to a treaty on general and complete disarmament...."

Article VI. "Each of the Parties to the Treaty undertakes to pursue negotiations in good faith on effective measures relating to cessation of the nuclear arms race at an early date and to nuclear disarmament, and on a treaty on general and complete disarmament under strict and effective international control." (ACDA 1982:91-93)

Treaty on the Prohibition of the Emplacement of Nuclear Weapons and Other Weapons of Mass Destruction on the Seabed and the Ocean Floor and in the Subsoil Thereof
Seabed Treaty
U.S. signed 1971, ratified 1972; in force 1972

Preamble, Paragraph 5. "Convinced that this Treaty constitutes a step towards a Treaty on general and complete disarmament under strict and effective international control, and determined to continue negotiations to this end...." (ACDA 1982:102)

Convention on the Prohibition of the Development, Production and Stockpiling of Bacteriological (Biological) and Toxin Weapons and on Their Destruction
Biological Weapons Convention
U.S. signed 1972, ratified 1975; in force 1975

Paragraph 2. "Determined to act with a view to achieving effective progress towards general and complete disarmament, including the prohibition and elimination of all types of weapons of mass destruction, and convinced that the prohibition of the development, production and stockpiling of chemical and bacteriological (biological) weapons and their elimination ... will facilitate the achievement of general and complete disarmament...." (ACDA 1982:124)

Treaty Between the United States of America and the Union of Soviet Socialist Republics on the Limitation of Anti-Ballistic Missile Systems
SALT I ABM Treaty
U.S. signed 1972, ratified 1972; in force 1972

Preamble, Paragraphs 5,6. "Mindful of their obligations under Article VI of the Treaty on the Non-Proliferation of Nuclear Weapons,

"Declaring their intention to achieve at the earliest possible date the cessation of the nuclear arms race and to take effective measures toward reductions in strategic arms, nuclear disarmament, and general and complete disarmament...." (ACDA 1982:139)

Article XI. "The Parties undertake to continue active negotiations for limitations on strategic offensive arms." (ACDA 1982:141)

SALT I Interim Agreement Between the United States of America and the Union of Soviet Socialist Republics on Certain Measures With Respect to the Limitation of Strategic Offensive Arms
SALT I
U.S. signed 1972, "approved" 1972; in force 1972

Introduction, Paragraph 4. "Mindful of their obligations under Article VI of the Treaty on the Non-Proliferation of Nuclear Weapons...." (ACDA 1982:150)

Treaty Between the United States of America and the Union of Soviet Socialist Republics on the Limitation of Underground Nuclear Weapons Tests
Threshold Test Ban
U.S. signed 1974; awaiting Senate action

Introduction, Paragraphs 2-3. "Declaring their intention to achieve at the earliest possible date the cessation of the nuclear arms race and to take effective measures toward reductions in strategic arms, nuclear disarmament, and general and complete disarmament under strict and effective international control.

"Recalling the determination expressed by the Parties to the 1963 Treaty Banning Nuclear Weapon Tests ... to seek to achieve the discontinuance of all test explosions of nuclear weapons for all time, and to continue negotiations to this end...."

[Comprehensive Test Ban talks—apparently encompassing extensive on-site inspection provisions—were early casualties of the failure of detente.—Eds.]

Article 1, Paragraph 3. "The Parties shall continue their negotiations with a view toward achieving a solution to the problem of the cessation of all underground nuclear weapon tests." (ACDA 1982:167)

Treaty Between the United States of America and the Union of Soviet Socialist Republics on Underground Nuclear Explosions for Peaceful Purposes
Peaceful Nuclear Explosions Treaty
U.S. signed 1976; awaiting Senate action

Introduction, Paragraph 3. "Reaffirming their adherence to the objectives and principles of the Treaty Banning Nuclear Weapon Tests... the Treaty on Non-Proliferation... and the Treaty on the Limitation of Underground Nuclear Weapon Tests, and their determination to observe strictly the provisions of these international agreements...." (ACDA 1983:173)

Convention on the Prohibition of Military or Any Other Hostile Use of Environmental Modification Techniques
Environmental Modification Convention
U.S. signed 1977, ratified 1979

Introduction, Paragraphs 1-3. "The Parties to this Convention,
"Guided by the interest of consolidating peace, and wishing to contribute to the cause of halting the arms race, and of bringing about general and complete disarmament under strict and effective international control, and of saving mankind from the danger of using new means of warfare....
"Determined to continue negotiations with a view to achieving effective progress towards further measures in the field of disarmament...." (ACDA 1982:193)

Treaty Between the United States of America and the Union of Soviet Socialist Republics on the Limitation of Strategic Offensive Arms
SALT II
U.S. signed 1979 (after President Gerald Ford's signature in 1974); not ratified by U.S.

Introduction, Paragraphs 4,6,9,10. "Attaching particular significance to the limitation of strategic arms and determined to continue their efforts begun with the (ABM) Treaty... and the (SALT I) Interim Agreement...,
"Mindful of their obligations under Article VI of the Treaty on the Non-Proliferation of Nuclear Weapons,
"Reaffirming their desire to take measures for the further limitation and for the further reduction of strategic arms, having in mind the goal of achieving general and complete disarmament,
"Declaring their intention to undertake in the near future negotiations further to limit and further to reduce strategic offensive arms...." (ACDA 1982:246)

II. Outer-Space–Related Commitments

The Outer Space Treaty of 1967 unambiguously prohibits military uses of space, which would seem to bring into question much of the activity of the U.S. space shuttle and of comparable Soviet systems, as well as of the military applications of the satellite systems of both superpowers and possibly of the regional powers. The treaty makes no distinction between purported defensive and offensive systems in its prohibitions of the militarization of space, which would therefore appear to prohibit the emplacement of Star Wars prototype ballistic missile defense systems based in space, as advocated by the Reagan administration in the United States.

Treaty on Principles Governing the Activities of States in the Exploration and Use of Outer Space, Including the Moon and Other Celestial Bodies
Outer Space Treaty
U.S. and USSR signed and ratified 1967; in force 1967

Preamble, Paragraphs 1,3,7,8. "The States Parties to this Treaty,
  "Recognizing the common interest of all mankind in the progress of the exploration and use of outer space for peaceful purposes,
  "Recalling resolution 1962 (XVIII), entitled 'Declaration of Legal Principles Governing the Activities of States in the Exploration and Use of Outer Space,' which was adopted unanimously by the United Nations General Assembly on 13 December 1963,
  "Recalling resolution 1884 (XVIII), calling upon States to refrain from placing in orbit around the Earth any objects carrying nuclear weapons or any other kinds of weapons of mass destruction or from installing such weapons on celestial bodies, which was adopted unanimously by the United Nations General Assembly on 17 October 1963 . . . ." (ACDA 1982:51)

Article II. "Outer space, including the moon and other celestial bodies, is not subject to national appropriation by claim of sovereignty, by means of use or occupation, or by any other means." [This would seem to suggest that exclusive use of space for a space-based ballistic missile defense system would be difficult for any government to claim.—Eds.]

Article IV. "States Parties to the Treaty undertake not to place in orbit around the Earth any objects carrying nuclear weapons or any other kinds of weapons of mass destruction, install such weapons on celestial bodies, or station such weapons in outer space in any other manner.
  "The moon and other celestial bodies shall be used by all States Parties to the Treaty exclusively for peaceful purposes. The establishment of military bases, installations and fortifications, the testing of any type of weapons and the conduct of military maneuvers on celestial bodies shall be forbidden . . . ." (ADCA 1982:52)
  [Article IV, Paragraph 1 appears to pose legal difficulties for the type of new superweapon apparently envisioned by Edward Teller, as these would apparently work only in space. See Richard Garwin, Chapter 3.—Eds.]

III. Selected BMD-Related Commitments

President Reagan's Star Wars speech of March 1983 announced a program for space-based ballistic missile defense that would directly oppose provisions of the 1972 ABM Treaty, nonexhaustively summarized below. The treaty does not prohibit research, but it does prohibit development and testing, despite some White House denials. Article V, Paragraph 1 is clear on this point. Tests planned by the United States for late 1985 may thus contravene specific provisions of the treaty and appear to pose problems for the 1967 Outer Space Treaty as well. The ABM Treaty has no expiration date.

Treaty Between the United States of America and the Union of Soviet Socialist Republics on the Limitation of Anti-Ballistic Missile Systems
ABM Treaty
U.S. signed and ratified [Senate Vote: overwhelming 88 to 2] 1972; in force 1972

Article I, Paragraphs 1,2. "Each Party undertakes to limit anti-ballistic missile (ABM) systems . . . in accordance with the provisions of this Treaty.

"Each Party undertakes not to deploy ABM systems for a defense of the territory of its country and not to provide a base for such a defense, and not to deploy ABM systems for defense of an individual region except as provided for in Article III of this Treaty." (ACDA 1982:139)

Article V, Paragraph 1. "Each Party undertakes not to develop, test, or deploy ABM systems or components which are sea-based, air-based, space-based, or mobile land-based." (ACDA 1982:140)

Article VI, Paragraph b. ". . . not to deploy in the future radars for early warning of strategic ballistic missile attack except at locations along the periphery of its national territory and oriented outward." (ACDA 1982:141)

[Although a working ABM breakout system would have to be composed of many such radars, this provision would seem to present several difficulties to the Soviet Union because of the phased-array radar at Krasnoyarsk, and perhaps equally to the United States because of phased-array radars under construction since 1978 in Georgia and Texas, radars that are neither on the U.S. border nor mainly outward-looking. The Soviet Union has offered on-site inspection at Krasnoyarsk if this complaint is not resolved via the usual channels.—Eds.]

Article XV, Paragraph 1. "This Treaty shall be of unlimited duration." (ACDA 1982:142)

IV. Selected Verification Provisions

National technical means (aerial surveillance, photographic and electronic; seismic detection; and HUMINT [human intelligence from sources such as espionage, defectors and other informants] inter alia) are generally relied upon for verification of treaty compliance. However, there are a number of provisions in existing treaties that provide for on-site inspection. Recent failures of arms control cannot be attributed to Soviet refusals to allow such provisions in arms control draft treaties, especially in light of the dramatic developments on this issue in the Soviet Union since 1979, and as there has been no U.S. action on drafts before the Senate that include on-site inspection provisions.

The Antarctic Treaty

U.S. and USSR signed 1959, ratified 1960; in force 1961

Article VII, Paragraphs 3 and 4. "All areas of Antarctica, including all stations, installations and equipment within those areas, and all ships and aircraft at points of discharging or embarking cargoes or personnel in Antarctica, shall be open at all times to inspection by any observers designated in accordance with Paragraph 1 of this Article.

"Aerial observation may be carried out at any time over any or all areas of Antarctica by any of the Contracting Parties having the right to designate observers." (ACDA 1982:24)

Outer Space Treaty

Article XII. "All stations, installations, equipment and space vehicles on the moon and other celestial bodies shall be open to representatives of other States Party to the Treaty on a basis of reciprocity. Such representatives shall give reasonable advance notice. . . ." (ACDA 1982:54)

Treaty Between the United States of America and the Union of Soviet Socialist Republics on Underground Nuclear Explosions for Peaceful Purposes.
Peaceful Nuclear Explosions Treaty
U.S. and USSR signed 1976

Article IV, Paragraph 1. "For the purpose of providing assurance of compliance with the provisions of this Treaty, each party shall:
    (a) use national technical means of verification. . . .
    (b) provide to the other Party information and access to sites of explosions and furnish assistance in accordance with the provisions set forth in the Protocol of this Treaty." (ACDA 1982:174)

Protocol to the PNE Treaty

Article III, Paragraph 2. "For any explosion with a planned aggregate yield exceeding 100 kilotons . . . if the parties . . . deem it appropriate for the confirmation of the yield of the explosion . . . the Party carrying out the explosion shall allow designated personnel within the areas and at the locations described in Article V to exercise the following rights and functions:

(a) confirmation that the local circumstances . . . are consistent with the stated peaceful purposes;

(b) confirmation of the validity of the geological and geophysical information provided in accordance with Article II through the following procedures:
- (1) examination by designated personnel of research and measurement data of the Party carrying out the explosion. . . .
- (2) examination by designated personnel of rock core or rock fragments as they become available. . . .
- (3) observation by designated personnel of implementation by the Party carrying out the explosion of the following four procedures. . . .
  - (i) construction of . . . each emplacement hole. . . .
  - (iii) removal of rock core or rock fragments from the wall of each emplacement hole at locations specified. . . .

(c) observation of the emplacement of each explosive. . . .

(d) unobstructed visual observation of the area of the entrance to each emplacement hole. . . .

(e) observation of each explosion."

Article III, Paragraph 3. "Designated personnel . . . shall have the right . . . to determine the yield of each individual explosion. . . ."

Article III, Paragraph 4. "Designated personnel . . . shall have the right [to] . . . a local seismic network. . . . Radio links may be used for the transmission of data and control signals. . . ."

Article III, Paragraph 5. "Designated personnel shall have the right to . . . acquire photographs . . . of the following:

exterior views of facilities and installations associated with the conduct of the explosion. . . .

geological samples. . . .

emplacement and installation of equipment and associated cables . . . for yield determination. . . .

emplacement and installation of the local seismic network. . . .

emplacement of the explosives and the stemming of the emplacement hole. . . .

visual displays and records. . . . 7. . . . a local seismic network . . . shall be emplaced, installed and operated. . . ." (ACDA 1982:179-182)

Article VII, Paragraphs 1-2. "Designated personnel with their personal baggage and their equipment . . . shall be permitted to enter the territory of the Party carrying out the explosion... to remain for the purpose of fulfilling their rights and functions... and to depart...

"... their persons, property, personal baggage, archives and documents as well as their temporary official and living quarters shall be accorded the same privileges and immunities as provided in... the Vienna Convention on Diplomatic Relations...." (ACDA 1982:188)

Comprehensive Test Ban (Draft)

Evidently provisions for sweeping measures of on-site inspection and other verification measures had been included in a draft of the CTB.

Parting Shots

These brief excerpts suggest that serious questions can be raised regarding arms control treaty compliance. It would not be productive to predicate arms control discussions on a one-sided demand for satisfaction of these issues raised outside the Standing Consultative Commission(s), as questions of compliance can be raised on both the U.S. and Soviet sides, and as the United States has declared its intent to proceed with programs that at some point contravene provisions of existing treaties, including the 1967 Outer Space Treaty and the ABM Treaty, depending on interpretation. There is also the possibility of exceeding the offensive weapons systems limits provided in SALT II, which have been tacitly and then verbally recognized despite the failure of the United States to ratify. This recognition may have represented declaratory policy only.

GLOSSARY

Selected Deterrence-Theoretical Terms

First strike: In one definition, a strike designed to destroy practically all of the opponent's nuclear forces before any retaliation can be launched; by definition, a counterforce attack, although it is not impossible that an actual first strike would be a countercity strike.

Second strike: A strike launched in retaliation; in classical deterrence theory, a second strike is launched after riding out an initial strike by the opponent, it is usual to project a second strike as countervalue, but it may mix the two targeting doctrines. Also called, somewhat more clearly, "strike-back" (see Snyder, 1961).

Stable nuclear deterrence: Both sides must possess relatively invulnerable weapons (see below). This assures each the ability to ride out a surprise attack and still retaliate with force sufficient to destroy the opponent, or at least to inflict unacceptable damage. Attack is deterred by means of the threat of reciprocal attack. (Clearly there is a question of societal relativity raised by this definition, as some U.S. analysts did not feel that Soviet inability to retaliate against the United States directly during the 1950s and early 1960s necessarily produced deterrence instability).

Acronyms and Other Shorter Terms

AA: antiaircraft

Glossary

AAM: air-to-air missile(s)

ABM: antiballistic missile (a missile designed to shoot down another missile) or missile system

AEW: airborn early warning

AFV: armored fighting vehicle(s)

ALBM: air-launched ballistic missile (ballistic missile launched from a specially designed airplane)

ALCM: air-launched cruise missile [see below] (cruise missile launched from a specially designed airplane)

APC: armored personnel carrier(s)

ASAT: anti-satellite war and associated weapons and communications systems

ASM: air-to-surface missile(s)

ASW: antisubmarine warfare

ATGW: antitank guided weapon(s)

AWACS: airborne warning and control system (Boeing 707 carrying radars and advanced computers and communications system capable of locating enemy aircraft and directing friendly aircraft to intercept them)

AWX: all-weather fighter(s)

BMD: ballistic missile defense (methods of defending missile launch sites from enemy attack, of which ABM is one type)

CBW: chemical and biological warfare

CEP: circular error probable (a measure of warhead accuracy given as the radius of a circle within which 50 percent of the warheads will fall)

COIN: counterinsurgence

comms: communications

Glossary

counterforce:	targeting strategy designed to attack military targets such as missile silos or submarine pens
countervalue or countercity:	targeting strategy designed to attack civilian and industrial targets
CM:	cruise missile (a small jet-powered missile; current U.S. designs are capable of extreme accuracy and approximately 2,000-mile range, with some plans for much greater range)
CW:	chemical warfare
DOD:	Department of Defense
ECCM:	electronic counter-countermeasures (offensive electronic devices used to defeat ECM)
ECM:	electronic countermeasures (defensive electronic devices used to defeat, hide, or confuse enemy attempts at radar or radio detection)
ELINT:	electronic intelligence
ERW:	enhanced radiation warhead; the neutron bomb (a nuclear device designed to kill by an intense pulse of short-lived radiation; fireball and blast effects are minimal) is an example
EW:	early warning
FAC(G):	fast attack craft (gun)
FAC(M):	fast attack craft (missile)
FAC(P):	fast attack craft (patrol)
FAC(T):	fast attack craft (torpedo)
GDP:	gross domestic product
GLCM:	ground-launched cruise missile(s)
GNP:	gross national product
GP:	general-purpose
GPS:	global positioning [satellite] system (satellite system able to pinpoint any target on earth with 10 to 20 meter accuracy)

GW: guided weapon(s)

ICBM: intercontinental ballistic missile

invulnerable
weapons: strategic weapons made difficult or impossible to destroy by means of hardening them in underground silos; hiding them by some camouflage system or underwater; moving them around (mobile missiles or those on submarines); scattering them; defending them with a BMD system; launching them on warning that an attack may be on the way

IRBM: intermediate-range ballistic missile(s)

KT: kiloton (1,000 tons TNT-equivalent explosive power)

LNO: limited nuclear options (war-fighting doctrine that entails a nuclear exchange other than a massive spasm; a select number of missiles fired at a few targets for demonstration or political effect; sometimes pictured as a slow-motion counterforce duel)

Look down/
shoot down: radar/computer system capable of locating a plane flying beneath the plane carrying the radar, then directing a missile to the target

MAD: mutual assured destruction (the ability of both sides to launch strikes of unacceptably destructive force after receiving an initial strike from the opponent)

MARV: maneuverable reentry vehicle (several separate warheads carried initially on the same missile but capable of independent maneuvering as they approach their targets)

M(B)FR: mutual [balanced] forced reductions (talks between NATO and WTO to reduce the number of troops and weapons in Europe)

MCM: mine countermeasures

MIRV: multiple independently targetable reentry vehicle (several separate warheads carried on the same missile and capable of being independently aimed at different targets)

MRBM: medium-range ballistic missile(s)

MRL: multiple rocket launcher(s)

MRV:		multiple reentry vehicle (several warheads carried on the same missile but not capable of independent targeting; a shotgun approach to aiming)
MT:		megaton (1 million tons TNT-equivalent explosive power)
nm:		nautical mile(s) = 6,080 feet
PGM:		precision-guided munitions (missiles, bombs, artillery shells or torpedoes capable of extreme accuracy; usually guided to target by means of wire, laser designator, infrared, optical or television sensors)
PSI:		pounds per square inch (used to measure missile silo hardness)
R&D:		research and development
RV:		reentry vehicle(s)
SAC:		Strategic Air Command
SAM:		surface-to-air missile (air defense missile)
SLBM:		sea-launched ballistic missile (ballistic missile launched from submarines)
SLCM:		sea-launched cruise missile (cruise missile launched from surface ships or the torpedo tubes of submarines)
SRAM:		short-range attack missile(s)
SRBM:		short-range ballistic missile(s)
SSBN:		submarine designed to launch SLBMs
SSM:		surface-to-surface missile(s)
SSN:		submarine(s), nuclear
Triad:		the historically accidental configuration of U.S. strategic forces, apparently in three parts (submarines carrying SLBMs, ICBMs, and strategic bomber force and refueling tankers), but actually in six (also including air defense, a minor ABM capability, and a group of systems for warning, command, control of communications, intelligence, and surveillance)

INDEX

Antiballistic missile (ABM). *See* Ballistic missile defense
ABM Treaty. *See* SALT-I under SALT Treaty; *also see Appendix*
Aircraft
 bombers, 15
 B-1, 56, 69
 stealth aircraft, 56
Arms Accords, 2; also Chapters 3 and 8
Antinuclear movement, 18. *See also* Nuclear freeze
Antisatellite weapons (ASAT). *See* Weapons
Antisubmarine warfare (ASW), 54, 61; also Chapter 3
Antisubmarine weapons. *See* Weapons
Antitank warfare, 28, 43
Arms Control and Disarmament Agency (ACDA), 152, 157
Arms control negotiations, 1-5, 7-9, 153; also Chapters 1, 8, and Appendix
 unilateral action as substitute for, 7, 12; also Chapters 3 and 8
Arms race, 1, 4, 6, 7, 54
Assured destruction, 34. *See also* Deterrence theory
Atomic Energy Commission (AEC), 28

Balance of power, 103; also Chapter 4
Balance of terror, 25, 49

Ballistic missiles. *See* Weapons
Ballistic missile defense (BMD), 4, 54, 65, 161; also Chapters 1, 3, and 8
Baruch Plan, 14
Berlin Crisis, 24
Biological war. *See* Chemical and biological war
Blast effects, 144. *See also* Nuclear explosion

Carter Administration, 69, 101, 109
Casualty estimates
 nuclear war, Chapter 2 and illustrations, especially Figure 7
 nuclear atmospheric testing, Chapters 7 and 8
Central Intelligence Agency (CIA), 9, 24, 167
Central Nuclear War (CNW), 78-80, 82, 85, 102; also Chapter 4
Chemical and biological war, Chapters 1 and 6
Civil Defense, Chapter 7
Collateral damage, 49, and Figures 2, 13-15
Command and control issues, Chapter 3. *See also* Theater nuclear war
Counterforce capability, 10, 100
Comprehensive Test Ban Treaty, 2, 3, 55, 67, and Appendix
Crisis escalation, Chapter 4

191

Cruise missiles. *See* Missiles
Cuban Missile Crisis, Chapters 2 and 8

Defense Council (of USSR), 2
Defense Economic Impact Modelling System (DEIMS), Chapter 5
Delivery vehicles, 3, 5
  accuracy, 2
  See also Weapons
Dense Pack proposal, 57, 63; also Chapter 3
Detente, 5; also Chapter 1
Deterrence theory, 7
  central nuclear war, Chapter 4
  common security, 7
  countervalue strike, 10
  escalation ladder, 26
  exchange ratio, Chapter 3
  finite deterrence position, Chapter 1
  first strike, 6, 8, 15, 23, 37, 41, 92; also Chapter 7
  margin of superiority, 12; also Chapter 7
  massive attack, 70
  mobilization war scenario, 105
  mutual assured destruction (MAD), 77, 90, 93; also Chapter 4
  nuclear use theories (NUTs), 77, 90, 93
  overlap on ground of counterforce and countervalue targets, Chapters 2 and 4; also illustrations
  preemptive attack, 26; also Chapter 3
  protracted crisis scenario, 105; also Chapters 4 and 7
  second strike (strike-back), 11, 55, 84, and Glossary

Eisenhower Administration, 110, 171
Electromagnetic pulse (EMP), 26, 129
End-of-the-World hypothesis, 102
Environmental effects of nuclear war, Chapters 2 and 6
  atomic tidal wave, 58
  earthquake trigger, 135-139; also Chapter 6
  See also Nuclear Explosion, effects of
Environmental war, Chapter 6
Equal security, 5

Equivalent megatonnage (EMT), 41, n. 1 in Chapter 2, and Chapter 4
Escalation ladder, 26. *See also* Deterrence theory
Europe, 22 (n. 3), and Chapter 2 (especially Figures 13-15); also Chapters 4 and 8
Eurostrategic talks, 3

Fallout, 49, 135-139, and Figure 7. *See also* Nuclear explosion, effects of
False nuclear war alerts, 70; also Chapter 4
Federal Emergency Management Agency (FEMA), 28; also Chapter 7
Fratricide, 49; also Chapters 1 and 3

Gedanken experiment, 95-97, 99
Geneva Protocol, 13; also Chapters 1 and 2

High Frontier, 66. *See also* Ballistic missile defense
Hiroshima and Nagasaki, Chapters 2, 4, 6, and 7
Hot line, 95; also Appendixes
Human rights, 4. *See also* Arms control negotiations; Jackson Amendment

Independent Commission on Disarmament and Security Issues, 7
India, 21

Jackson Amendment, 5; also Chapter 8
Joint Chiefs of Staff, U.S., 2, 24-25; also Chapter 8

Kennedy Administration, 25

Limited nuclear war. *See* Theater nuclear war
Low-frequency transmitters, 64

Manhattan Project, 10
Military Spending, U.S., 141; also Chapters 4, 5, and 8
  R & D sectoral effects, 112
Military-related technologies, 117; also Chapter 5

MIRVs, 2, 12, 165; also Chapters 7 and 8
Missiles
   ABM. *See* Ballistic missile defense
   ballistic missiles, 3
   Cruise missiles, 2, 16, 18, 55; also
      Chapters 3 and 8
   ICBMs, 5, 15, 23, 35-36, 56, 72, 100, 170
   land-based missiles, 15, 55
   launchers, 5; also Chapters 3 and 8
   medium range missiles, 3
   Minuteman, 36, 55, 57-58, 60, 69, and Figures 5a and 5b
   MX missiles, 10, 34, 56-57, 59-60, 62; also Chapter 3
   Pershing-II, 2-3, 19, 34; also Chapter 8
   SS-4, 18
   SS-5, 18
   SS-20, 3, 18
   throwweight, 2
   Titan II, Figure 1
   See also Weapons
Missile Gap, 11; also Chapter 8
Mutual assured destruction (MAD), 77, 90, 93. *See also* Deterrence theory
Mutual balanced force reductions (MBFR, or MFR), 1, 168; also Chapter 8

Nagasaki. *See* Hiroshima
National Aeronautics and Space Administration (NASA), 117; also Chapter 5
National Security Council (U.S.), 110
NATO, 2-3, 43, 87, 168
Negotiations. *See* Arms control negotiations
Nevada test site, 28
No-First-Use declaration, 3, 88, 98; also Chapter 4
Non-proliferation, 19, 21, 88; also Chapter 8
Nuclear explosion, effects of, Figures 3, 4, and 7 in Chapter 2 and Chapters 3, 6, and 7. *See also* Blast effects; Environmental effects; Fallout
Nuclear freeze, 3, 9, 11, 14, 16, 19, 73, 92, 100, 173; also Chapters 1, 3, 4, and 8

Nuclear pacifism, 90, 92; also Chapter 4
Nuclear threats, Chapter 2
Nuclear weapons. *See* Weapons
Nuclear winter, 133; also Chapter 6

Office of Technology Assessment (OTA), 35

Partial Test Ban, 7, 150, 169; also Chapter 8 and Appendix
Peaceful Nuclear Explosion Treaty, 1, 3, 17, 150; also Chapter 8 and Appendix
Physicians for Social Responsibility, 49; also Chapter 7
Post-attack scenario, 146; also Chapter 4
Precision guided munitions (PGMs), 45
Psychological overkill, 91; also Chapters 2 and 7

Quemoy-Matsu crisis, 24

Radiation. *See* Nuclear explosion, effects of
Reagan Administration, 3, 27, 36, 72

SALT Treaty
   SALT-I, 8, 12, 16-17, 72, 158, 164-165
   SALT-II, 3-5, 10, 16-17, 72, 158, 167-168
Satellite surveillance, 14, 171. *See also* Verification
Seismic detection systems. *See* Verification
Skowcroft Commission, 60; also Chapter 8
Soviet Union (USSR), Chapter 4 and *passim*
   Defense Council of, 2
Space
   ban on weapons in, Chapters 3 and 8
   militarization of, 2-3; also Chapters 3 and 8
Sputnik, 11
START proposals, 5, 18, 22 (n. 4), 158
Stealth. *See* Aircraft
Strategic surprise, 9; also Chapter 1. *See also* Deterrence theory

Submarine basing systems (SUMs), 58, 61; also Chapter 3

Technology
  and cost of enemy casualties, Chapter 5
  civilian sector innovations, Chapter 5
  effects of on arms acquisitions, Chapters 3 and 8
Theater nuclear force talks, 1; also Chapter 2
Theater nuclear war, 28; also Introduction and Chapters 2 and 4
Treaty ratification, Chapter 8

United Nations Committee on Disarmament, 56
United States government
  ACDA, 152, 157
  Arms Control Institute, Chapter 3
  Department of Commerce, 80
  Department of Defense, 35, 58, 117, 152
  Department of State, 152, 157
  export competitiveness, Chapter 5
  forward-based systems, 4; also Chapter 8
  House of Representatives Science and Technology Committee, 69
  TRIAD, Chapter 7 and *passim*

Verification and treaty compliance, 2, 7, 14, 171; also Chapters 1 and 8

Warning time, 2, 22 (n. 3); also Chapters 1 and 3
Wars
  American Revolution, 124
  Cold War, 6, 103
  Crimean War, 15
  "fatalistic inevitability" of, Chapter 4
  Korean War, 24, 106, 126
  Middle East war, 2
  Modern war, 10
  Star wars, 3
  Thermonuclear war, 28, 142; also Chapter 4
  U.S. Civil War, 124-125
  Vietnam War, 115, 126
  World War-I, 13, 28, 82-83, 104
  World War-II, 10, 23, 35, 93, 115, 123, 126, 169
Warsaw Treaty Organization, 43
Weapons
  antisatellite weapons (ASAT), 56; also Chapter 3
  antisubmarine weapons, Chapter 3
  conventional build-up, 15; also Chapter 4
  neutron bomb, Chapters 2 and 6
  new weapons, 9, 173
  nuclear weapons, 1-3, 5, 10, 13, 35-37, 41; also Chapter 6. *See also* Nuclear explosion
  strategic nuclear weapons, 37
  super weapons (third-generation nuclear weapons), 67; also Chapter 3
  tactical nuclear weapons, 43, 45-46; also Chapter 2, including Figures 10 and 11
Window of vulnerability, 37, 57, 84, and Figures 8 and 9; also Chapters 2 and 4. *See also* Missiles, ICBMs

Zero Option, 18

ABOUT THE BOOK AND EDITORS

Presenting a wide range of views, scientists, theoreticians, and public officials of international reputation explore the dynamics of the arms race, the potential costs of arms racing without short-term boundaries, and the prospects for arms control. Among the topics covered are the use of limited nuclear options as a foreign policy instrument, the technological and the strategic imperatives in arms development, the impact on U.S. export competitiveness of continual increases in the U.S. military budget, and the possible environmental and medical repercussions of nuclear war. A thought-provoking, critical analysis of arms control achievements completes the main text.

Two appendixes provide a glossary of terms and selections from recent arms control accords of special relevance to verification, space war, and other contemporary issues.

Theresa C. Smith is author of *Trojan Peace,* a study of deterrence relations, as well as numerous articles on international negotiations and the arms race. She has taught in the Department of Political Science and the Russian and East European Institute at Indiana University, and is now on the faculty of Macalester College. **Indu B. Singh** is the author of three books and several articles on international communications and information resource management, and he is editor-in-chief of the journals *Telematics and Informatics* and *Advances in Telematics.* Dr. Singh is vice president of Spectrum Planning, Inc. He previously was director of the International Communications Program at Rutgers University.